THIS BOOK
BELONGS
TO

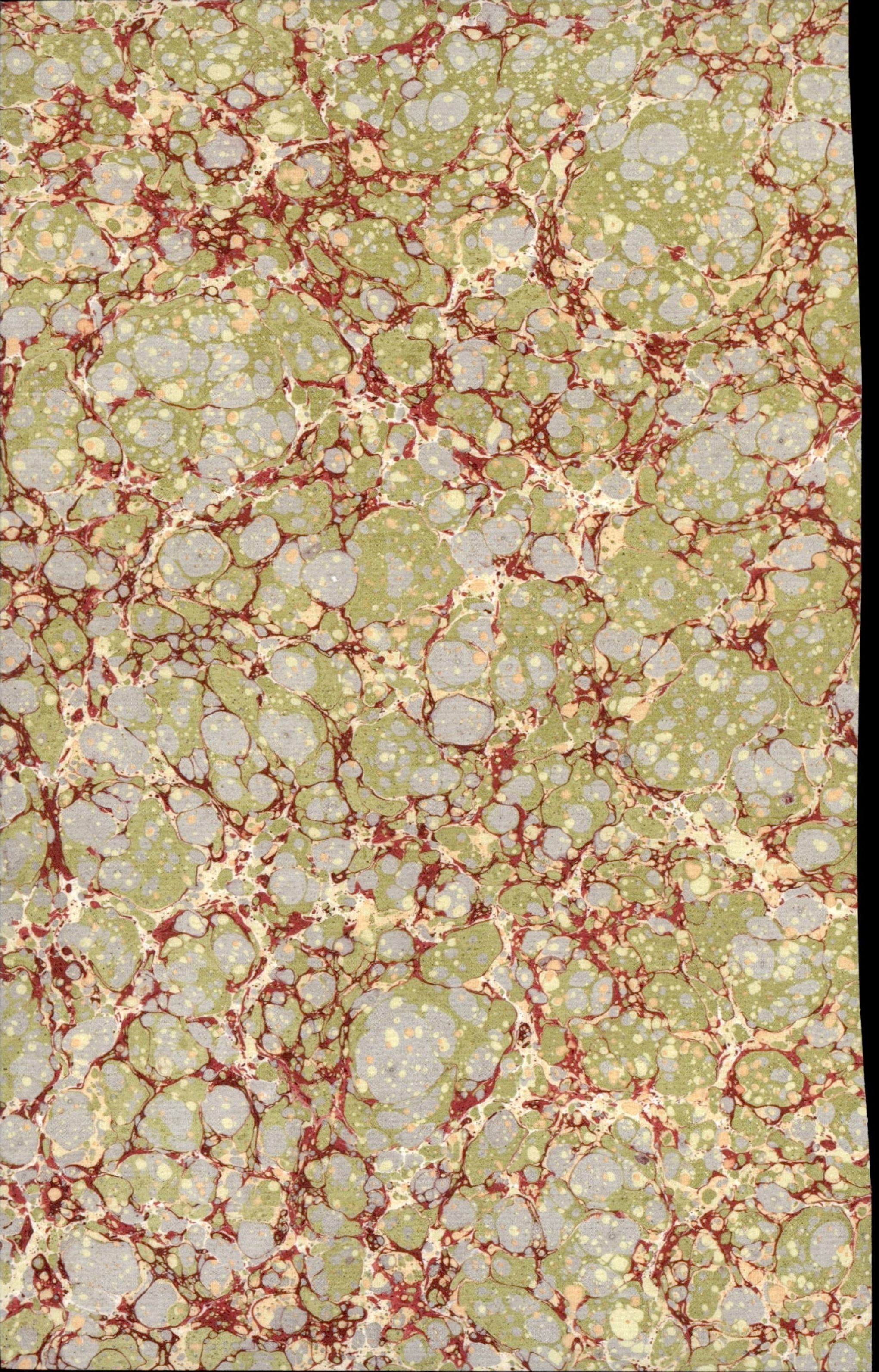

FOREVER
PARIS

Book design and typesetting
Marie-Lou Étienne
with Cécile Joly

Design principle and cover
Romain Chirat

With the editorial collaboration of
Salomé Bruneau
Anne-Sophie Leroux
Kate van den Boogert
Anne-Charlotte Dancourt

Editorial directors
Kate Mascaro & Julie Rouart

Editorial administration manager
Delphine Montagne

Editor, English edition
Helen Adedotun, assisted by Thomas Fitzpatrick

Editors, French edition
Mélanie Puchault & Yaël Rusé, assisted by Agathe Lo Presti

Translation from the French
Kate Robinson

Production
Élodie Conjat

Color separation
Les Artisans du Regard, Paris

Printed in China by C&C Offset

This book is typeset in Adobe Caslon Pro, Chambord, Vunder Script & De Vinne.

Simultaneously published in French as *Mon Paris de toujours*

Éditions Flammarion
82 rue Saint-Lazare
75009 Paris

editions.flammarion.com
@flammarioninternational

26 27 28   5 4 3

ISBN: 978-2-08-048245-7

Legal deposit: 11/2025

Flammarion is actively committed to reducing the ecological footprint of its publications. The book you hold in your hands was printed on paper made from wood sourced from sustainably managed forests, using mineral oil-free inks, by a printer committed to environmental protection, and is compliant with European Union Deforestation Regulation (EUDR). Send regulation (EU) 2023/988 inquiries to latelier@flammarion.fr

FOREVER PARIS

A Guide to the Timeless
Soul of the City

Pulvis
Amyli
Alcool
EXTRA
VANILLE
MIGNON
PETIT BEURRE
PARIS
CRAYONS
COULEURS
LANGUE
LANGUE
LANGUE

FOREVER PARIS

When I arrived in Paris at nineteen years old, without a map or reference points of any kind, I explored the city from end to end in search of its secrets. I stepped inside unassuming workshops, wandered down hidden passages, and peeked into little-known courtyards. There, I met dedicated women and men—frame-makers, costume designers, metalsmiths, bookbinders, and more—who express their craft using their hands, with incredible humility, to safeguard their invaluable knowledge from being lost.

These are the people who shaped my Paris: a Paris of living postcards, of skills passed down with patience, of savoir faire infused with love. This book is more than a collection of addresses; it is a tribute to a way of living, creating, traversing time, and holding steady in a tumultuous world.

It is also a journey back in time. All of the addresses featured have been in operation for decades, some of them for several centuries. I have kept them to myself for a long time, like precious treasures that lead me to the very soul of Paris. They embody the spirit of my "forever Paris," the same spirit that compelled me to find a home for my own boutique in a space steeped in history—a former tapestry workshop run for a century by the Péquignot family.

As Jean Cocteau said, "Of all the cities in the world, Paris is the most conspicuous and the most invisible." This book is my declaration of love to this invisible Paris.

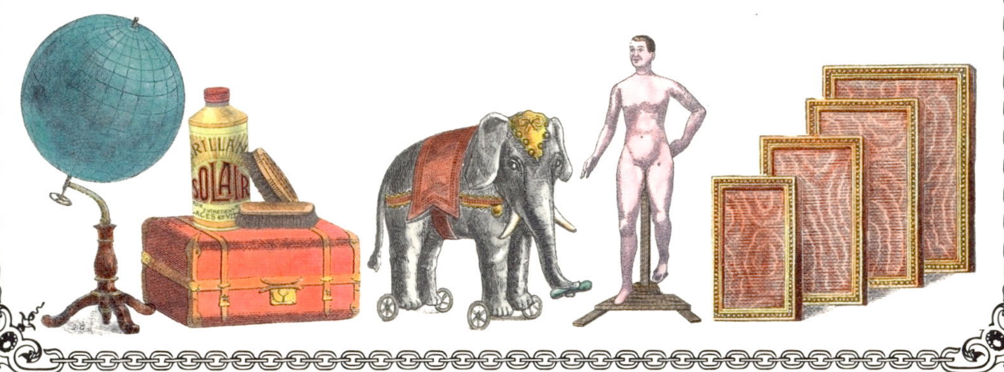

CONTENTS

N° 0291

N° 0292

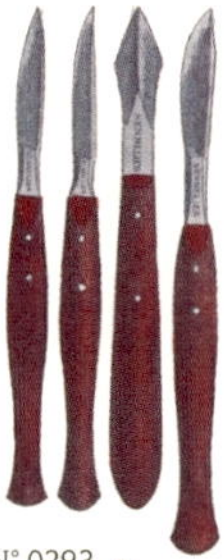

N° 0293

N° 0294

N° 0295

N° 0296

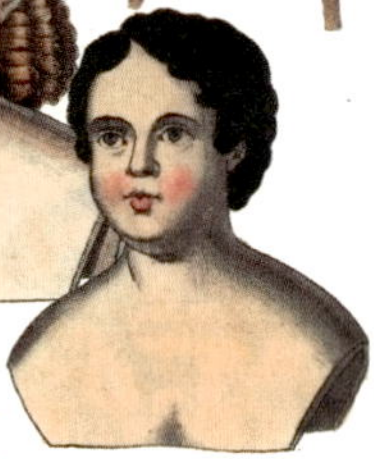

N° 0297

N° 0298

N° 0299

CONTENTS

N° 0310

N° 0311

N° 0312

N° 0313

N° 0314

N° 0315

N° 0318

N° 0319

N° 0316

ADDRESS CATEGORIES: COLOR KEY

- Art & culture
- Outdoor activities
- Shops
- Food shops & markets
- Restaurants, cafés & bars
- Entertainment, wellness & hotels

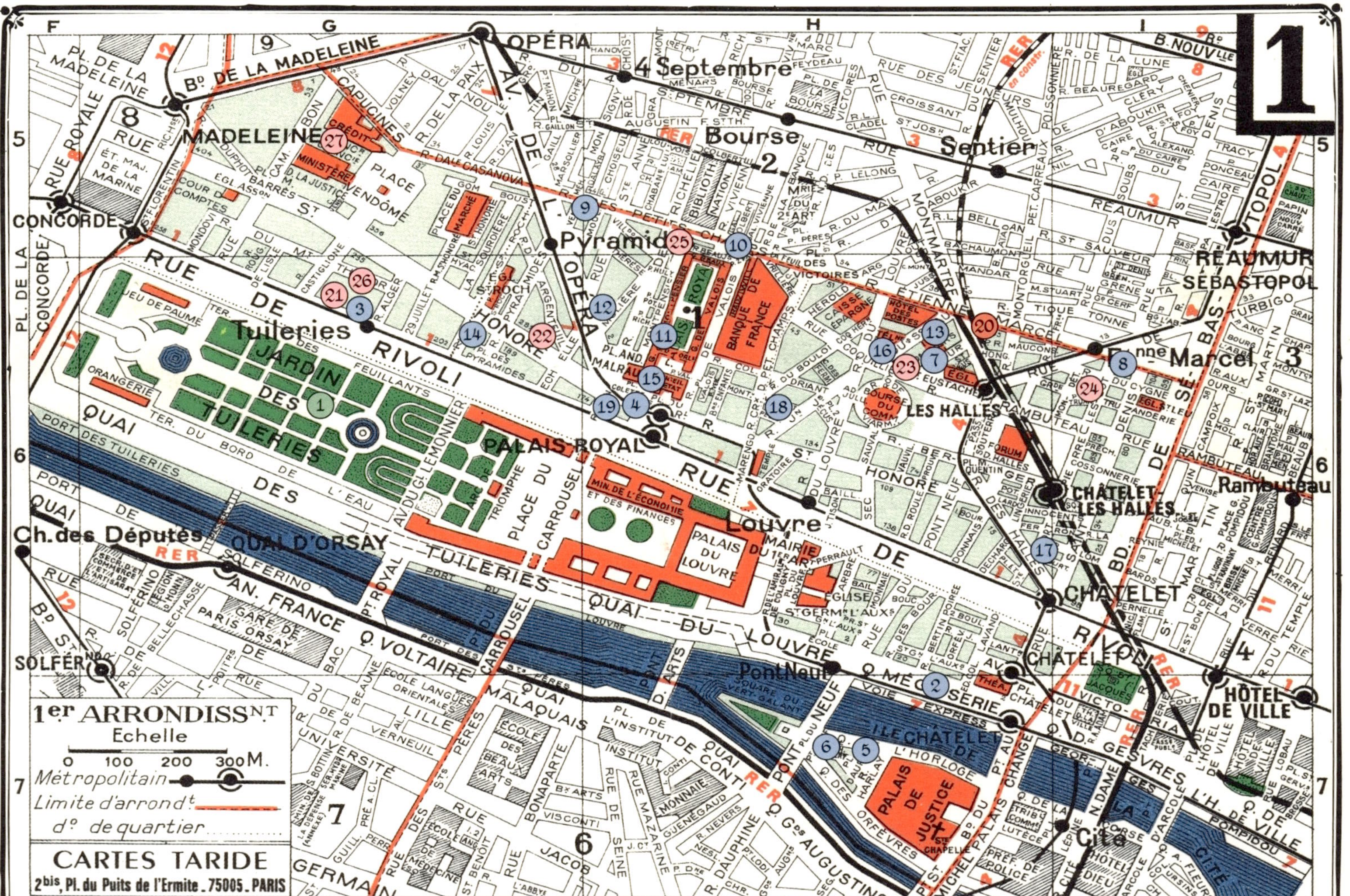
1
1er ARRONDISSNT
Echelle
0 100 200 300M.
Métropolitain
Limite d'arrondt
do de quartier
CARTES TARIDE
2bis, Pl. du Puits de l'Ermite . 75005 . PARIS
OPÉRA
4 Septembre
Bourse
Sentier
Réaumur Sébastopol
Madeleine
Concorde
Pyramides
Tuileries
Palais-Royal
Louvre
Les Halles
Châtelet-Les Halles
Châtelet
Rambuteau
Étienne Marcel
Hôtel de Ville
Pont Neuf
Cité
Ch. des Députés
Solférino
JARDIN DES TUILERIES
RUE DE RIVOLI
PALAIS DU LOUVRE
BANQUE DE FRANCE
PALAIS DE JUSTICE
QUAI D'ORSAY
QUAI DU LOUVRE

1ER ARRONDISSEMENT

1. Jardin des Tuileries & Fête Foraine
Entrances rue de Rivoli, place de la Concorde
2. Bouquinistes
Quai de la Mégisserie
3. Galignani
224 rue de Rivoli
4. Librairie Delamain
155 rue Saint-Honoré
5. GG Bookbinding
16 place Dauphine
6. Gaubert
41 quai de l'Horloge
7. La Droguerie
9–11 rue du Jour
8. Declercq Passementiers
15 rue Étienne-Marcel
9. Annie Bouquet
7 rue des Moulins
10. Maison Bonnet
5 rue des Petits-Champs
11. Bacqueville
6-7-8 galerie de Montpensier, Jardin du Palais-Royal
12. Antoine
10 avenue de l'Opéra
13. Fifi Chachnil
68 rue Jean-Jacques-Rousseau
14. Au Nain Bleu
14 rue Saint-Roch
15. Les Drapeaux de France – Boutique Noxa
Place Colette
16. E. Dehillerin
18–20 rue Coquillière
17. Aurouze
8 rue des Halles
18. Galerie Casanova
17 galerie Véro-Dodat
19. À la Civette
157 rue Saint-Honoré
20. Le Comptoir de la Gastronomie
34 rue Montmartre
21. Angelina
226 rue de Rivoli
22. Verlet
256 rue Saint-Honoré
23. Au Pied de Cochon
6 rue Coquillière
24. Le Petit Bouillon Pharamond
24 rue de la Grande-Truanderie
25. Bar de l'Entracte
47 rue de Montpensier
26. Au Petit Bar
7 rue du Mont-Thabor
27. Bar Hemingway – Ritz Paris
38 rue Cambon

JARDIN DES TUILERIES

JARDIN DES TUILERIES & FÊTE FORAINE

1

Entrances rue de Rivoli, place de la Concorde
M° Tuileries / Concorde

The oldest park in Paris—designed by Louis XIV's famous gardener Le Nôtre—attracts Parisians year-round with its majestic alleyways lined with centuries-old trees, its fountains, and its statues. But what I love the most is when, each summer and Christmas, this historic park is transformed into a magical fairground. Indulging my inner child, I ride the Ferris wheel for a breathtaking view over the city, visit the fun house for unforgettable laughs, and tuck into a hot waffle. At holiday time, I take my niece and nephew to see Santa soar high above the park in his sleigh.

N° 1327

BOUQUINISTES

2

Quai de la Mégisserie
M° Châtelet / Pont Neuf

Dozens of *bouquinistes*—second-hand booksellers plying their trade out of large, traditional green boxes—line the Quai de la Mégisserie. They first set up shop in the early 17th century, on Pont-Neuf, before relocating to the quays in the 19th century. Since then, they have overlooked the Seine, sharing with passersby their collections of used and antique books, magazines, posters, and engravings, which are a source of inspiration for my illustrations.

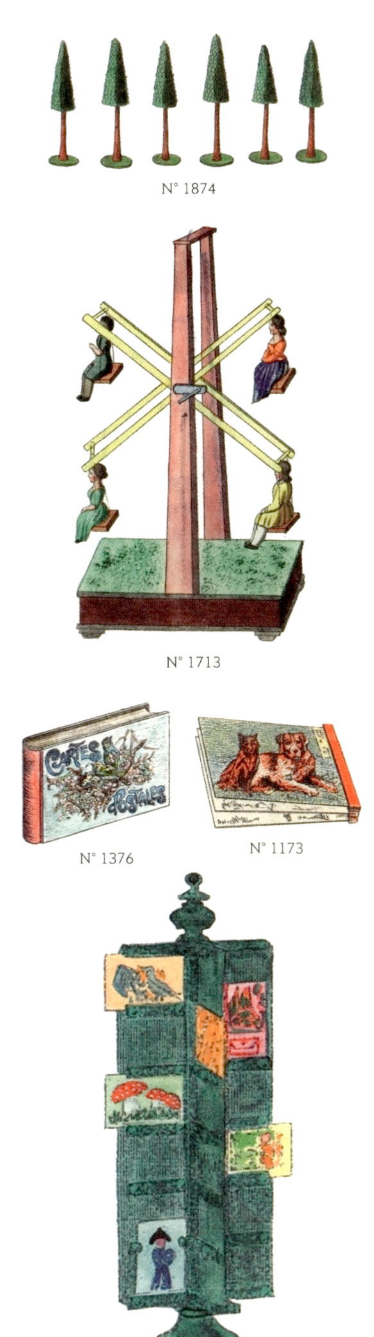

N° 1874

N° 1713

N° 1376

N° 1173

N° 1256

N° 1385

N° 1373

N° 1385

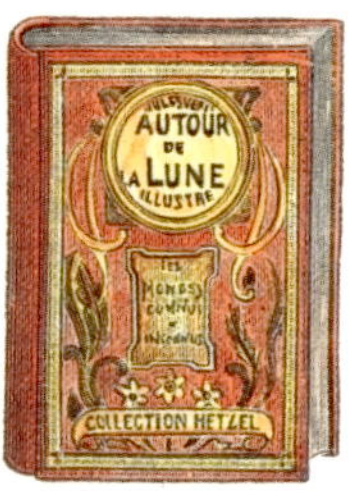

N° 1380

N° 1412

N° 1409

N° 1359

N° 1319

N° 1334

N° 1337

GALIGNANI

3

224 rue de Rivoli
M° Tuileries
01 42 60 76 07
galignani.fr • @librairiegalignani

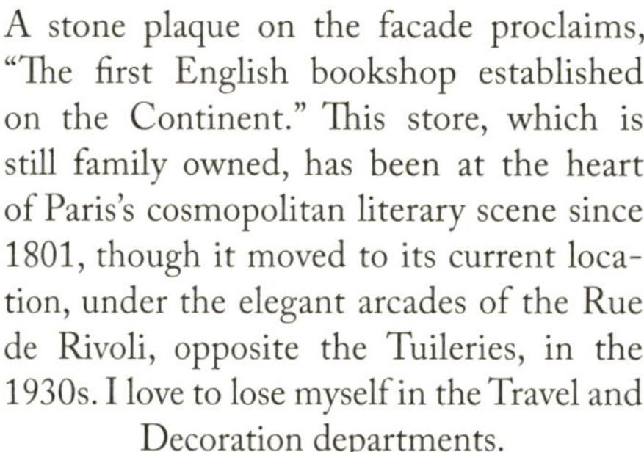

A stone plaque on the facade proclaims, "The first English bookshop established on the Continent." This store, which is still family owned, has been at the heart of Paris's cosmopolitan literary scene since 1801, though it moved to its current location, under the elegant arcades of the Rue de Rivoli, opposite the Tuileries, in the 1930s. I love to lose myself in the Travel and Decoration departments.

LIBRAIRIE DELAMAIN

4

155 rue Saint-Honoré
M° Palais-Royal – Musée du Louvre
01 42 61 48 78
librairie-delamain.com •
@librairie_delamain_paris

Located near the Palais-Royal since 1708, Librairie Delamain is the oldest bookstore in Paris. After a century under the arches of the Palais-Royal, the store moved to a location across from the Comédie-Française following a fire. For more than three centuries, the bookstore has played host to the greatest writers and actors who come in search of inspiration. In this magical place, the wisdom of the old never overshadows the power of the new.

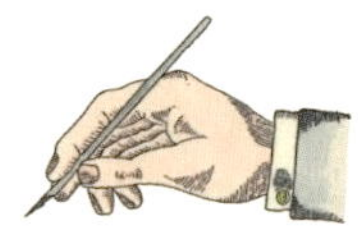

GG BOOKBINDING

16 place Dauphine
M° Pont Neuf
01 46 34 06 32

This bookbinding workshop has been in operation on Place Dauphine, just behind the Palais de Justice on the Île de la Cité, for 150 years. Perpetuating the historic trade, Greg has been at the helm here since 2012, repairing old books for bibliophiles or binding other documents into book form, such as legal journals for the lawyers working across the way.

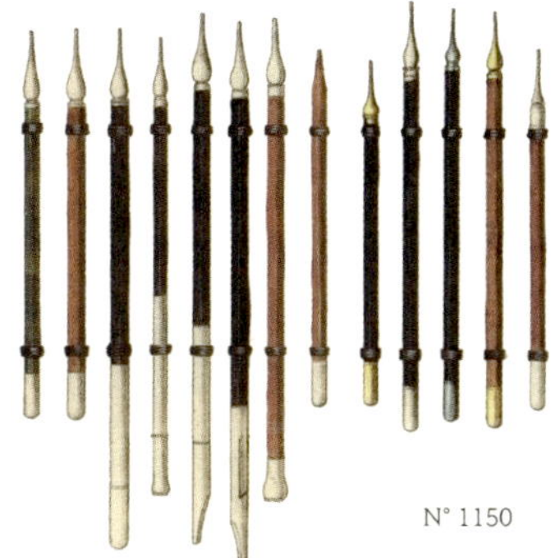

N° 1150

GAUBERT

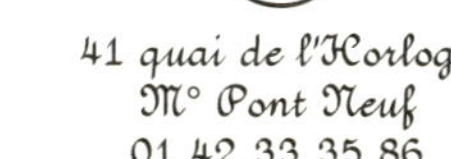

41 quai de l'Horloge
M° Pont Neuf
01 42 33 35 86
gaubert.calipage.fr

Crossing Place Dauphine, it would be impossible to miss Gaubert's iconic green storefront. Once inside, weave your way among the many lawyers who come for office supplies, and ogle stationery that would enrich any collection. Nestled here since 1830, this store, with its period staircase and eccentric decor, has stood the test of time to become a genuine institution for the area's legal experts (as well as others).

N° 1446

N° 1129

N° 1397 N° 1520

N° 1520

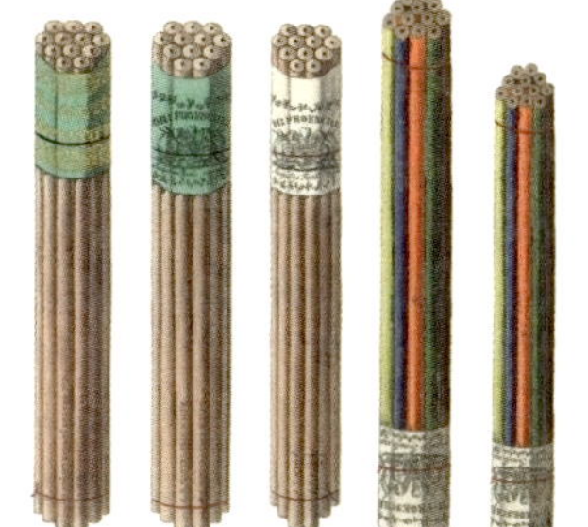

N° 1520

N° 1831

N° 1832

N° 1833

N° 1834

N° 1835

N° 1311

N° 1852

N° 1853

N° 1854

N° 1855

◈ LA DROGUERIE ◈

7

9–11 rue du Jour
M° Les Halles; RER Châtelet – Les Halles
01 45 08 93 27
ladroguerie.com/en/paris/ • @ladrogueriepari s

This notions store, with its air of a candy shop, has stocked all kinds of colorful ribbons, buttons, and other materials for sewing and creative pastimes since 1975. I like coming here because the place whisks me back to my childhood, when my mom would take me with her to pick out buttons for my school smock. What a delight it was to examine each little shape—from animals to pencils to fish—before deciding which one I wanted.

N° 1852

N° 1161

N° 1853

❖ DECLERCQ PASSEMENTIERS ❖

8

15 rue Étienne-Marcel
M° Étienne Marcel
01 44 76 90 70
declercqpassementiers.fr • @declercqpassementiers

The art of passementerie is a family affair. This story begins in 1852, when Joseph Bertaud opened a small workshop in the heart of Paris. Since then, thanks to seven generations, several relocations, and a lot of love, this traditional craft that embellishes the most beautiful upholstery fabrics has been maintained. Entering the boutique is like stepping into a theater set, where everything is fashioned by the imagination.

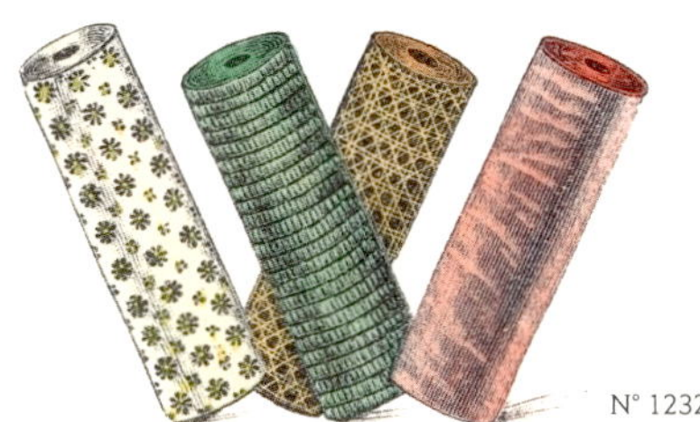

N° 1232

❖ ANNIE BOUQUET ❖

9

7 rue des Moulins
M° Pyramides / Quatre-Septembre
01 42 60 65 67
anniebouquet.com/en/ • @annie.bouquet

Since the late 1990s, Annie has been indulging her love of embroidery in her small boutique-studio on rue des Moulins. In fact, she happens to be one of the last cartoon painters in France. The charming little blue storefront beckons; Annie offers a warm welcome as we step inside, and the tinkling of the little bell recalls boutiques of old. An address that is a delight for the eyes as well as for all embroidery aficionados.

N° 1311 N° 1312

MAISON BONNET

10

5 rue des Petits-Champs
M° Palais-Royal – Musée du Louvre / Bourse
01 42 96 46 35
maisonbonnet.com/en • @maisonbonnet

Without a doubt, this place has glasses to suit every face. Bonnet makes bespoke frames using expertise that is practically unique in the world. It all began in the 1930s, when Alfred Bonnet established a small workshop in the Jura region. His son brought this savoir faire to Paris, and since then, a whole host of celebrities has come here seeking the perfect pair—among them Yves Saint Laurent, whose glasses helped create a legend.

N° 1348

N° 1128

N° 1113

N° 1583

N° 1584

BACQUEVILLE

11

6-7-8 galerie de Montpensier, Jardin du Palais-Royal
M° Palais-Royal – Musée du Louvre
01 42 96 26 90
commerce.bacqueville-medailles.com

This is the kind of boutique worth the trip just for the visit itself, even if you leave empty-handed. Bacqueville is one of the last three stores in France to hold the *droit de frappe*, or right to mint French medals and decorations (such as the Legion of Honor, among others). Since 1790, it has been minting the country's highest honors in the heart of the Palais-Royal—a location central to French history.

N° 1107

N° 1931

N° 1113

N° 1136

ANTOINE

(12)

10 avenue de l'Opéra
M° Pyramides
01 42 96 01 80
antoine1745.com/en/ • @antoine1745

Established in 1745, Antoine has supplied Parisian gentlemen with walking canes and umbrellas in its timeless boutique here since 1885. Alongside the hundreds of luxury canes and brollies, you'll also find hats, gloves, fans, and bowties—all the accoutrements of a dandy! The heritage Scottish umbrellas are my favorites, for a touch of British chic, and for my niece and nephew I like the retro models with wooden handles shaped like rabbits or bears.

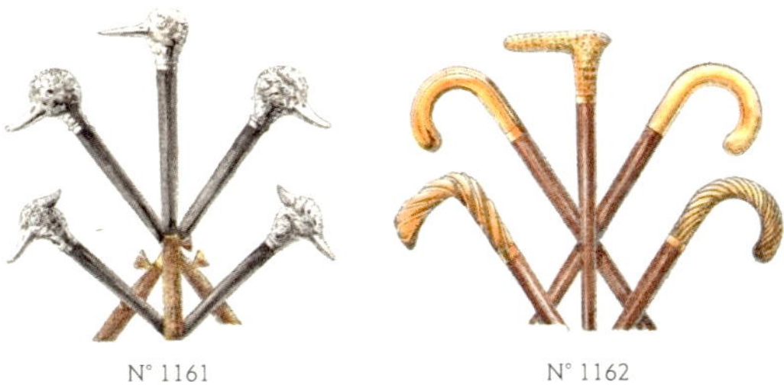

N° 1161 N° 1162

FIFI CHACHNIL

(13)

68 rue Jean-Jacques-Rousseau
M° Les Halles / Étienne Marcel
01 42 21 19 93
fifichachnil.com/en • @maisonfifichachnil

Paris's very own '50s inspired pinup girl, Fifi Chachnil has been sharing her frivolous and fun attitude to life through va-va-voom lingerie and ready-to-wear collections for four decades. Her boutique-atelier, which she opened in 1986, is a veritable boudoir, overflowing with candy pink fabric and lace, and I adore her unique, colorful approach to fashion. She's a fabulous singer, too!

N° 1191

N° 1213

N° 1106

N° 1140 N° 1191

CHEVAUX
MÉCANIQUES

AU

VOITURES
POUR ENFANTS

NAIN BLEU

JOUETS 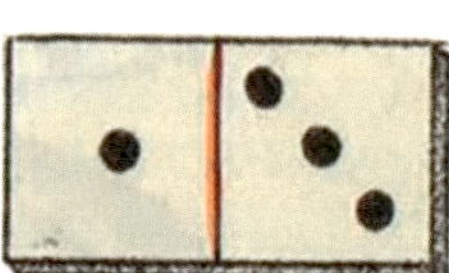 & JEUX

AU 14, RUE SAINT-ROCH - PARIS 1ER

EXPOSITION ET MISE EN VENTE

AU NAIN BLEU

14

14 rue Saint-Roch
M° Tuileries
09 75 89 28 43
aunainbleu.com/gb/ • @aunainbleuofficiel

Au Nain Bleu has been offering customers exceptional plushies and traditional toys since 1836. After several relocations, from boulevard des Capucines to rue Saint-Honoré, the store recently settled on rue Saint-Roch. I come here for genuine old-fashioned teddy bears that I like to give to close friends as baby gifts. These are toys to be kept for a lifetime.

N° 1103

LES DRAPEAUX DE FRANCE – BOUTIQUE NOXA

15

Place Colette
M° Palais-Royal – Musée du Louvre
01 40 20 00 11
lesdrapeauxdefrance.com • @lesdrapeauxdefrance

This is where dreams withstand the test of time. Since 1949, Les Drapeaux de France has been recounting history's biggest moments in miniature. In this store that feels like a cabinet of curiosities, the drawers are filled with more than 300,000 tin figurines of historical characters. From Roman conquests to the Napoleonic Wars, and from the world of the circus to Alice's Wonderland, I love to escape here to be transported across the ages.

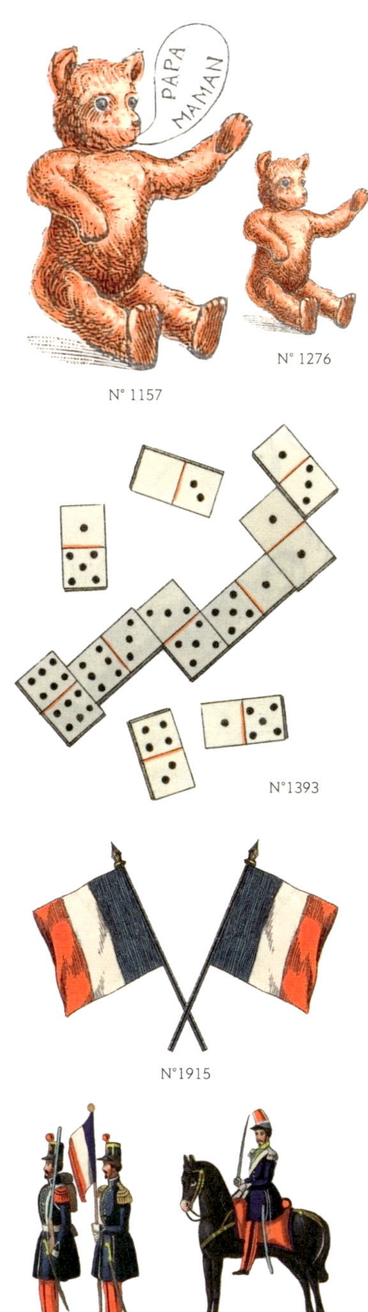

N° 1157

N° 1276

N°1393

N°1915

N° 1866

N° 1816

E. DEHILLERIN

16

18–20 rue Coquillière
M° Les Halles; RER Châtelet – Les Halles
01 42 36 53 13
edehillerin.fr/en/ • @e_dehillerin

One of the last vestiges of the Les Halles market district, this legendary kitchen supply store has hardly changed since it opened back in 1820. Utensils hang from the ceiling, copper pots adorn the walls, and knives are piled high in metal boxes. I come here for the wooden spoons of all sizes, but budding chefs will find everything they need, from rolling pins to piping tips to oyster and snail forks.

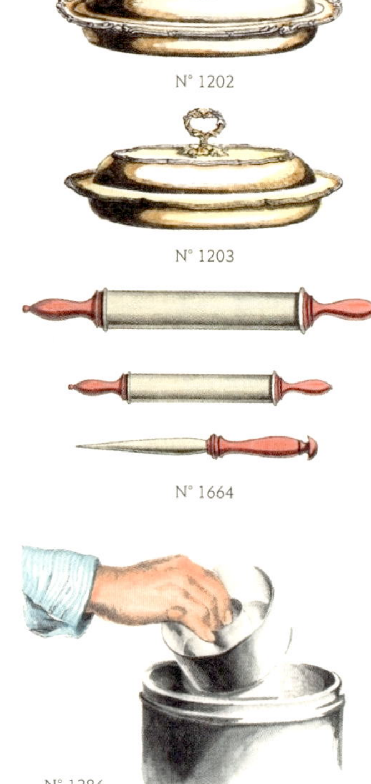

N° 1202

N° 1203

N° 1664

N° 1386

N° 1657

AUROUZE

17

8 rue des Halles
M° Châtelet
01 40 41 16 20
maison-aurouze.fr • @maisonaurouze

N° 1300

Aurouze has been helping Parisians to get rid of pests like rats, cockroaches, and bedbugs since 1872. The exterminator's superb green facade harks back to old-time Paris, but the real curiosities hang in the shop window: stuffed rats of impressive size have been proudly displayed like trophies for over a century. The store is a scamper into the past—and into the movie *Ratatouille*, which featured a storefront inspired by this place.

Eugène Dehillerin
Acier Phénix
Aciers Granits
Hygiène, Économie, Solidité
Acier Granit
Acier Phénix
AUX
ACHETEURS
D'USTENSILES
DE CUISINE
ACHETEZ L'ACIER PHÉNIX
OU LES ACIERS GRANITS
EXCLUSIVEMENT CHEZ
DEHILLERIN
Acier Granit
supérieur
Acier Granit Supérieur
MAGASIN DE VENTE
AU 18-20 RUE COQUILLIÈRE À PARIS 1ER

N° 1482

N° 1483

N° 1484

GALERIE CASANOVA

18

17 galerie Véro-Dodat
M° Palais-Royal – Musée du Louvre
01 42 33 38 93
galerie-casanova.com/en/ • @galeriecasanova

N° 1481

N° 1485

To find this workshop, you'll need to step inside the Véro-Dodat passage—one of my favorite covered passages—which opened in 1826. Beneath its glass roof, time seems to stand still, captured in charming period storefronts and rounded arcades. Entering the gallery is like walking onto a movie set. Number 17 is home to Galerie Casanova, where Jérôme, an expert luthier, repairs, embellishes, and restores guitars and other string instruments from across the ages.

N° 1366

N° 1367

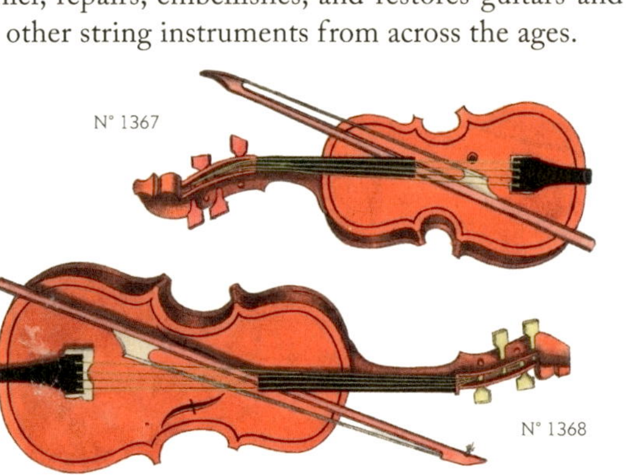

N° 1368

N° 1369

◈ À LA CIVETTE ◈

19

157 rue Saint-Honoré
M° Palais-Royal – Musée du Louvre
01 42 96 04 99
alacivette.com • @alacivette

This tobacco shop has the honor of being the oldest and most respected of its kind in France (and perhaps the world). Founded in 1716 near the Comédie-Française, the boutique has seen countless Parisians and well-known personalities drop by to stock up on high-end tobacco, carefully selected by the founders and the teams who have come in their wake. I come for the elegant Dupont lighters, but also to let myself be swept up in the scent of Havanas, which leaves few unmoved.

N° 1345

◈ LE COMPTOIR DE LA GASTRONOMIE ◈

20

34 rue Montmartre
M° Étienne Marcel; RER Châtelet – Les Halles
01 42 33 31 32
comptoirdelagastronomie.com •
@comptoirdelagastronomie

Le Comptoir de la Gastronomie, established in 1894, exudes the authenticity and charm of 19th-century Les Halles, the belly of Paris. The menu at this gourmet grocery store and its bistro includes French classics such as foie gras, *pâté en croûte*, and *bouchées à la reine*. I love the old-fashioned Parisian ambience here, as well as the products, the wood paneling, and the shop windows that recall a bygone era.

N° 1178

N° 1452

N° 1103

N° 1129

N° 1157

N° 1112

N° 1604

N° 1320

N° 1330

N° 1447

N° 1285

N° 1226

N° 1273

N° 1988

N° 1807

N° 1323

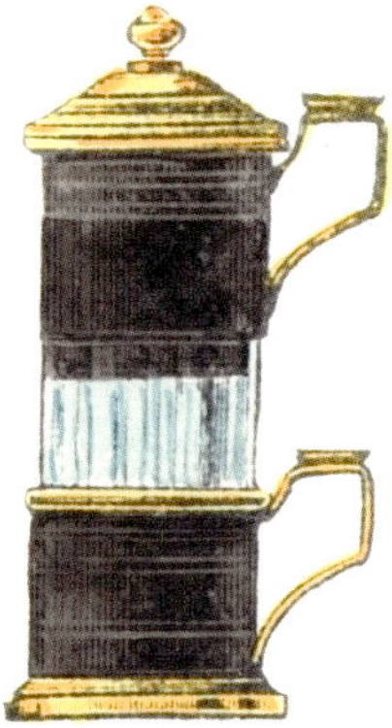

N° 1265

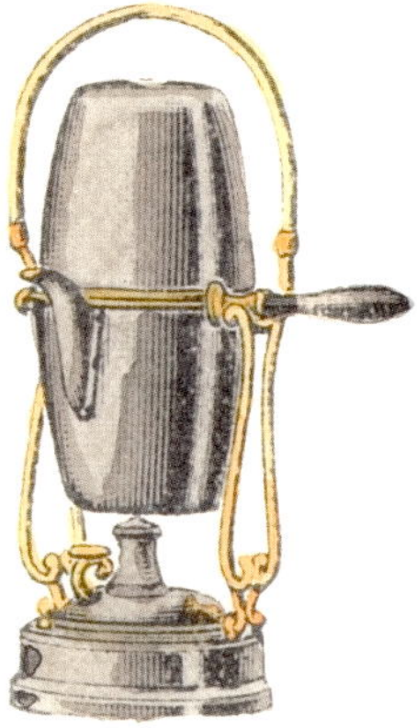

N° 1237

◈ ANGELINA ◈

21

226 rue de Rivoli
M° Tuileries
01 42 60 82 00
angelina-paris.fr • @angelina_paris

A mecca for gourmands since 1903, Angelina belongs to that select circle of must-visit addresses that are popular with both Parisians and tourists. Like everyone else, I come here for the thick, velvety old-fashioned hot chocolate and the iconic Mont-Blanc pastry—a perfect combination of meringue, airy whipped cream, and chestnut-cream vermicelli.

◈ VERLET ◈

22

256 rue Saint-Honoré
M° Pyramides
01 42 60 67 39
verlet.fr • @verletparis

At Verlet, the inviting scent of sweet treats wafts out onto the sidewalk, stopping passersby in mid-step. Inside, the fragrances of more than 35 kinds of coffee tempt the nose, along with some 50 teas, cookies, speculaas, and candied fruit. Here, visitors take a step back in time, as the place has hardly changed since Auguste Woehrlé opened it in 1880.

DEPUIS 1880

VERLET

COMPTOIR DE CAFÉS ET DE THÉS, D'ÉPICES
ET DE FRUITS CONFITS CHOISIS

NOTRE BOUTIQUE ET SALON DE THÉ

AU 256 RUE SAINT-HONORÉ

À PARIS (PROCHE DU LOUVRE)

Tous les chemins mènent

Au Pied de Cochon

Ouvert jour et nuit

HALLES CENTRALES DE PARIS ENTRE
LA BOURSE DU COMMERCE ET SAINT-EUSTACHE

6 rue Coquillière à Paris

◈ AU PIED DE COCHON ◈

23

6 rue Coquillière
M° Les Halles; RER Châtelet – Les Halles
01 40 13 77 00
pieddecochon.com/en/ • @pieddecochon

From 8 a.m. to 5 a.m., Au Pied de Cochon serves classic French cuisine, and has been doing so since 1947. And if you aren't sure what the house specialty is, the name should give you a clue (*cochon* means "pig" in French). I like coming here late at night after a party, when my stomach is easy to please. I usually get *escargots*, onion soup, or rib steak with Béarnaise sauce, which I just love eating amid the quintessential Paris decor.

N° 1340 N° 1378

◈ LE PETIT BOUILLON PHARAMOND ◈

24

24 rue de la Grande-Truanderie
M° Étienne Marcel
01 40 28 45 18
petitbouillonpharamond.com •
@lepetitbouillonpharamond

Since 1832, the Maison Pharamond has been serving traditional Normandy dishes to enthusiastic Parisians. Proudly declaring its origins across its half-timbered facade—"À la Petite Normande"—the restaurant here was opened in 1879; redecorated in art nouveau style for the 1900 Exposition Universelle, it has retained its unique Belle Époque decor full of stained glass and wood paneling. I come for the *œuf mayo*, *jambon purée*, and Normandy specialty *tripes à la mode de Caen*.

N° 1300
N° 1301
N° 1302
N° 1303
N° 1304
N° 1305
N° 1306
N° 1307
N° 1308

N° 1180

N° 1181

BAR DE L'ENTRACTE

25

47 rue de Montpensier
M° Pyramides
01 42 97 57 76

N° 1233

N° 1236

When I was studying art history near the Palais-Royal, I often came to this postage-stamp-sized bar for a drink or to share a charcuterie board amid the slightly antiquated decor, surrounded by actors from the theater next door. And for good reason: this place prides itself on being the oldest bar in Paris. Created in 1614, it was originally called La Pissote, because all the coach drivers in Paris came here for a rest and to relieve themselves before heading back to work.

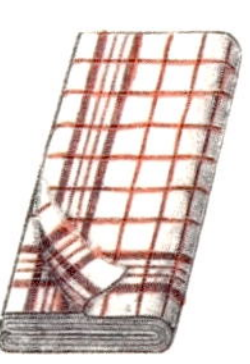

N° 1243

N° 1244

N° 1109

N° 1216

N° 1217

N° 1110

N° 1719

N° 1720

AU PETIT BAR

7 rue du Mont-Thabor
M° Tuileries
01 42 60 62 09

This "little bar" is a veritable relic of a bygone age—no credit cards accepted or Wi-Fi access here. Jean and Marie have been at the helm of this cozy bistro since 1966, and today their two sons have joined the family business. For as long as anyone can remember, it's been serving the same simple weekly menu. I often pop in to grab a freshly prepared *jambon-beurre* sandwich standing at the original Formica counter.

BAR HEMINGWAY – RITZ PARIS

38 rue Cambon
M° Madeleine
01 43 16 33 74
ritzparis.com/hotel/paris/bars-restaurants/bar-hemingway

Opened in 1898, this plush intimate cocktail bar tucked away at the back of the Ritz is a temple to the great writer—and drinker!—Ernest Hemingway, who made it his HQ before the war. Legend has it he even helped liberate the place from the Nazis. Today, the "feast" continues, as patrons lounge on upholstered leather chairs, sipping an iconic Serendipity—which was invented right here—and other signature or bespoke cocktails.

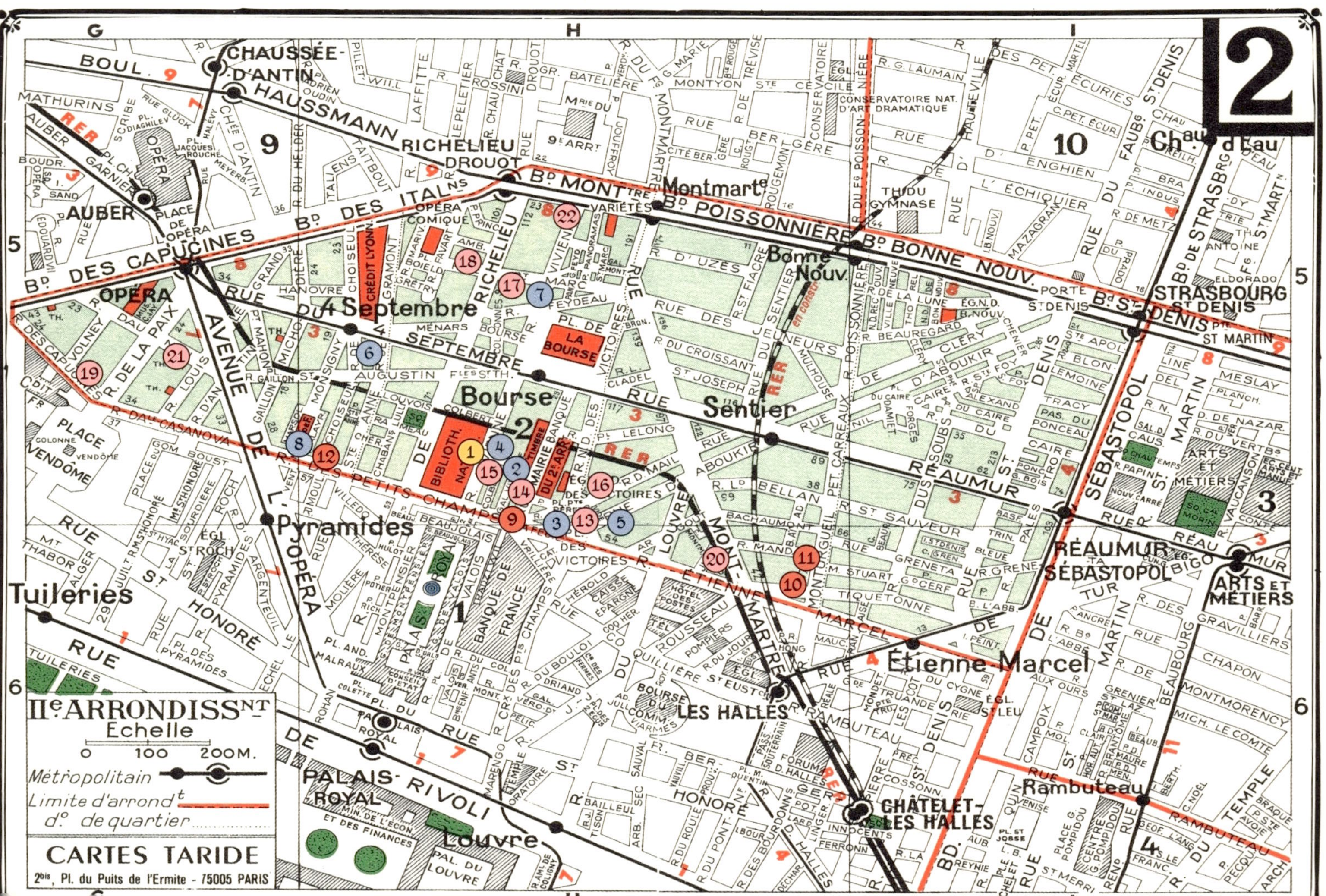

2
IIe ARRONDISSnt
Echelle
0 100 200M.
Métropolitain
Limite d'arrondt
do de quartier
CARTES TARIDE
2bis, Pl. du Puits de l'Ermite - 75005 PARIS
Bourse
Sentier
4 Septembre
Opéra
Pyramides
Tuileries
Louvre
Palais Royal
Étienne Marcel
Les Halles
Châtelet-Les Halles
Réaumur Sébastopol
Arts et Métiers
Strasbourg St Denis
Bonne Nouv.
Montmartre
Richelieu Drouot
Chaussée-d'Antin
Auber
Rambuteau
Ch. d'Eau
Biblioth. Nat.
La Bourse
Crédit Lyon.
Mairie du 2e Arr.
Banque de France
Bd des Capucines
Bd des Italns
Bd Montmartre
Bd Poissonnière
Bd Bonne Nouv.
Bd St Denis
Bd de Strasbourg
Bd Sébastopol
Boul. Haussmann
Avenue de l'Opéra
Rue du 4 Septembre
Rue Réaumur
Rue de Rivoli
Rue St Honoré
Rue Montmartre
Rue Étienne Marcel
Rue Rambuteau
Rue de la Paix
Rue Richelieu
Place Vendôme
G
H
I
5
6

2E ARRONDISSEMENT

1. Bibliothèque Nationale de France – Richelieu
58 rue de Richelieu & 5 rue Vivienne
2. Librairie Jousseaume
45–46–47 galerie Vivienne
3. Au Cœur Immaculé de Marie – Librairie Catholique
8 rue des Petits-Pères
4. Galerie Athanase / Gribaudo Vandamme
6 rue Vivienne
5. Design et Nature
4 rue d'Aboukir
6. Ultramod
3 & 4 rue de Choiseul
7. Armurerie de la Bourse
37 rue Vivienne
8. Courty & Fils
44 rue des Petits-Champs
9. Legrand Filles et Fils
1 rue de la Banque
10. G. Detou
58 rue Tiquetonne
11. Stohrer
51 rue Montorgueil
12. Tetrel
44 rue des Petits-Champs
13. Boulangerie Pâtisserie Victoires & Bar du Moulin
10 place des Petits-Pères
14. Le Bougainville
5 rue de la Banque
15. Le Grand Colbert
2 rue Vivienne
16. Chez Georges
1 rue du Mail
17. Le Gavroche
19 rue Saint-Marc
18. Aux Lyonnais
32 rue Saint-Marc
19. Le Petit Vendôme
8 rue des Capucines
20. Brasserie Le Tambour
41 rue Montmartre
21. Harry's Bar
5 rue Daunou
22. Chez Carmen
53 rue Vivienne

◈ BIBLIOTHÈQUE NATIONALE DE FRANCE – RICHELIEU ◈

58 rue de Richelieu & 5 rue Vivienne
M° Bourse / Quatre-Septembre
01 53 79 59 59
bnf.fr/en/richelieu • @labnf

Opened in 1691, this gorgeous library houses a dazzling collection including the manuscript of *Les Misérables*. I search for old documents here to illustrate my books with Flammarion. The majestic Salle Ovale, basked in golden light and hushed silence, is open to the public. The striking Salle Labrouste—the library of the Institut National d'Histoire de l'Art—is for members only, but visitors can (must!) peek inside to see its nine magnificent cupolas and painted murals—can you spot the hidden monkey to the left of the entrance?

N° 2903

N° 2606

N° 2607

N° 2608

◈ LIBRAIRIE JOUSSEAUME ◈

(2)

45-46-47 galerie Vivienne
M° Bourse
01 42 96 06 24
librairiejousseaume.fr • @librairie_jousseaume

With its antique black lacquered facade, arched windows, and original mosaic tiled floor, this secondhand bookshop—located inside the enchanting galerie Vivienne—is steeped in history. Acquired by current owner Francois Jousseaume's great-grandfather, a passionate bibliophile, in 1890, it has remained a cultural landmark on the Right Bank, proposing thousands of used books, both ancient and more recent.

N° 2125

N° 2303

◈ AU CŒUR IMMACULÉ DE MARIE – LIBRAIRIE CATHOLIQUE ◈

3

8 rue des Petits-Pères
M° Bourse
01 42 60 97 87
aucoeurimmaculedemarie.site-solocal.com •
@aucoeurimmacule

Located on the small square across from the basilica of Notre-Dame-des-Victoires, this bookshop is where I come for all things spiritual. Featuring its original burgundy storefront, it has been offering visitors a variety of catholic books for all ages since 1850, as well as a whole array of religious objects. A comforting address to soothe your ills and lift your soul.

N° 2289 N° 2281 N° 2283

◈ GALERIE ATHANASE / GRIBAUDO VANDAMME ◈

4

6 rue Vivienne
M° Bourse
07 44 89 57 32
@athanase_vivienne

As an avid collector of old globes and maps, this boutique created in the late 1980s is an absolute treasure trove for me. Vintage engravings are organized by category in wooden cases up to the ceiling, while posters and ancient maps are carefully arranged in marbled portfolios. The glass floor provides the ultimate vitrine for antique books, maps, and globes showcased below visitors' feet. Look out for the winged pigs in the store window!

N° 2779 N° 2208

N° 2851 N° 2379

N° 2583

N° 2283

DESIGN ET NATURE

5

4 rue d'Aboukir
M° Bourse
01 43 06 86 98
designetnature.fr • @design_et_nature

I've always loved collecting taxidermy animals for my curiosity cabinets; a preserved flamingo or parrot inspire and transport me to distant worlds when I'm working in my atelier. Taxidermy specialist Anne Orlowska creates magnificent panoramas of the animal, plant, and mineral kingdoms—respecting all CITES regulations protecting endangered species—and her expertly curated window displays are well worth a detour.

◆ ULTRAMOD ◆

6

3 & 4 rue de Choiseul
M° Quatre-Septembre
01 42 96 98 30
ultramod.fr • @ultramodmerceriepari s

Cross the threshold of Ultramod and step into a chapter of fashion history. Established in the 19th century in the heart of the milliners' district, the shop sold all kinds of ribbons, felt, and other hat making supplies. Today, this notions shop bursting with vintage and heritage pieces is a delight to behold and an indispensable address for those in search of quality sewing materials.

◆ ARMURERIE DE LA BOURSE ◆

7

37 rue Vivienne
M° Bourse / Grands Boulevards
01 42 36 79 83
armureriedelabourse.com

Don't be put off by the storefront! Created in 1870 by the famous armorer Auguste Lefaucheux, the Armurerie de la Bourse is packed with hidden treasures. I come here exclusively for clothes and accessories of exceptional quality. I particularly recommend the toasty warm hunting socks for winter, as well as my ultimate favorite: the very chic English cartridge bag by Antique Sauvage.

◈ COURTY & FILS ◈

8

44 rue des Petits-Champs
M° Pyramides / Quatre-Septembre
01 42 96 59 21
couteaux-courty.com/en/

Founded in 1875, this boutique—one of the oldest in Paris—was renamed by the Courty family in the 1950s and has been synonymous with quality knives ever since. With 500 articles in its catalog, it's as much a museum as a store. The antique windows and displays are stacked with military and hunting knives, colorful Opinel kitchen knives, or Auvergne shepherd's knives, as well as classic and one-off models.

N° 2381

◈ LEGRAND FILLES ET FILS ◈

1 rue de la Banque
M° Bourse / Pyramides
01 42 60 07 12
caves-legrand.com • @caveslegrandparis

The Maison Legrand has been dedicated to fine wine for six generations, since 1880. Following World War II, pioneering wine merchant Lucien Legrand began to select his wines directly from winegrowers to sell in this stylish boutique in the Passage Vivienne, and today it proposes almost 10,000 references. You can also enjoy a meal from the elegant seasonal menu, surrounded by hundreds of bottles—the beef wellington is superb.

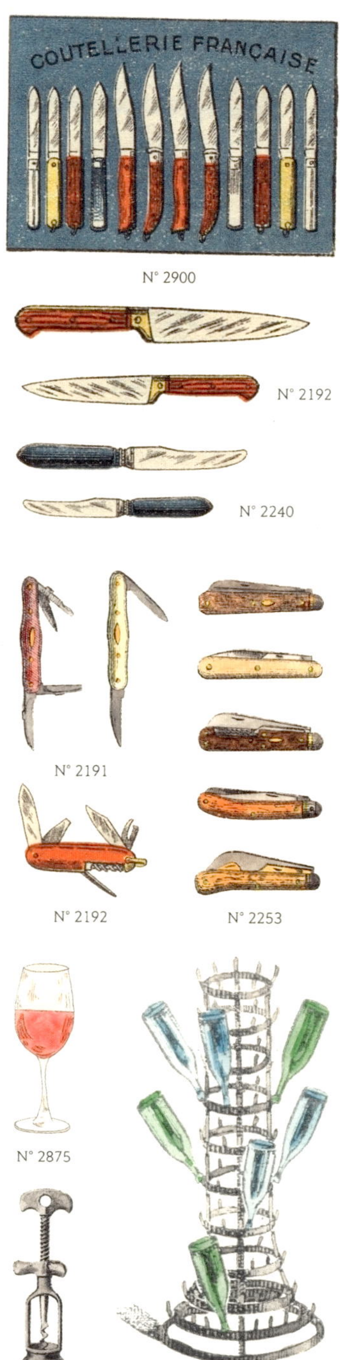

N° 2900

N° 2192

N° 2240

N° 2191

N° 2192

N° 2253

N° 2875

N° 2566

N° 2266

G. DETOU

10

58 rue Tiquetonne
M° Étienne Marcel / Les Halles
01 42 36 54 67
@epiceriegdetou

A gourmet destination for food lovers and chefs since 1951. It supplies hard-to-find baking ingredients: praline to add crunch to gâteaux, egg white powder to make light and airy macarons, or tonka beans to give crème brulées a flavorsome twist. And for those with an oven phobia, there's a gourmet grocery stocked with French specialties like Pommery mustard, La Belle-Iloise sardines, and Sabaton candied chestnuts.

N° 2271 N° 2374 N° 2345 N° 2344 N° 2673 N° 2588 N° 2459 N° 2221 N° 2124 N° 2306 N° 2461 N° 2143 N° 2169 N° 2224 N° 2313 N° 2333 N° 2259

STOHRER

11

51 rue Montorgueil
M° Étienne Marcel / Sentier
01 42 33 38 20
stohrer.fr • @stohrer

This institution on rue Montorgueil, established in 1730 by Louis XV's former pastry chef, Nicolas Stohrer, has attracted Parisians for centuries thanks to the pâtissier's most famous invention—the baba au rhum! The oldest pastry shop in Paris, it features a beautiful historically listed decor from 1864, and although the baba is the star, you'll find exquisite versions of all the French classic desserts.

N° 2319

N° 2347

N° 2346

N° 2348

N° 2349

N° 2357

N° 2750

N° 2665

N° 2666

N° 2715

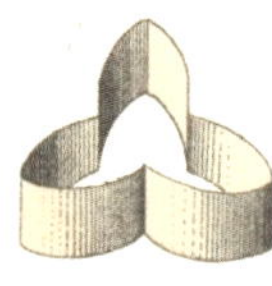

N° 2716

N° 2717

TETREL

12

44 rue des Petits-Champs
M° Pyramides / Quatre-Septembre
01 42 96 59 58

Founded a century ago by the owner's grandparents, this candy/gourmet grocery/wine shop has retained all of its charm, including its art deco store front and interior. Shelves and vitrines display a mouth-watering panorama of traditional confectionery from around France: Montélimar nougat, pralines from Montargis, calissons from Aix, and more. And for those with less of a sweet tooth, there are plenty of wines and other gourmet products to enjoy.

N° 2262

N° 2525

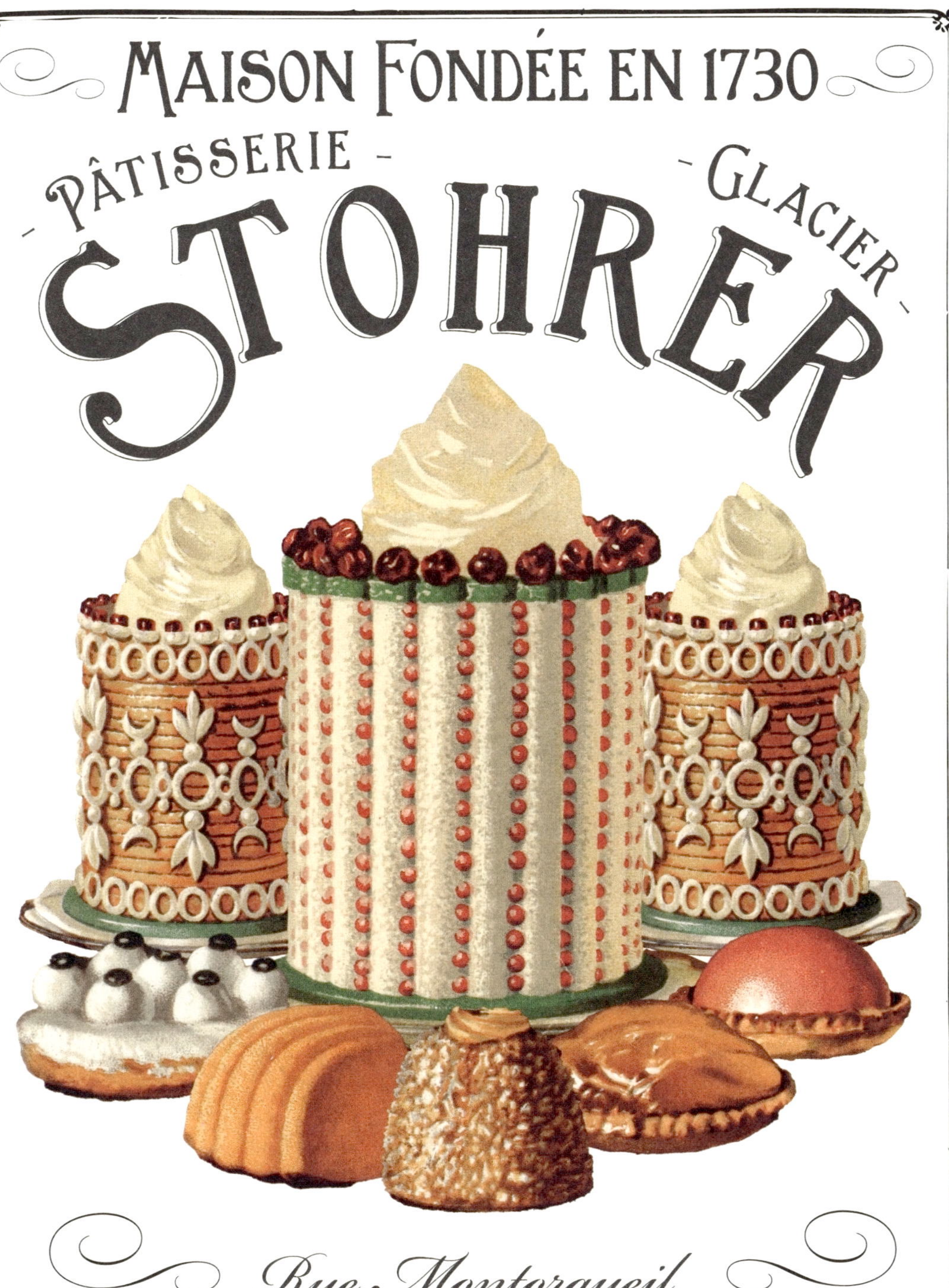
Maison Fondée en 1730
- Pâtisserie -
Stohrer
- Glacier -
Rue Montorgueil,
au pied de Saint-Eustache, à Paris

BOULANGERIE PÂTISSERIE VICTOIRES & BAR DU MOULIN

13

10 place des Petits-Pères
M° Bourse
09 53 11 23 90

On place des Petits-Pères, you could be forgiven for thinking that you've been transported to a small Tuscan village. The charming little church is the very soul of the place, but there's also this neighborhood café just opposite, where you can sit and admire the view. I come here at lunchtime for a savory tartine on the terrace. Next door is the bakery, a listed historic monument that is as pretty as its mouthwatering pastries, especially the delicious *viennoiseries*.

N° 2578 N° 2723 N° 2692 N° 2865

LE BOUGAINVILLE

14

5 rue de la Banque
M° Bourse
01 42 60 05 19
bougainville-restaurant.fr • @lebougainville

Located in the galerie Vivienne, this authentic bistro was opened in 1962. Formica tables and bar, red faux-leather banquettes, a mosaic tiled floor—everything has been preserved to take diners back in time to the 1960s. The menu, too, is reminiscent of a past era, featuring homemade French classics that ensure a full house at lunchtimes. But don't despair if you can't get a table right away—the place is open all day, every day!

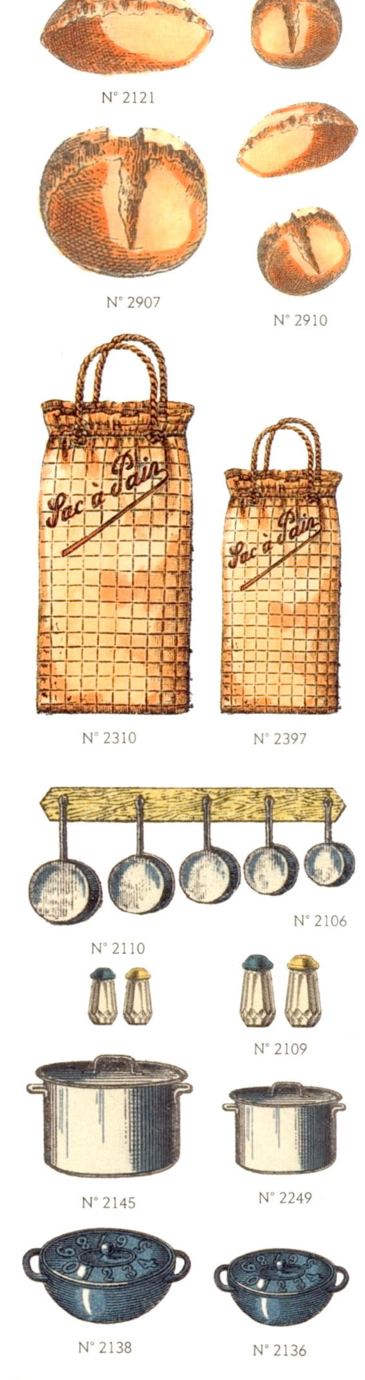

N° 2121 N° 2907 N° 2910 N° 2310 N° 2397 N° 2106 N° 2110 N° 2109 N° 2145 N° 2249 N° 2138 N° 2136

N° 2656

N° 2584

◈ LE GRAND COLBERT ◈

2 rue Vivienne
M° Bourse / Pyramides
01 42 86 87 88
legrandcolbert.fr/en/ • @legrandcolbert

Established in 1900, this iconic Parisian brasserie was restored to its original splendor in 1985, along with the galerie Colbert. Its elegant decor—complete with pristine white tablecloths, shiny brass lamps, gilded mirrors, black leather banquettes, and luxuriant palm trees—transports you back to the Belle Époque. I like to order the famous roast chicken, or else the sole meunière, and I just can't resist the baked Alaska for dessert.

N° 2432 N° 2463 N° 2428

N° 2656

N° 2687

◈ CHEZ GEORGES ◈

1 rue du Mail
M° Bourse
01 42 60 07 11
@chezgeorgesruedumail

This archetypal French bistro has been serving traditional French cuisine since 1964: house-made *jambon persillé*, celery root remoulade, and the famous Pavé du Mail pepper steak are just a few of the classic dishes on the menu handwritten in colorful ink. I come here for the inimitable atmosphere, as aproned waitresses work the two old-fashioned yet elegant dining rooms, taking diners back to the good old days of the 1950s and '60s.

N° 2707 N° 2534 N° 2584

◈ LE GAVROCHE ◈

17

19 rue Saint-Marc
M° Bourse / Grands Boulevards
01 42 96 89 70
@legavroche75002

This pint-sized bistro, with its Zolaesque atmosphere, has been humming to the music of tinkling glasses and clinking plates since 1924. It was one of my haunts when I was studying art history: steak tartare, packed tables, and lively discussions filled our evenings here. Open until 2 a.m., this merry watering hole is perfect for that notorious "last" drink—which it rarely is.

◈ AUX LYONNAIS ◈

18

32 rue Saint-Marc
M° Richelieu – Drouot
01 42 96 65 04
auxlyonnais.com • @aux_lyonnais

This legendary *bouchon* restaurant, founded in 1890, is a veritable temple to authentic Lyon-style cuisine, in the heart of Paris. Diners come from far and wide to sample fresh and modern interpretations of the great Lyon classics, from pike quenelles or *pâté en croûte* to pink praline tart. I especially love the vintage decor, with its pretty moldings and floral friezes in faience.

N° 2190

N° 2174

◈ LE PETIT VENDÔME ◈

19

8 rue des Capucines
M° Opéra / Madeleine
01 42 61 05 88
lepetitvendome.fr/en •
@le_petit_vendome

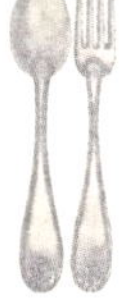

N° 2175

N° 2194

N° 2191

N° 2195

Since 1958, friends, locals, and coworkers have flocked to this tiny bistro for its generous, unpretentious menu of authentic French dishes, including *œufs mayonnaise*, onion soup, and pigs' trotters in cider vinaigrette. Also popular are the on-demand sandwiches made with cheese and charcuterie from the Auvergne region—ideal for a quick bite on the go.

N° 2192

N° 2196

N° 2193

N° 2197

N° 2450

N° 2291

N° 2289

N° 2349

N° 2209

BRASSERIE LE TAMBOUR

20

41 rue Montmartre
M° Sentier / Étienne Marcel
01 42 33 06 90
brasserieletambour.fr • @brasserieletambour

Since the 1970s, this restaurant has been the HQ for partygoers in the area because it serves food until the wee hours of the morning. The establishment recently changed hands but continues to offer generous French dishes and good wine. The welcoming atmosphere makes this brasserie a neighborhood favorite.

N° 2358

N° 2357

HARRY'S BAR

21

5 rue Daunou
M° Quatre-Septembre / Opéra
01 42 61 71 14
harrysbar.com • @harrysbar_theoriginal

A popular haunt for American expats since 1911, this renowned cocktail bar—which claims to have invented the Bloody Mary, Side Car, and Blue Lagoon—was brought over from 7th Avenue in New Yok and reconstructed here in Paris, in the run up to Prohibition. Today, patrons like nothing better than pulling up a stool at the old mahogany bar and enjoying one of the 400 cocktails or 350 whiskys on offer, served by white jacketed barmen.

CHEZ CARMEN

22

53 rue Vivienne
M° Grands Boulevards / Richelieu – Drouot
01 42 36 45 41

This is where I come to keep the party going after a night out at a club. Night owls shimmy on the dancefloor of this micro-bar on the Grands Boulevards as an old jukebox blares Claude François's hits until closing time—at noon. After decades of wild nights, Carmen, who opened the bar in 1982, still plays host to the most party-loving Parisians.

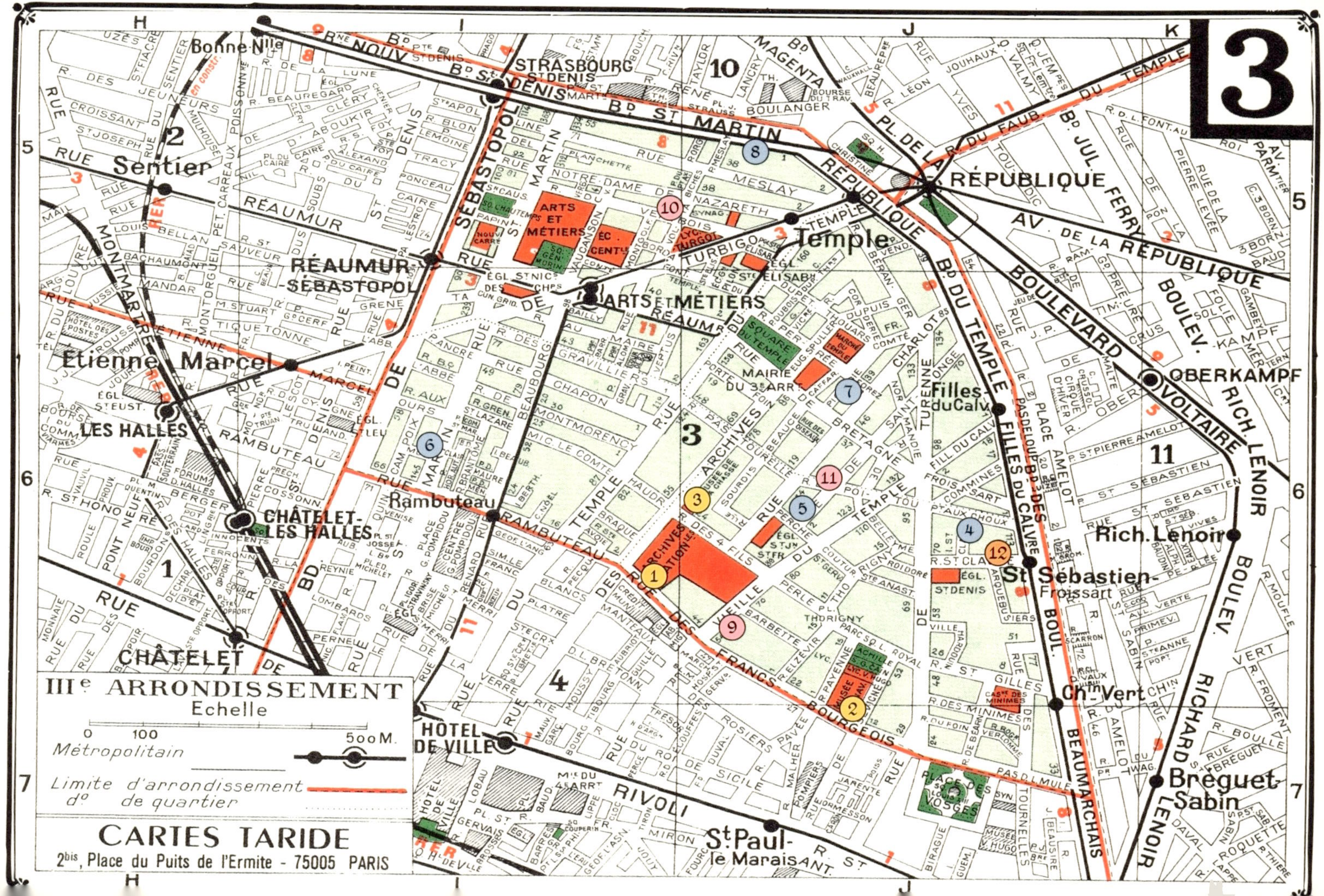
3
IIIe ARRONDISSEMENT
Echelle
0 100 500 M.
Métropolitain
Limite d'arrondissement
do de quartier
CARTES TARIDE
2bis, Place du Puits de l'Ermite - 75005 PARIS
Sentier
Réaumur-Sébastopol
Etienne Marcel
Les Halles
Châtelet-Les Halles
Châtelet
Strasbourg St Denis
Bonne Nlle
Arts et Métiers
Temple
République
Oberkampf
Filles du Calv.
Rambuteau
Hôtel de Ville
St Paul-le Marais
St Sébastien-Froissart
Rich. Lenoir
Ch.in Vert
Bréguet-Sabin
Bd St Martin
Bd du Temple
Boulevard Voltaire
Boulev. Richard Lenoir
Beaumarchais
Rivoli
Sébastopol
Réaumur
Archives
Turbigo
Rue du Temple
Bretagne
Boulev. Rich. Lenoir
Av. de la République
Rue des Francs Bourgeois
Square du Temple
Mairie du 3e arrt
Archives nationales
Arts et Métiers
Place des Vosges

3[E] ARRONDISSEMENT

1. Archives Nationales
60 rue des Francs-Bourgeois
2. Musée Carnavalet
23 rue Madame-de-Sévigné
3. Musée de la Chasse et de la Nature
62 rue des Archives
4. Tartaix
13 rue du Pont-aux-Choux
5. Artmetal Framex
3 rue de Saintonge
6. L'Écritoire
26 passage Molière
7. Rêve de Gosse
18 rue de Picardie
8. Au Clown de la République
11 boulevard Saint-Martin
9. Robert et Louise
64 rue Vieille-du-Temple
10. Chez l'Ami Louis
32 rue du Vertbois
11. Chez Nénesse
17 rue de Saintonge
12. Alain Maître Barbier
8 rue Saint-Claude

ARCHIVES NATIONALES

1

60 rue des Francs-Bourgeois
M° Rambuteau
01 75 47 20 02
archives-nationales.culture.gouv.fr • @archivesnatfr

If Hogwarts were in Paris, it would probably be housed here, among the soaring bookshelves steeped in the scent of wood polish. Visiting France's national archives is like climbing inside a time machine to experience history alongside the Knights Templar and François I. Ease back into the present with a stroll through the small garden hidden within the archive's outer walls, far from the busy streets of the Marais district.

N° 3331

N° 3422

N° 3168

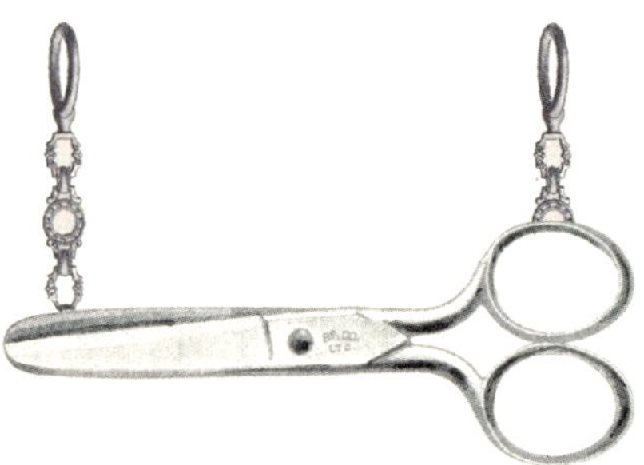

N° 3151

MUSÉE CARNAVALET

2

23 rue Madame-de-Sévigné
M° Saint-Paul / Chemin Vert
01 44 59 58 58
carnavalet.paris.fr/en • @museecarnavalet

This museum is well worth a visit, especially for the gallery displaying signs from defunct Parisian stores. Wrought-iron lettering and painted wood panels evoke a bygone era in the capital. It was here that I had the idea for the sign on my own boutique, inspired by those of a knife-grinder and a wine merchant. Recover your spirits after this jaunt through time with a *goûter* in the marvelous hidden garden.

N° 3309

N° 3374

MUSÉE DE LA CHASSE ET DE LA NATURE

3

62 rue des Archives
M° Rambuteau
01 53 01 92 40
chassenature.org/en • @museechassenature

I've always loved this museum dedicated to the relationship between humans and nature. With a cabinet of curiosity feel, it has staged taxidermy animals since 1967, alongside artworks from all periods, in 17th- and 18th-century-style decors. A fox sleeps peacefully on a Louis XIII chair, a 10-foot (3-m) polar bear stands guard, and the owl installation by Jan Fabre (my favorite) mesmerizes visitors. Try and spot the hidden mouse painted on a baseboard!

TARTAIX

4

13 rue du Pont-aux-Choux
M° Saint-Sébastien – Froissart
01 42 72 02 63
tartaix.com • @tartaixmetaux

This century-old company knows how to handle any metal of any length for any project. Surrounded by cubbyhole cabinets that have hardly changed since 1919, when the store opened, the team of expert metalsmiths cut, pierce, coil, mill, and weld various metals according to clients' wishes. I bring tubes of brass here to be cut into curtain rods. A precious craft skill in the heart of Paris.

N° 3182

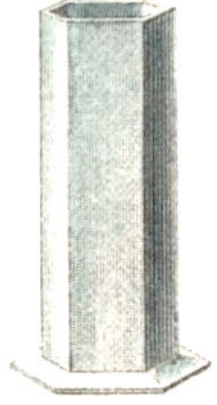

N° 3257

N° 3232

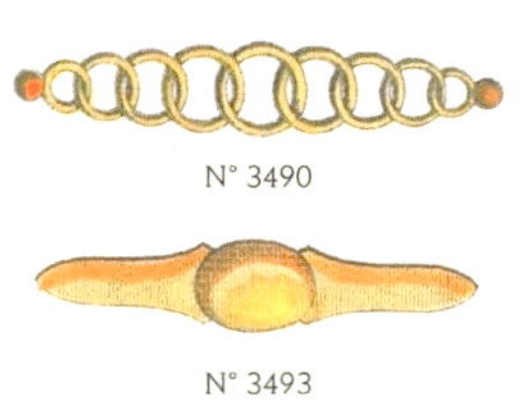

N° 3490

N° 3491

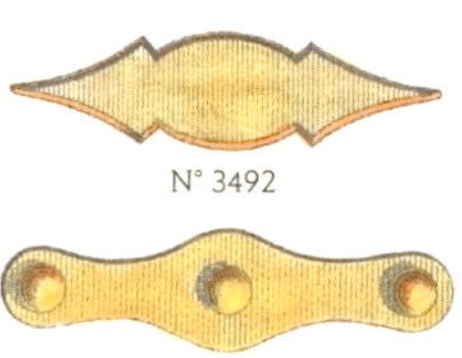

N° 3492

N° 3493

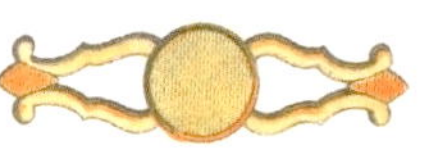

N° 3494

N° 3495

N° 3496

N° 3497

N° 3498

ARTMETAL FRAMEX

5

3 rue de Saintonge
M° Saint-Sébastien – Froissart / Rambuteau
01 42 72 14 11
artmetal-framex.com/en/ • @artmetal_framex_paris

This family-owned company has been specializing in metal stamping since 1840, and, more recently, in buttons. Tucked away in the Marais, under an elegant glass ceiling, it proposes more than 120,000 stamps—one of the largest collections in the world—in all shapes and sizes. I can spend hours here, alongside jewelry, fashion, and costume designers, leafing through the store's catalogs that show the patina of age.

N° 3695

N° 3694

N° 3210

N° 3222

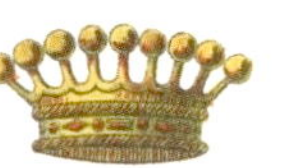

N° 3211

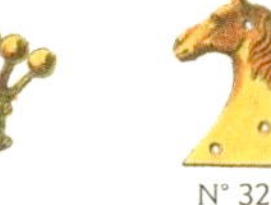

N° 3223

N° 3212

N° 3224

N° 3087

N° 3459

L'ÉCRITOIRE

6

26 passage Molière
M° Rambuteau
01 42 78 01 18
lecritoireparis.com/en/ • @lecritoireparis

N° 3605

I come here for red wax, seals, and beautiful writing paper, and I especially like their collection of Eiffel Tower-shaped pewter bookmarks. In 1975, Sofie created this temple of *belles lettres* for all those who love writing. In 2022, the shop moved to passage Molière, taking its ink-stained counter along with it—an enduring record of the stationer's history.

N° 3606

N° 3689

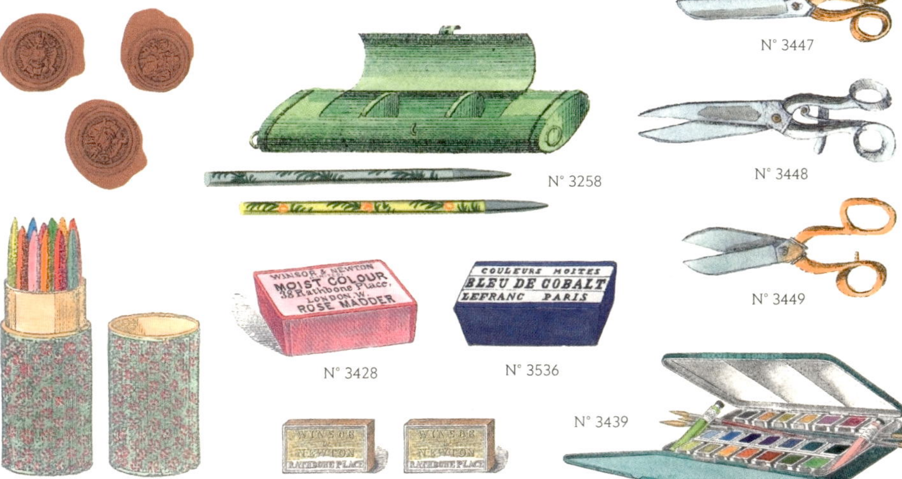

N° 3447

N° 3258

N° 3448

N° 3449

N° 3428

N° 3536

N° 3439

N° 3618

N° 3922

◈ RÊVE DE GOSSE ◈

7

18 rue de Picardie
M° Filles du Calvaire
06 63 75 07 73
@revedegosse

"Cloth poet" Emmanuel, owner of this vintage clothing store, tells stories through garments: maybe patching and painting on a 1930s suit, or lining old work jackets with recycled fur. Emmanuel took over the boutique from Daniel Saadetian—a distinguished tailor who continued the business his father established in 1926—and inherited a store imbued with history and ancestral savoir faire, which he strives to uphold.

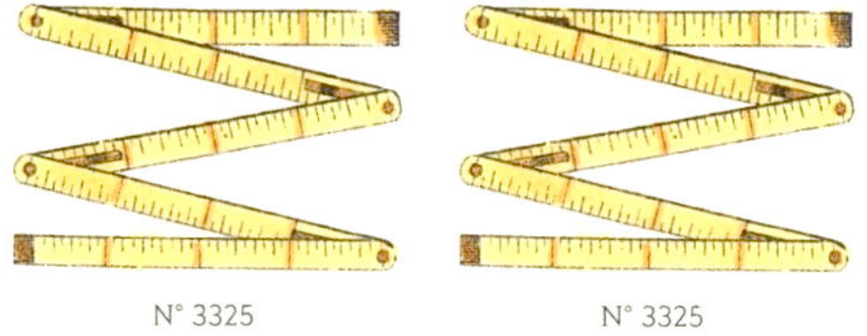

N° 3325 N° 3325

◈ AU CLOWN DE LA RÉPUBLIQUE ◈

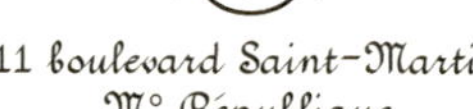

8

11 boulevard Saint-Martin
M° République
01 42 72 73 73
aumondedelafete.fr/en • @auclowndelarepublique

This store has been costume central for more than 50 years. I've known about it forever, and no matter what theme I have in mind, I'm certain to find the perfect outfit in this extensive dress-up trunk. You can buy or rent costumes here, but I come mainly to unearth some outlandish accessory or for decorative elements. If you go the day before Halloween, plan to take your time—you'll be there along with half the neighborhood.

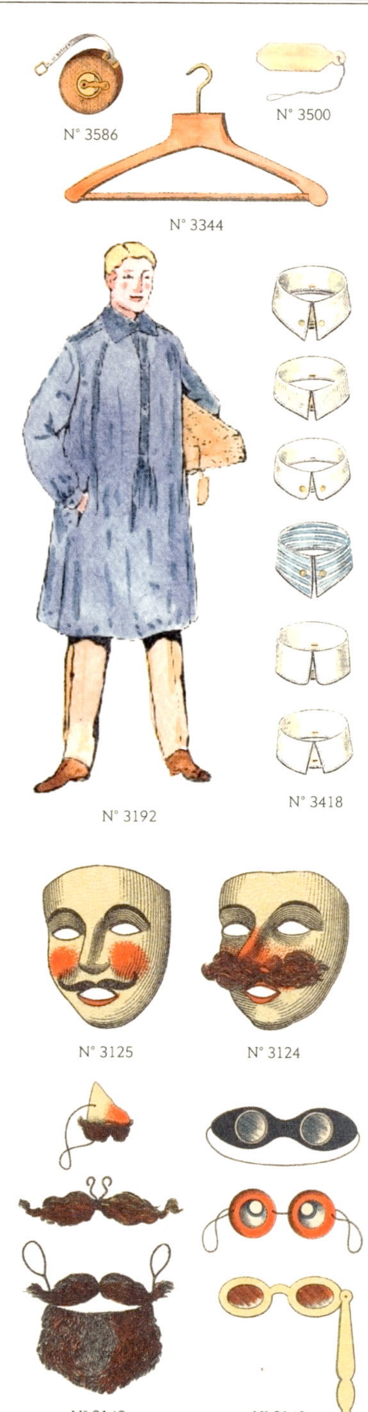

N° 3586 N° 3500 N° 3344 N° 3192 N° 3418 N° 3125 N° 3124 N° 3149 N° 3140

ROBERT ET LOUISE

9

64 rue Vieille-du-Temple
M° Rambuteau / Saint-Paul
01 42 78 55 89
robertetlouise.com/en/

The crackling fire; the old-fashioned wooden tables shared with strangers; the bottle of red wine that brings everyone together—Robert et Louise has offered refuge from the frenzy of the Marais since 1958. It also invites you to reconnect with your carnivorous side. I especially enjoy the entrecôte steak cooked over a wood fire, as well as the impressive cheese selection.

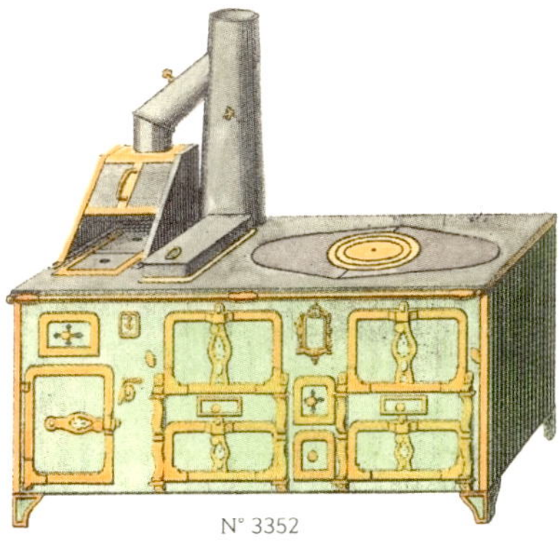

N° 3352

CHEZ L'AMI LOUIS

10

32 rue du Vertbois
M° Arts et Métiers
01 48 87 77 48
@ami_louis_restaurant_

This veritable institution, complete with copper pots, rotisserie, and range cooker, was founded in 1924 by Antoine Magnin, with his signature red scarf. The chef has changed, but the menu and the setting remain the same at heart. I'm partial to the frog legs, the duck confit, and the mountain of shoestring fries. Brad Pitt, Catherine Deneuve, and Bill Clinton have all dined here.

N° 3228

N° 3749

N° 3255

N° 3107

N° 3345

N° 3199

CHEZ NÉNESSE

17 rue de Saintonge
M° Filles du Calvaire / Saint-Sébastien – Froissart
01 42 78 46 49
@cheznenesse

I've been coming to this old bistro ever since I moved to Paris. Established in 1960, it's one of the rare places in the Marais that's never changed, remaining true to its '50s–'60s village spirit, with red checkered tablecloths, home-style cuisine, and an old wood-burning stove right in the center of the dining room. Everything on the chalkboard menu is fresh and prepared to order; I like to come on Thursdays for the ever-popular *steak frites*.

N° 3107

ALAIN MAÎTRE BARBIER

8 rue Saint-Claude
M° Saint-Sébastien – Froissart
01 42 77 55 80
alain-maitrebarbiercoiffeur.com

This barber shop is a living museum of the traditional wet shave. Everything—the scent of beard soap, the snip-snipping of scissors, the velvet chairs—exudes the elegance of a forgotten craft. I love admiring the antique objects that recount the history of the trade. And what a pleasure it is to place your face in the hands of a true master barber! A timeless experience in which each gesture is performed with precision.

N° 3317

N° 3105 N° 3103 N° 3119

N° 3211

N° 3212

N° 3213

N° 3157

N° 3611

N° 3690

N° 3379

N° 3281

N° 3202

N° 3830

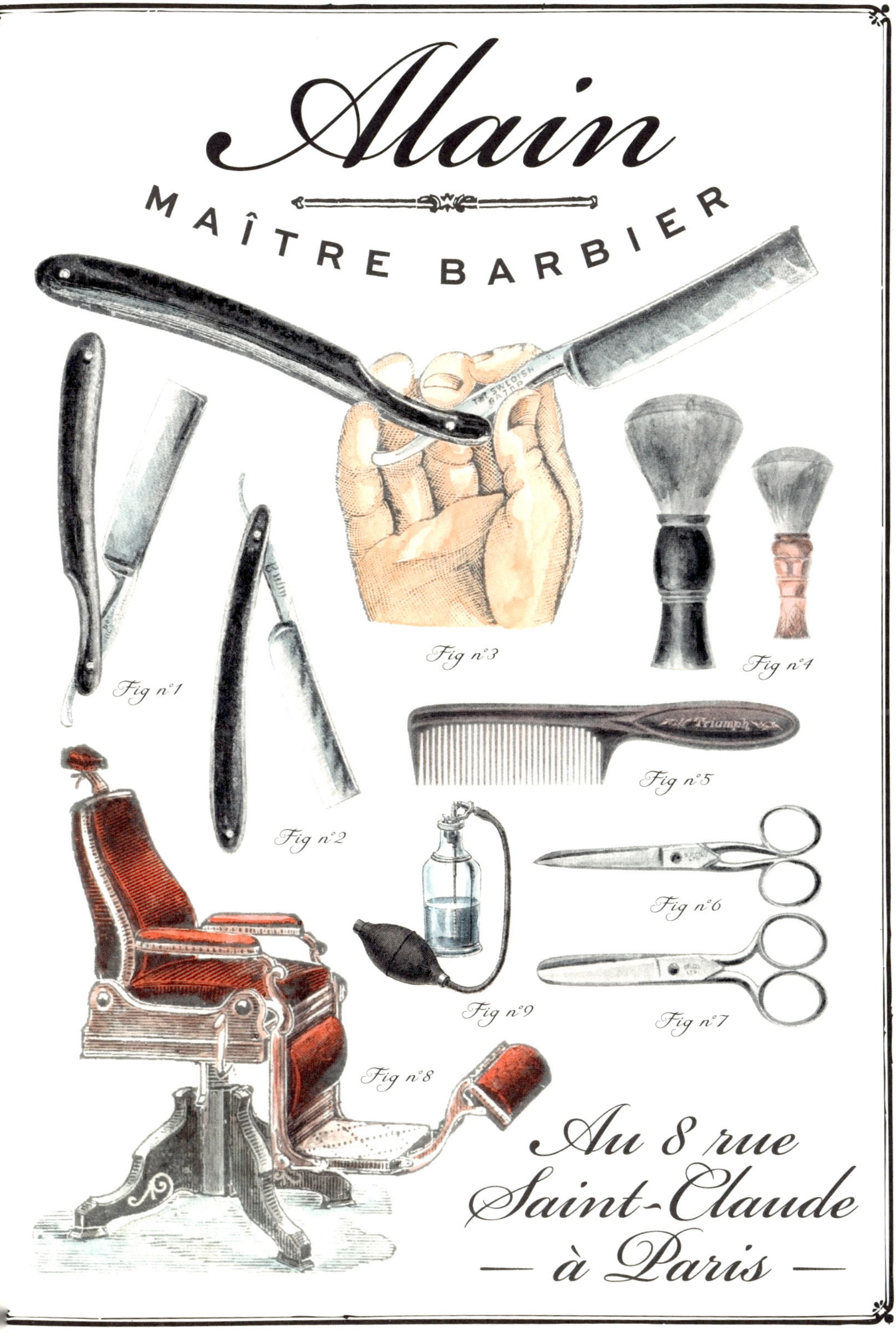

Alain

MAÎTRE BARBIER

THE SWEDISH RAZOR

Fig n°1

Fig n°2

Fig n°3

Fig n°4

Triumph

Fig n°5

Fig n°6

Fig n°7

Fig n°8

Fig n°9

Au 8 rue
Saint-Claude
— à Paris —

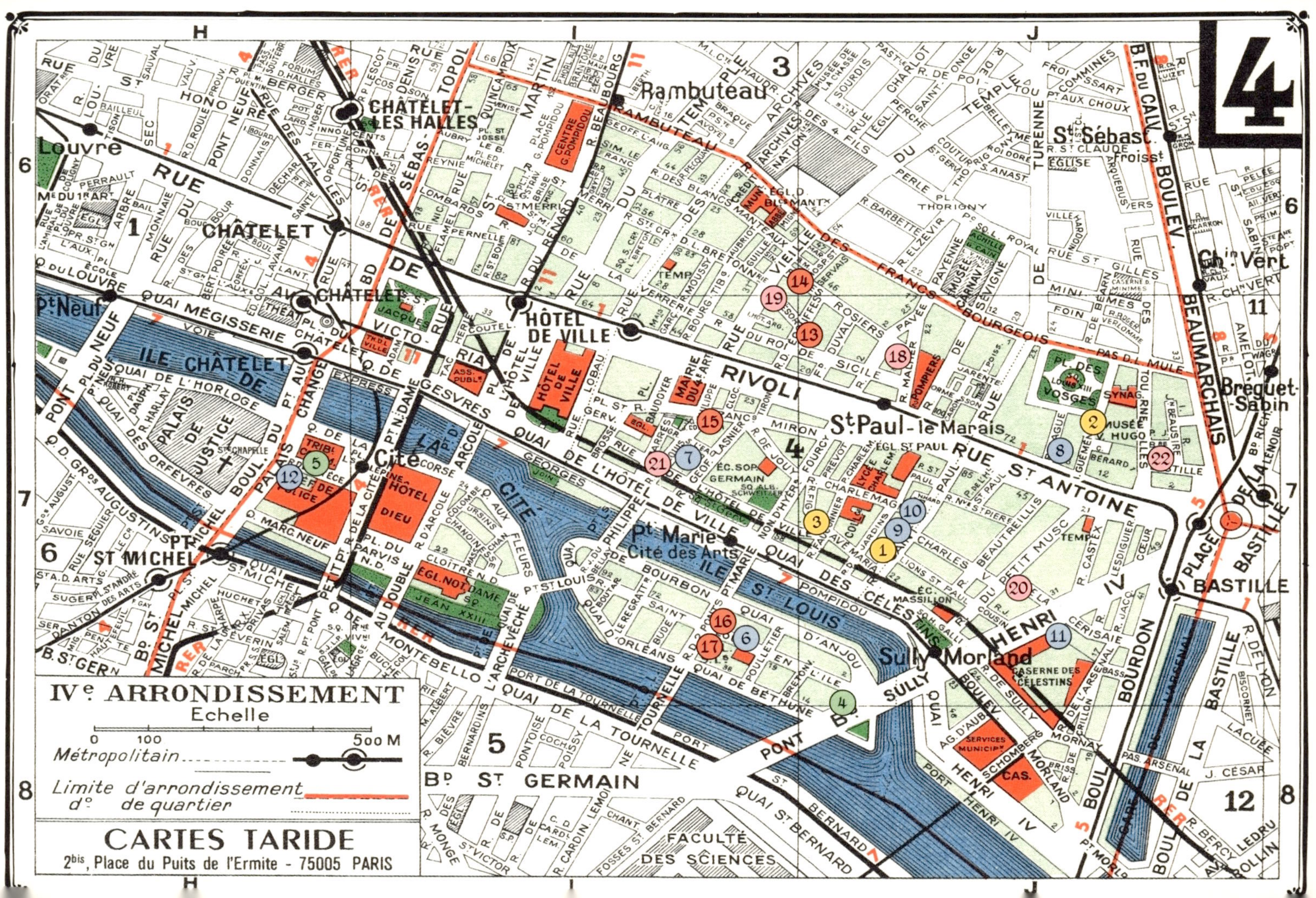
4
IVe ARRONDISSEMENT
Echelle
0 100 500 M
Métropolitain
Limite d'arrondissement
d° de quartier
CARTES TARIDE
2bis, Place du Puits de l'Ermite - 75005 PARIS
Louvre
Châtelet-Les Halles
Châtelet
Hôtel de Ville
Rambuteau
St Sébast. Froissart
Ch.in Vert
Breguet-Sabin
Bastille
St Paul-le Marais
Pt Marie Cité des Arts
Cité
St Michel
Sully Morland
Pt Neuf
RUE DE RIVOLI
RUE ST ANTOINE
BOULEV. BEAUMARCHAIS
BD DE SÉBASTOPOL
QUAI DE LA MÉGISSERIE
ILE DE LA CITÉ
ILE ST LOUIS
PALAIS DE JUSTICE
HÔTEL DIEU
HÔTEL DE VILLE
CENTRE G. POMPIDOU
ÉGL. NOTRE DAME
CASERNE DES CÉLESTINS
BD ST GERMAIN
BOULEV. HENRI IV
BOULEV. BOURDON
FACULTÉ DES SCIENCES

4ᴱ ARRONDISSEMENT

1. Musée de la Magie
   11 rue Saint-Paul
2. Maison Victor Hugo
   6 place des Vosges
3. Bibliothèque Forney
   1 rue du Figuier
4. Garage de l'Île Saint-Louis
   5 boulevard Henri-IV
5. Marché aux Fleurs Reine-Elizabeth-II
   Place Louis-Lépine, allée Célestin-Hennion
6. Librairie Ulysse
   26 rue Saint-Louis-en-l'Île
7. Mélodies Graphiques
   10 rue du Pont-Louis-Philippe
8. Argenterie d'Antan
   6 rue de Birague
9. Au Débotté
   19 rue Saint-Paul
10. EW Objets Anciens
    21 rue Saint-Paul
11. Bazar d'Électricité
    34 boulevard Henri-IV
12. Maison Bosc
    3 boulevard du Palais
13. Maison David
    6 rue des Écouffes
14. Sacha Finkelsztajn – La Boutique Jaune
    27 rue des Rosiers
15. Izraël
    30 rue François-Miron
16. Boucherie Gardil
    44 rue Saint-Louis-en-l'Île
17. Berthillon
    29–31 rue Saint-Louis-en-l'Île
18. Le Loir dans la Théière
    3 rue des Rosiers
19. Au Petit Fer à Cheval
    30 rue Vieille-du-Temple
20. Le Temps des Cerises
    31 rue de la Cerisaie
21. Chez Julien
    1 rue du Pont-Louis-Philippe
22. Bofinger
    5–7 rue de la Bastille

MUSÉE DE LA MAGIE

1

11 rue Saint-Paul
M° Pont Marie / Saint-Paul
01 42 72 13 26
museedelamagie.com • @museedelamagie

The scene is set right from the entrance: this is a museum of magic masquerading as a vintage joke and novelty shop. Established in 1993, it holds one of the largest collections of historical and modern-day magic paraphernalia. In addition to the optical illusions, automatons, and other props on display that will capture your imagination, you'll be amazed by magic tricks performed by an illusionist during your visit.

N° 4253

N° 4238

N° 4262

N° 4242

N° 4245

N° 4072

MAISON VICTOR HUGO

6 place des Vosges
M° Bastille
01 42 72 10 16
maisonsvictorhugo.paris.fr/en •
@maisonsdevictorhugo

Since 1903, one of my favorite museums in Paris has welcomed visitors into the private world of Victor Hugo, whose writing marked his century. I'm most inspired by the decoration—the Chinese salon's carpeting, the wallpaper, the extensive plate collection. My secret treat: having a drink in the hidden cafe, while mingling with the spirit of the genius himself.

BIBLIOTHÈQUE FORNEY

1 rue du Figuier
M° Pont Marie
01 42 78 14 60
bibliothequeforney.wordpress.com • @bibforney

Located in the Hôtel de Sens, which resembles a small château, this library specializes in fine arts, graphic arts, and decorative arts—all of my favorites. The collection is truly incredible and brings together books, periodicals, and catalogs, as well as wallpaper, fabric samples, and design models. A precious source of inspiration for anyone who loves beautiful things.

◈ GARAGE DE L'ÎLE SAINT-LOUIS ◈

4

5 boulevard Henri-IV
M° Sully - Morland
01 43 54 55 64
gisl.fr • FB: Garage de l'île Saint Louis

This car repair shop has been tucked away in the heart of Île Saint-Louis since 1939. Nearly everything has been conserved: the storefront, tools, furniture, and even a few spare parts from classic cars. You might feel like time has stood still here, but the mechanics are all up to speed and can fix new cars just as well as older models.

N° 4198

N° 4698

N° 4703

N° 4108

N° 4114

◈ MARCHÉ AUX FLEURS REINE-ELIZABETH-II ◈

5

Place Louis-Lépine, allée Célestin-Hennion
M° Cité
paris.fr/lieux/marche-aux-fleurs-reine-elizabeth-ii-4506

Beneath the pavilions from 1900, stalls overflow with peonies in spring, pine trees at Christmas, and orchids all year long. I like to wander, following my nose, but if you're looking for something specific, the florists will be delighted to show you where to find it, even if it's one row over. At the end of the walkways, you'll find the Seine and Notre-Dame cathedral. Sights fit for a queen.

N° 415

N° 4148

LIBRAIRIE ULYSSE

6

26 rue Saint-Louis-en-l'Île
M° Pont Marie
01 43 25 17 35
ulysse.fr • @librairie_ulysse

The journey begins in Asia and, several books later, touches down in North Africa. Every volume in this bookshop, opened in 1971, is an invitation to travel. You have to make an appointment with Catherine, the founder, to enter this paradise for globetrotters of all stripes. I come here to find inspiration for my next trip abroad, or to read up on a country I plan to visit.

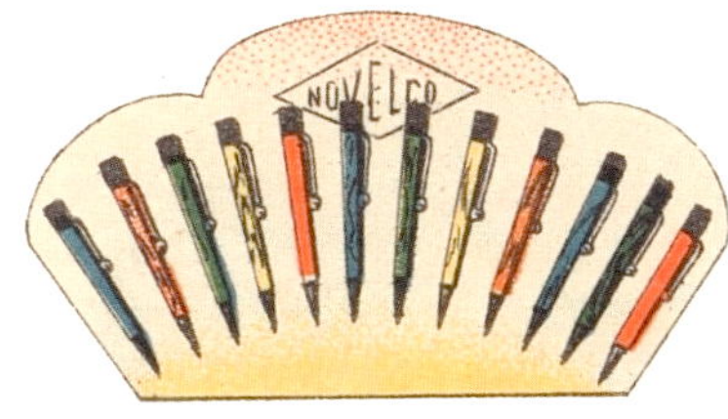

N° 4644

MÉLODIES GRAPHIQUES

7

10 rue du Pont-Louis-Philippe
M° Pont Marie
01 42 74 57 68
melodies-graphiques.com • @melodiesgraphiques

From behind its black-and-gold storefront, this boutique has been providing *belles lettres* enthusiasts with calligraphy essentials since 1986. It also stocks beautiful paper and writing accessories. I particularly like their vintage products and their high-quality writing paper. And the store itself looks like a pretty, little old-fashioned jewel box.

N° 494

N° 4473

N° 4158

N° 4442

N° 4891

N° 4502

N° 4403

N° 4633

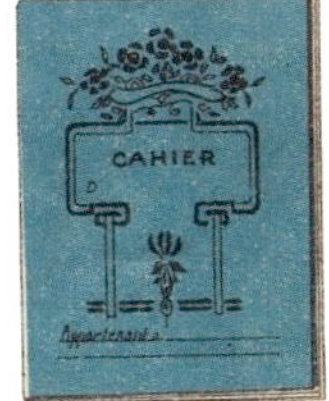

N° 4634

ARGENTERIE D'ANTAN

8

6 rue de Birague
M° Bastille
01 42 71 31 91
argenterie-dantan.com • @argenterie.dantan

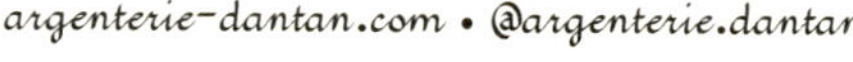

Argenterie d'Antan buys and sells exceptional silver and gold flatware dating from the 18th century up to the present day. The pieces are sourced from personal collections and prestigious hotels, and have been carefully selected by Corinne, the owner with an expert eye. If forks could talk, the stories they would surely tell. You'll be planning your next dinner party by the time you leave.

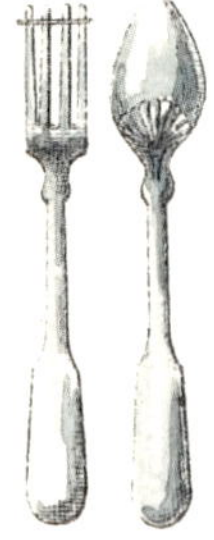

N° 4419

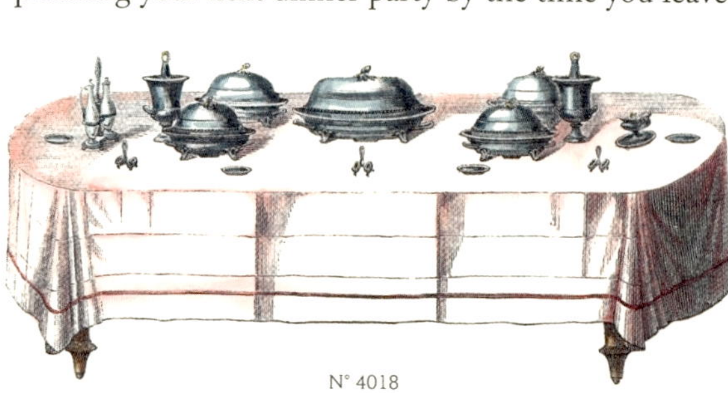

N° 4018

N° 4419

◈ AU DÉBOTTÉ ◈

19 rue Saint-Paul
M° Saint-Paul / Pont Marie
06 07 97 00 43
audebotte.fr

The effect is immediate—like plunging your hand into a beautiful antique jewelry box. Claudine Murat has been collecting and selling French and European antiques in her shop, which feels like an 18th-century hôtel particulier, since the 1990s. The magnificent, perfectly preserved furniture provides a window onto the past.

◈ EW OBJETS ANCIENS ◈

21 rue Saint-Paul
M° Sully – Morland / Saint-Paul
01 42 77 55 11
@ew_paris

All the items for sale in this miniature *brocante* are small in size. It's hard to know where to start in this micro-boutique, abounding with treasures, near the Village Saint-Paul shopping district. I could spend several hours gazing at all the relics of my childhood and of my memories—but also at the pretty plates, which sometimes find their way home with me.

N° 4290 N° 4358 N° 4421 N° 4589 N° 4537 N° 4653 N° 4315 N° 4511 N° 4201 N° 4275 N° 4276 N° 4591

BAZAR d'ÉLÉCTRICITÉ

34, Boul^d Henry IV
(Bastille)

1

Applique pour 2 lampes
Saillie 13 c/m Prix : **18 francs**

2

Applique
Louis XV pour 2 lampes
Saillie 30 c/m Prix : **35 fr.**

3

Applique tube uni carré
Saillie 25 c/m Prix : **6 fr. 50**

4

Applique, saillie 23 c/m
Prix : **5 fr. 75**

5

Saillie 25 cent.
Prix : **6 fr.**

6

Applique, saillie 19 c/m
Prix : **5 fr. 50**

7

Bras, saillie 23 cent.
Prix : **4 fr. 50**

8

Applique, saillie 25 c/m
Prix : **6 fr. 50**

9

Saillie 35 c/m
Prix : **11 francs**

0

Applique, saillie 32 c/m
Prix : **12 francs**

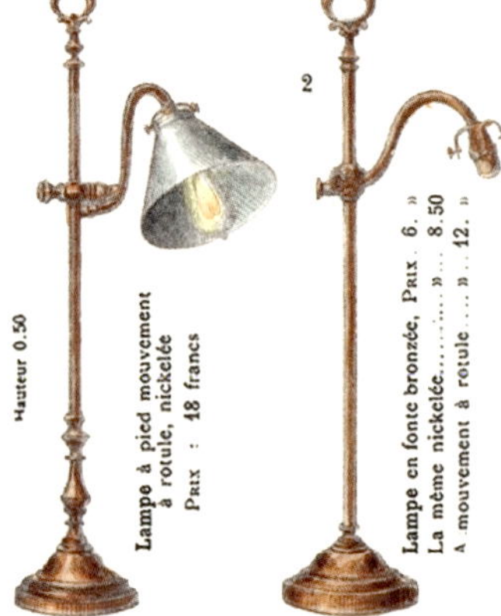

Hauteur 0.50

Lampe à pied mouvement à rotule, nickelée
Prix : **18 francs**

2

Lampe en fonte bronzée, Prix 6. »
La même nickelée .... » ... 8.50
A mouvement à rotule .... » ... 12. »

4

Hauteur totale 33 c/m

Prix sans abat-jour : **35 fr.**

BAZAR D'ÉLECTRICITÉ

11

34 boulevard Henri-IV
M° Bastille / Sully – Morland
01 48 87 83 35
bazarelec.com • @bazardelec

The Bazar d'Électricité set up shop in the heart of the Bastille neighborhood in 1884. Since then, it has kept up with the latest technological innovations, and offers its clients all manner of modern, design-forward light fixtures and electrical installations. The store can also repair lighting appliances or bring them up to standard.

N° 4181

MAISON BOSC

12

3 boulevard du Palais
M° Cité
01 43 54 16 50
maisonbosc.com/gb/ • @maisonbosc

In 1845, Maison Bosc began making legal robes for the judicial professions in France and abroad. Ever since, this exceptional establishment has helped to keep the world's oldest clothing tradition alive. Lawyers, judges, and other legal professionals come here to order their custom-made gowns. And even if I never buy anything, I love this place for all the historical treasures it holds.

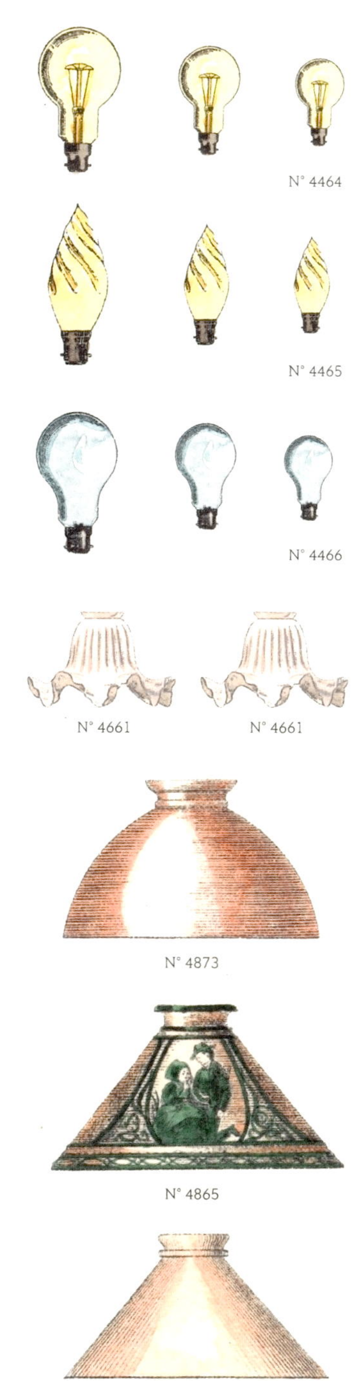

N° 4464

N° 4465

N° 4466

N° 4661 N° 4661

N° 4873

N° 4865

N° 4892

N° 4374

N° 4334

MAISON DAVID

13

6 rue des Écouffes
M° Saint-Paul
01 77 18 23 62
michel-kalifa.fr • @michelkalifa_marais

This deli, owned by Michel Kalifa, from Casablanca, and his wife Françoise, has been located just off rue des Rosiers, in the heart of the Pletzl—Paris's historic Jewish quarter—since 1975. Michel's an artisan butcher/charcutier who masters all the Ashkenazi Jewish specialties, from pastrami and chopped liver to his famous *Pickelfleisch*, or house-made harissa and Malossol pickles.

SACHA FINKELSZTAJN – LA BOUTIQUE JAUNE

14

27 rue des Rosiers
M° Hôtel de Ville / Saint-Paul
01 42 72 78 91
laboutiquejaune.fr • @laboutiquejauneparis

It's hard to walk down rue des Rosiers without noticing this sunny storefront. At the Boutique Jaune—or "yellow shop"—you'll find the best of Ashkenazi cuisine: strudel, pletzel, vatrouchka, and more. The store was founded in 1946 by Polish refugees Dora and Itzik Finkelsztajn. The product range has grown, but the expertise remains the same. I simply can't leave here without a delicious babka in my shopping bag.

◈ IZRAËL ◈

15

30 rue François-Miron
M° Saint-Paul / Pont Marie
01 42 72 66 23
@epicerieizrael

In the Izraël family since 1947, this grocery shop—a fragrant Aladdin's cave overflowing with fine Oriental and exotic ingredients—offers visitors a magic carpet ride out of the Marais to far-flung places. Jute bags filled with fragrant spices, rice, or lentils are stacked on the floor, preserved lemons and ginger are piled high on platters, and strings of dried chilis and sausage hang tantalizingly from the ceiling.

N° 4837

◈ BOUCHERIE GARDIL ◈

16

44 rue Saint-Louis-en-l'Île
M° Pont Marie
01 43 54 97 15

This butcher has pursued one mission since it opened in 1905: to supply meat of exceptional quality, with impeccable flavor, whose origin is clearly indicated. Both father and son are committed to these exacting standards, and their efforts have been rewarded with a flurry of awards and prizes. Their incredible veal cutlets never disappoint, and nor does their invaluable advice.

N° 4114 N° 4092 N° 4187 N° 4277 N° 4515 N° 4911 N° 4768

BERTHILLON

17

29–31 rue Saint-Louis-en-l'Île
M° Pont Marie
01 43 54 31 61
berthillon.fr • @berthillon_officiel

A summer in Paris without Berthillon ice cream? Impossible. As soon as the sun appears, I hurry to Île Saint-Louis with only one question on my mind: dark chocolate or salted-butter caramel? To be paired with sunglasses for a stroll along the river. In winter, combine it with a piping hot coffee in the other hand and *voilà*! Forever fashionable, no matter the season.

N° 410 N° 411 N° 412

LE LOIR DANS LA THÉIÈRE

3 rue des Rosiers
M° Saint-Paul
01 42 72 90 61
leloirdanslatheiere.com/en/ • @leloirdanslatheiereofficiel

It's easy to fall for the bohemian charm of this tearoom that feels straight out of *Alice's Adventures in Wonderland*. Since 1996, Paul and his family have been regaling their guests with fresh, seasonal dishes served against a backdrop of bric-a-brac treasures carefully selected over the years. My guilty pleasure is the gigantic lemon tart piled (nearly) ceiling-high with meringue.

N° 4269

N° 4295 N° 4260

N° 4286

N° 4169

N° 4275

N° 4481

SALON DE THÉ

LE LOIR DANS LA THÉIÈRE

AU 3 RUE DES ROSIERS - PARIS

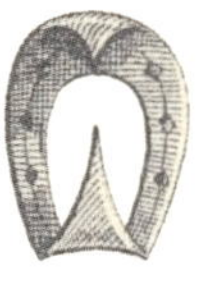

AU PETIT FER À CHEVAL

19

30 rue Vieille-du-Temple
M° Saint-Paul / Hôtel de Ville
01 42 72 47 47
rphunter.com/cafeine-reservations-3/

Taking its name from the marble-topped horseshoe-shaped bar, this restaurant, with its cheery green facade, has been a beacon of Parisian café culture in the Marais since 1989. In winter, customers enjoy classic French dishes, including specialties duck confit and steak tartare, in the cozy dining room at the back, while in summer tables are set out on the sidewalk, awaiting a ray of sunshine.

LE TEMPS DES CERISES

20

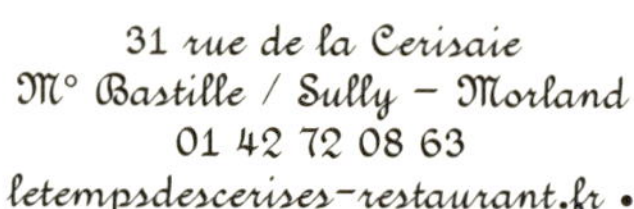

31 rue de la Cerisaie
M° Bastille / Sully – Morland
01 42 72 08 63
letempsdescerises-restaurant.fr •
@tempsdescerises

When this small house was built in the Middle Ages, it was surrounded by a cherry orchard. Today, Le Temps des Cerises is a neighborhood bistro featuring a typical 1930s decor: a mosaic facade, authentic zinc bar, and red booths. I just love the upper level, which looks like a small Parisian apartment; you can even book it for a soirée with friends.

◈ CHEZ JULIEN ◈

(21)

1 rue du Pont-Louis-Philippe
M° Pont Marie
01 42 78 31 64
chezjulien.paris/en/ • @chezjulienparis

The original restaurant located here dates back to 1780; today, the Belle Époque decor harkens back to its days as a former bakery. Soak up the sun on one of the terraces that give this listed historic monument its appeal. I like coming here for breakfast when the city is just waking up, or for dinner in the cozy, baroque-inspired private lounge upstairs.

N° 4183

N° 4490 N° 4496

N° 4345 N° 4346 N° 4347

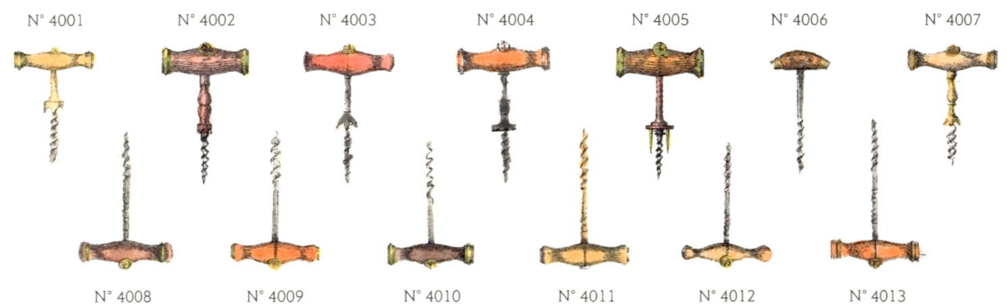

N° 4001 N° 4002 N° 4003 N° 4004 N° 4005 N° 4006 N° 4007

N° 4008 N° 4009 N° 4010 N° 4011 N° 4012 N° 4013

◈ BOFINGER ◈

(22)

5-7 rue de la Bastille
M° Bastille
01 42 72 87 82
bofingerparis.com/en/ • @brasserie_bofinger

Bofinger is the oldest Alsatian brasserie in Paris and was the first to serve beer on tap, attracting neighborhood craftsmen, who showed up toting their own steins. I like this place for its art deco ambience, impeccable service, and typical Alsatian menu—the choucroute is irresistible. If you can tear yourself away from your plate, the cupola overhead is well worth admiring.

N° 4997

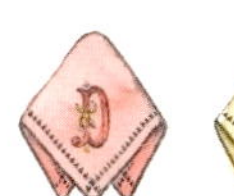

N° 420

N° 419

N° 418

N° 4001

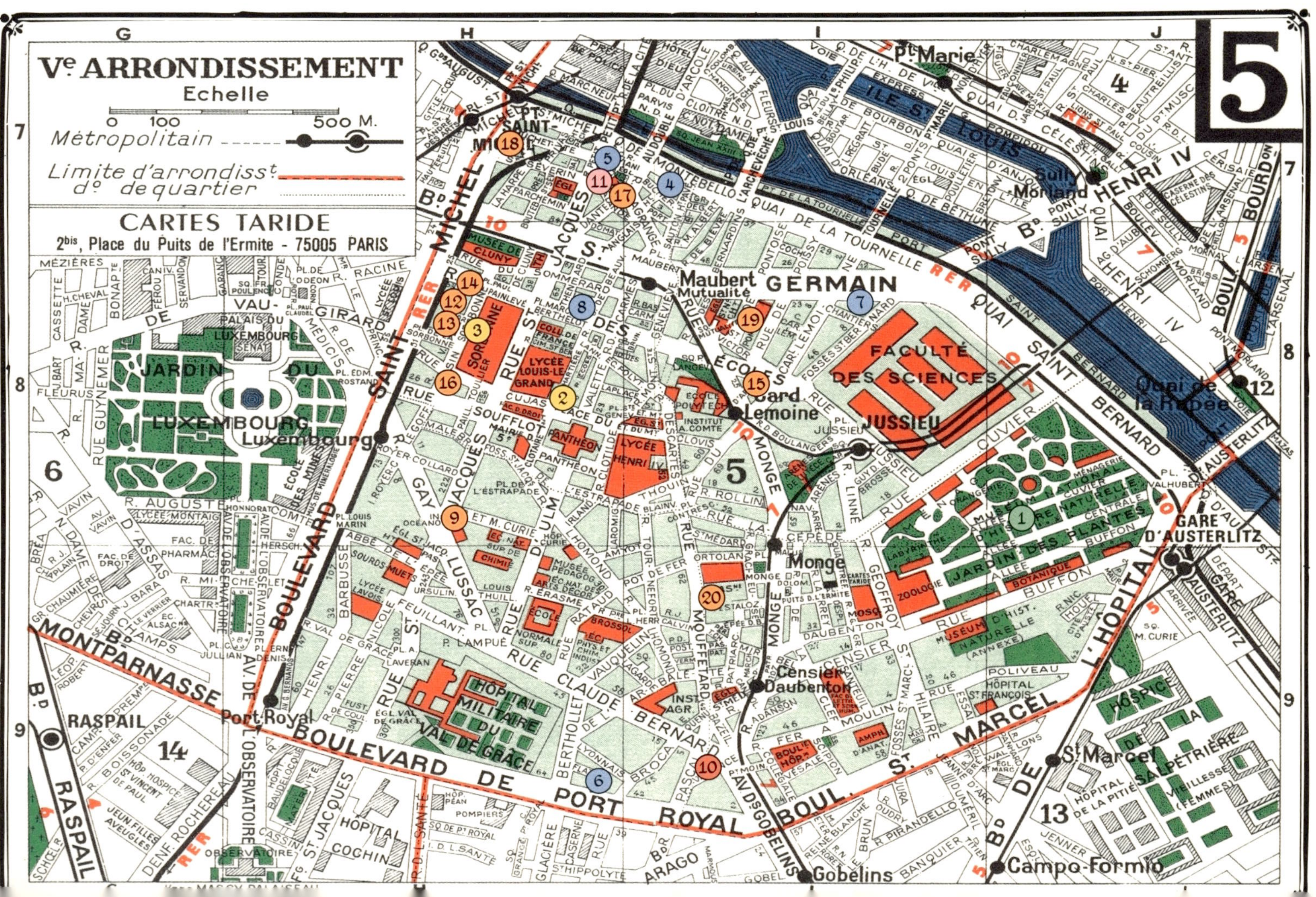

5
Ve ARRONDISSEMENT
Echelle
0 100 500 M.
Métropolitain
Limite d'arrondisst
do de quartier
CARTES TARIDE
2bis, Place du Puits de l'Ermite - 75005 PARIS
QUAI DE LA TOURNELLE
QUAI SAINT BERNARD
BD ST GERMAIN
BD SAINT MICHEL
BOULEVARD DE PORT ROYAL
BOULEVARD ST MARCEL
BD MONTPARNASSE
BD DE L'HOPITAL
JARDIN DU LUXEMBOURG
JARDIN DES PLANTES
FACULTÉ DES SCIENCES
JUSSIEU
PANTHÉON
SORBONNE
HÔPITAL MILITAIRE DU VAL DE GRÂCE
GARE D'AUSTERLITZ
ILE ST LOUIS
Maubert Mutualité
Cardinal Lemoine
Censier Daubenton
Monge
Luxembourg
Port Royal
Campo-Formio
Gobelins
St Marcel
Sully Morland
Pt Marie
Quai de la Rapée
RASPAIL

5E ARRONDISSEMENT

1. Jardin des Plantes
57 rue Cuvier
2. Bibliothèque Sainte-Geneviève
10 place du Panthéon
3. Bibliothèque de la Sorbonne
17 rue de la Sorbonne
4. Charbonnel
13 quai de Montebello
5. Shakespeare and Company
37 rue de la Bûcherie
6. Musée des Éclairages Anciens – Lumière de l'Œil
4 rue Flatters
7. La Quincaillerie
3, 4, 7 boulevard Saint-Germain
8. Crocodisc
40 & 42 rue des Écoles
9. Maison de l'Océan
195 rue Saint-Jacques
10. Brûlerie des Gobelins
2 avenue des Gobelins
11. The Tea Caddy
14 rue Saint-Julien-le-Pauvre
12. Reflet Médicis
3 rue Champollion
13. Filmothèque du Quartier Latin
9 rue Champollion
14. Le Champo – Espace Jacques Tati
51 rue des Écoles
15. Grand Action
5 rue des Écoles
16. Cinéma du Panthéon
13 rue Victor-Cousin
17. Studio Galande Béruchet
42 rue Galande
18. Espace Saint-Michel
7 place Saint-Michel
19. Espace Sportif Pontoise
19 rue de Pontoise
20. Bowling Mouffetard
73 rue Mouffetard

JARDIN DES PLANTES

N° 5209

◆ JARDIN DES PLANTES ◆

1

57 rue Cuvier
Entrances quai Saint-Bernard, rue Buffon,
rue Geoffroy-Saint-Hilaire, rue Cuvier
M° Place Monge / Jussieu / Censier – Daubenton;
M° / RER Gare d'Austerlitz
jardindesplantesdeparis.fr/en •
@jardindesplantesdeparis

N° 5379

N° 5245

N° 5309

Louis XIII's aim for the Jardin des Plantes—then known as the Jardin Royal—was to bring together "all things rare in nature." It may have changed many times over the last four centuries, but it remains a wonder in the heart of Paris. I come here to learn about flowers from far-flung locations, to unravel the mysteries of evolution, and to stroll the paths in search of trees sporting the Remarkable Trees label, including the Jussieu cedar planted in 1734. To me, this park is the perfect union of nature, knowledge, and poetry.

N° 5122

N° 5205

N° 5215

JARDIN ALPIN

N° 5451

If you take the rue Cuvier entrance, you'll come across the Jardin Alpin. Located between the menagerie and the large greenhouses, it is home to 2,000 species of mountain plants. The gardeners have done amazing work using the garden's recessed location to recreate alpine microclimates, offering a soothing change of scenery.

N° 5269

N° 5100

N° 5101

N° 5102

N° 5103

N° 5139

ZOO

The menagerie at the Jardin des Plantes is one of the oldest zoos in the world and occupies several acres. Nearly half of its 150 species are endangered and therefore protected here. This is a must-visit, and I always bring my niece and nephew to see the resident celebrities: the red flamingos. Make a detour to the vivarium if you want a bit of a fright.

MERRY-GO-ROUND

One of the garden's main attractions is its unique Dodo Manege. You won't find any wooden horses here; instead, children clamber atop a triceratops or a dodo. This carrousel, which features animals that have gone extinct or are endangered species, offers a gentle way to raise awareness about protecting wildlife.

N° 511 N° 512 N° 513

GREENHOUSES

I'm always impressed when I climb the large art deco staircase into the greenhouses. The metal and glass structure reminds me of the nave at the Grand Palais, but here, a tropical forest awaits. Another greenhouse, on the left, recreates a desert habitat, and the one a little further on whisks me to New Caledonia. These large greenhouses are a voyage in themselves, and the light is superb throughout.

N° 5832

N° 5357

N° 5240

N° 5154

N° 5240

N° 5286

N° 5139

MUSÉUM NATIONAL D'HISTOIRE NATURELLE

01 40 79 56 01
mnhn.fr/en • @le_museum

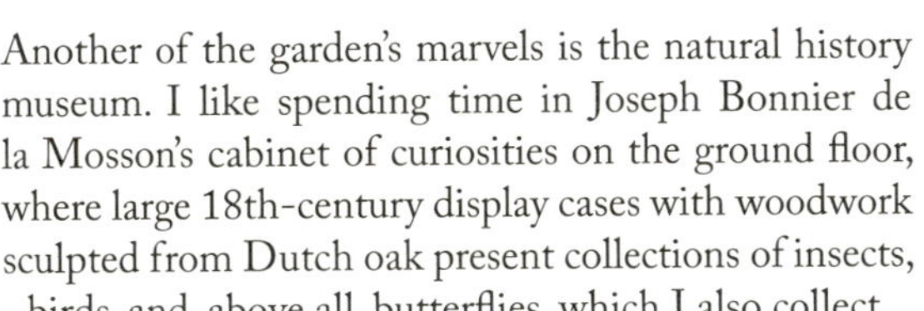
Another of the garden's marvels is the natural history museum. I like spending time in Joseph Bonnier de la Mosson's cabinet of curiosities on the ground floor, where large 18th-century display cases with woodwork sculpted from Dutch oak present collections of insects, birds, and, above all, butterflies, which I also collect.

For fans of drawing and history, the central library is home to priceless 18th-century parchments, as well as large botanical plates—a precious source of personal inspiration. And be sure to see the statues in the monumental stairwells.

The Grande Galerie de l'Évolution is fascinating for all ages, and my inner child thrills at the sight of the meteorites exhibited in the Galerie de Minéralogie.

Before leaving, I always visit the rose garden, which runs along this gallery. When its 300 varieties of roses are in full bloom, expect a tidal wave of color and fragrance.

N° 5287

N° 5288

N° 5289

N° 5151

N° 5154

N° 5198

N° 5804

N° 5762

N° 5455

N° 5123

N° 5641

N° 5483

◈ BIBLIOTHÈQUE SAINTE-GENEVIÈVE ◈

(2)

10 place du Panthéon
M° Cardinal Lemoine
01 44 41 97 97
bsg.univ-paris3.fr • @bibliothequesaintegenevieve

Facing the Panthéon, the Bibliothèque Sainte-Geneviève has welcomed students, readers, and other curious minds since 1851. Two incredible wrought iron vaults, 700 seats, and hundreds of thousands of tomes give the library its distinctive atmosphere. Here, readers consult books onsite, cocooned in a space virtually untouched by time, where a welcome silence replaces the bustle of the city.

◈ BIBLIOTHÈQUE DE LA SORBONNE ◈

(3)

17 rue de la Sorbonne
M° Cluny – La Sorbonne / Odéon
01 40 46 30 97
bis-sorbonne.fr • @bis_sorbonne

Since 1770, the library at the Sorbonne university has accommodated the world's most brilliant minds. I enjoy spending time in the large reading room on the second floor. At the end of each table stands a bookshelf, and at the end of the room hangs an imposing engraving of Richelieu examining the plans for the university. Everything here is conducive to study. With a little luck, the library will let you in on some of its secrets.

CHARBONNEL

13 quai de Montebello
M° Maubert – Mutualité
01 44 07 26 88
charbonnelshop.fr • @charbonnelparis

In 1862, F. Charbonnel set up shop here and developed his own art paper, which soon became a reference for the greatest painters of the day. Since then, the boutique has been committed to supplying products of exceptional quality by names like Lefranc Bourgeois, and I am never disappointed. Charbonnel also offers lithography and painting classes for all levels.

N° 5304

SHAKESPEARE AND COMPANY

37 rue de la Bûcherie
M° Saint-Michel; RER Saint-Michel – Notre-Dame
01 43 25 40 93
shakespeareandcompany.com • @shakespeareandcoparis

Created in 1951 in a former 17th-century monastery, this labyrinthine bookstore offers an extensive selection of English-language literature. Inside the incredible maze of *belles lettres*, attractive wood paneling commingles with hidden armchairs where I enjoy curling up with a book. Afterward, I like to go to the adjoining café and continue reading with a cup of tea.

N° 5522

N° 5233

N° 5234

N° 5234

N° 5159

N° 5151

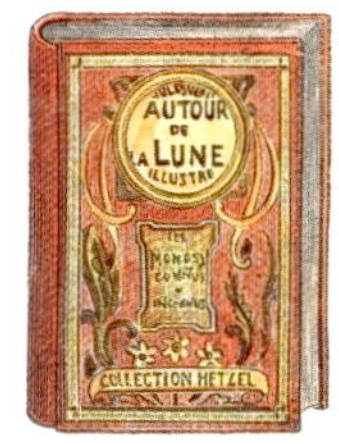

N° 5421

N° 5585

N° 5420

LUMIÈRE DE L'ŒIL

MAGASIN-ATELIER DE RESTAURATION
SPÉCIALISÉ DANS LES ÉCLAIRAGES ANCIENS

Musée des Eclairages Anciens

AU 4, RUE FLATTERS - PARIS Vᴱ

◈ MUSÉE DES ÉCLAIRAGES ANCIENS – LUMIÈRE DE L'ŒIL ◈

4 rue Flatters
M° Les Gobelins; RER Port-Royal
01 47 07 63 47
lumieredeloeil.com • @lumieredeloeil

I love collecting old lamps to create cozy ambiances in my interiors, and this place is my first stop! Behind a charming blue storefront lies an incandescent world of vintage lighting—a combination of boutique, workshop, and amateur museum run since 1981 by the fascinating Monsieur Ara, who invites you to discover his collection of oil, alcohol, and gas lamps from the end of the 18th to the early 20th century.

N° 5990

◈ LA QUINCAILLERIE ◈

7

3, 4, 7 boulevard Saint-Germain
M° Jussieu
01 46 33 66 71
laquincaillerie.com/en/ • @laquincailleriesaintgermain

When my antique workshop chests of drawers are missing handles, I look for replacements here. Created in 1958 in the very heart of the Saint-Germain neighborhood, La Quincaillerie has always been passionately dedicated to contemporary design and home accessories. Two stores located opposite each other offer a large selection of products, along with the best advice.

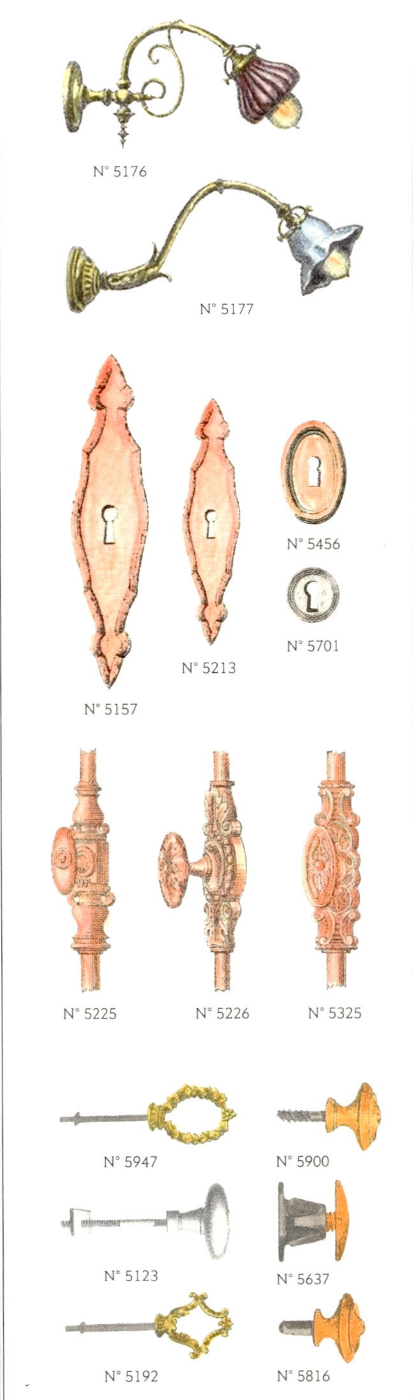

N° 5932

CROCODISC

8

40 & 42 rue des Écoles
M° Cluny – La Sorbonne
01 43 54 33 22 / 01 43 54 47 95
crocodisc.com • @crocodisc75

You don't look for a record here, you find one—or rather, it finds you. The two stores situated side by side on rue des Écoles, their bins bursting with vinyl, cassette tapes, and CDs, have been the haunt of music buffs since 1978. With the exception of classical music, every style is represented, and the time-burnished sleeves always inspire me. In this place, nostalgia is the order of the day.

N° 5745

MAISON DE L'OCÉAN

9

195 rue Saint-Jacques
RER Luxembourg
01 44 32 10 70
maison.oceano.org/en/

Founded in 1906 by Prince Albert I of Monaco, this institute exists to unite all those committed to protecting the oceans. The main feature of this historic building is its magnificent amphitheater bursting with paintings of maritime conquests. It regularly hosts concerts in a dreamlike atmosphere, illuminated by hundreds of candles placed across the stage floor.

N° 5883

N° 5342

N° 5235 N° 5235

N° 5324

N° 5649

❖ BRÛLERIE DES GOBELINS ❖

2 avenue des Gobelins
M° Les Gobelins
01 43 31 90 13
bruleriedesgobelins.fr • @bruleriedesgobelins

In 1957, residents of the Gobelins neighborhood began to notice the heady aroma of coffee drifting through the air. Since then, the Brûlerie des Gobelins has changed little, and continues to pass on the secrets of exceptional, organic, fair-trade coffee to its master roasters. I especially like their Harrar moka for its comforting notes of toast and caramel.

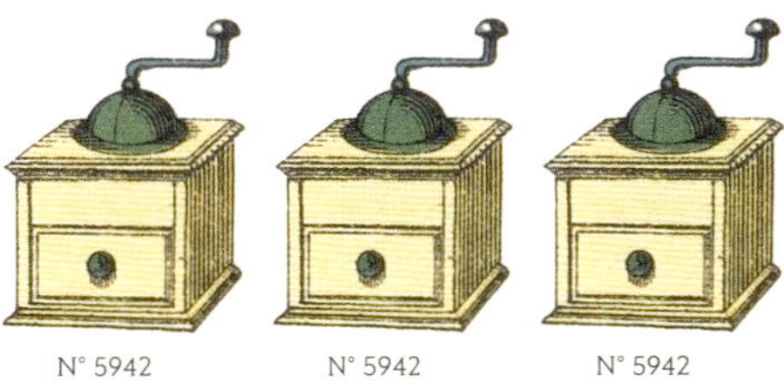

N° 5942 N° 5942 N° 5942

❖ THE TEA CADDY ❖

14 rue Saint-Julien-le-Pauvre
M° Cluny – La Sorbonne
01 43 54 15 56
the-tea-caddy.com

An oasis of British culture since 1928, this tearoom offers a wide selection of teas, properly prepared in teapots and served in quaint Blue Willow pattern teacups. The house-made scones and jam are perfect for a teatime *goûter*. Sitting in the long, narrow room, with its lattice windows overlooking the Square René Viviani, gives me the delightful impression of traveling across England in a train.

N° 509 N° 5089 N° 509

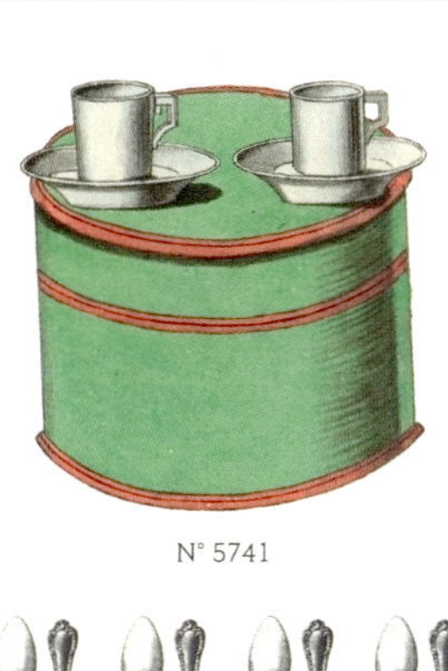

N° 5741

N° 5388

N° 5148 N° 5358

N° 5169 N° 5168

N° 5178

CINEMAS

N° 5205

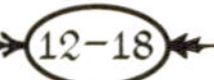

12–18

M° Cluny – La Sorbonne / Odéon / Cardinal Lemoine / Jussieu; RER Luxembourg / Saint-Michel – Notre-Dame

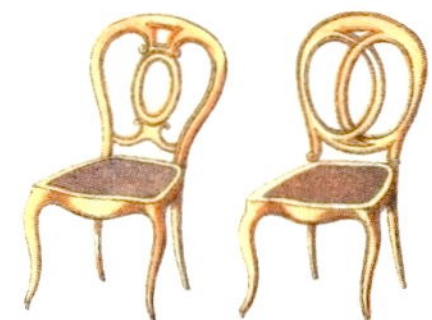

N° 5207

When I feel like escaping the hustle and bustle of the city for a while and losing myself in a good movie, I head over to the Latin Quarter. Rue Champollion—declared the "Mecca of cinema" by Quentin Tarantino—is home to three longstanding arthouse movie theaters. (12) **Reflet Médicis** (3 rue Champollion) dates to 1964. During the first week of June, I like to catch the rescreening of the Cannes Film Festival's innovative Un Certain Regard selection. (13) Converted into a cinema in 1956, **Filmothèque du Quartier Latin** (9 rue Champollion) shows an eclectic program of lesser-known films in its two screening rooms: the lush red "Marilyn" room—my favorite—and the smaller, blue "Audrey." (14) **Le Champo – Espace Jacques Tati** (51 rue des Écoles, on the corner of rue Champollion) took up residence in a former bookstore in 1938. With its art deco facade and programming that spotlights the classics, it has built up a loyal clientele. (15) Since 1970, small indie theater **Grand Action** (5 rue des Écoles) has attracted movie goers with its extensive programming and cozy love seats. (16) **Cinéma du Panthéon** (13 rue Victor-Cousin), dating back to 1907, proposes one of the most cutting-edge programs. My favorite spot is the pretty tearoom on the first floor, decorated by Catherine Deneuve and Christian Sapet. (17) Opened in 1973, **Studio Galande Béruchet** (42 rue Galande) is a tiny one-screen cinema. Since 1978, it has held weekly—and interactive—screenings of the legendary musical *The Rocky Horror Picture Show*. (18) Known for its bold, independent programming, **Espace Saint-Michel** (7 place Saint-Michel) was established in 1911 by Victor Gandon, and is still family run today.

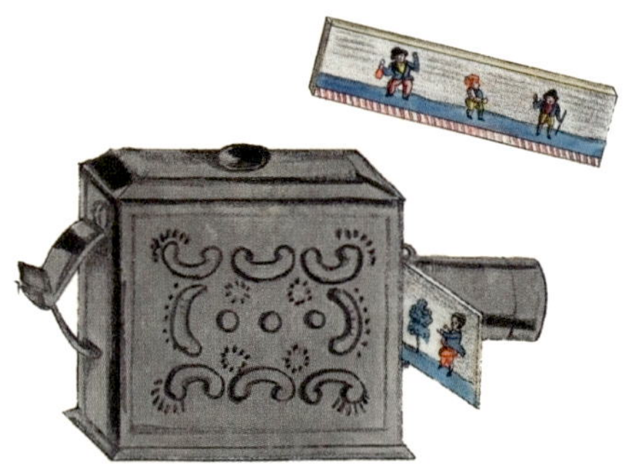

N° 5470

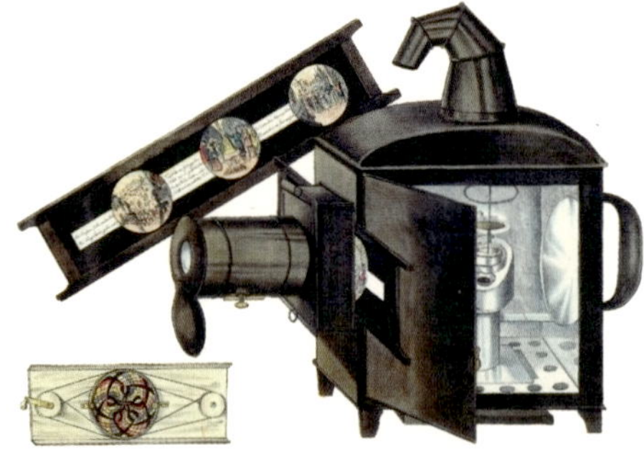

N° 5101

ESPACE SPORTIF PONTOISE

19

19 rue de Pontoise
M° Maubert – Mutualité
01 55 42 77 88
espace-sportif-pontoise-paris.fr •
@espacesportifpontoiseparis

This listed historical building, dating back to 1933, is one of the most beautiful swimming pools in Paris. Designed by Lucien Pollet in the art deco style, it was recently renovated and has retained all the charm of yesteryear. I came here to swim for many years, in winter and summer—I love its architecture, as well as the private changing rooms available for bathers, where you can leave your things. And for late-night swimmers, it's open until 11 p.m.!

N° 5253

BOWLING MOUFFETARD

20

73 rue Mouffetard
M° Place Monge
01 43 31 09 35
bowlingmouffetard.fr • @bowlingmouffetard

For a dose of good old American fun, I head here to get into the tenpin bowling spirit. It reminds me of *The Big Lebowski*! Opened in 1979, this bowling alley is a veritable institution in the Latin quarter, complete with bright lights and vintage decor. In addition to the eight bowling lanes, there are pool tables and retro arcade games, and the festivities go on until 2 a.m.

N° 5232

N° 5595

N° 5250

N° 5599

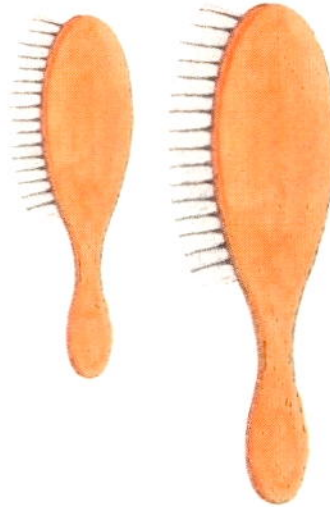

N° 5219

N° 5347

N° 5112

N° 5117

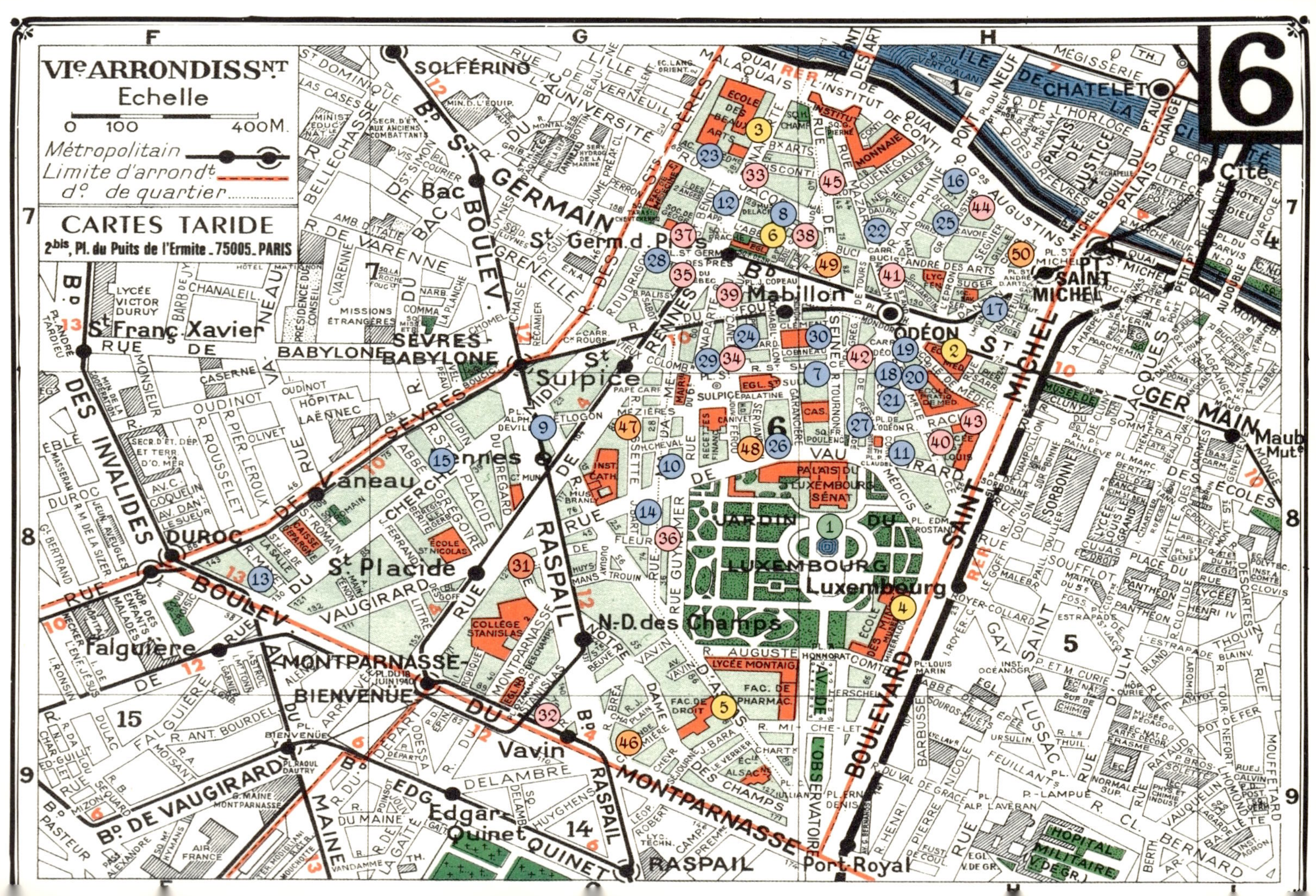

6
VIe ARRONDISSNT
Echelle
0 100 400M.
Métropolitain
Limite d'arrondt
do de quartier
CARTES TARIDE
2bis, Pl. du Puits de l'Ermite . 75005 . PARIS
F
G
H
7
8
9
SOLFÉRINO
Bac
St Germ. d. Prés
Mabillon
Odéon
St Michel
Saint Michel
Cité
Châtelet
Sèvres-Babylone
St Sulpice
Rennes
Vaneau
Duroc
St Placide
Falguière
Montparnasse-Bienvenüe
N.-D. des Champs
Vavin
Edgar-Quinet
Raspail
Port-Royal
Luxembourg
St Franç. Xavier
Bd St Germain
Boulevard Saint Michel
Boulevard Raspail
Boulev. Montparnasse
Bd des Invalides
Bd de Vaugirard
Rue de Vaugirard
Rue de Rennes
Jardin du Luxembourg
Palais du Luxembourg
Sénat
Sorbonne
Panthéon
Musée de Cluny
Institut
Monnaie
École des Beaux Arts
Île de la Cité
Palais de Justice
Collège Stanislas
Lycée Montaigne
Fac. de Pharmac.
Fac. de Droit
Hôpital Militaire (V. de Gr.)
Hôp. des Enfants Malades
Hôpital Laënnec
Missions Étrangères
Caserne

6ᴱ ARRONDISSEMENT

1. Jardin du Luxembourg
Entrances rue de Vaugirard, rue de Médicis, boulevard Saint-Michel, rue Guynemer
2. Musée d'Histoire de la Médecine
12 rue de l'École-de-Médecine
3. Beaux-Arts de Paris – Cour du Mûrier
14 rue Bonaparte
4. Musée de Minéralogie de l'École des Mines
60 boulevard Saint-Michel
5. Musée Zadkine
100 bis rue d'Assas
6. Musée National Eugène Delacroix
6 rue de Furstemberg
7. Galerie Jean-Claude Martinez
21 rue Saint-Sulpice
8. Yveline Antiques
4 rue de Furstemberg
9. Au Bain Marie
59 boulevard Raspail
10. Horloges & Pendules – François Hubert
43 rue Madame
11. Antiq Photo
11 & 16 rue de Vaugirard
12. Zuber
36 rue Bonaparte
13. Ateliers Lison de Caunes
20–22 rue Mayet
14. Marin Montagut
48 rue Madame
15. Cherche Midi Couleurs
58 rue du Cherche-Midi
16. Charvin
57 quai des Grands-Augustins
17. Relma
3 rue des Poitevins
18. Typodéon
6 rue Monsieur-le-Prince
19. Atelier Lambert Barnett
4 rue Monsieur-le-Prince
20. San Francisco Book Company
17 rue Monsieur-le-Prince
21. Librairie Rieffel
15 rue de l'Odéon
22. Librairie François Chanut
41 rue Mazarine
23. Librairie Alain Brieux
48 rue Jacob
24. Au Plat d'Étain
16 rue Guisarde
25. Galerie du Jouet Ancien
8 rue des Grands-Augustins
26. La Maison de Poupée
40 rue de Vaugirard
27. Au Cor de Chasse
25 rue de Condé
28. Kerstin Adolphson
157 boulevard Saint-Germain
29. Georges Thuillier
10 place Saint-Sulpice
30. Trudon
78 rue de Seine
31. Maison Verot
3 rue Notre-Dame-des-Champs
32. Le Select Montparnasse
99 boulevard du Montparnasse
33. Ladurée
21 rue Bonaparte
34. Café de la Mairie
8 place Saint-Sulpice
35. Brasserie Lipp
151 boulevard Saint-Germain
36. Le Fleurus
2 rue de Fleurus
37. Café de Flore
172 boulevard Saint-Germain
38. Guenmaï
6 rue Cardinale
39. Tsukizi
2 bis rue des Ciseaux
40. Polidor
41 rue Monsieur-le-Prince
41. Le Procope
13 rue de l'Ancienne-Comédie
42. La Crèmerie
9 rue des Quatre-Vents
43. Bouillon Racine
3 rue Racine
44. Lapérouse
51 quai des Grands-Augustins
45. La Palette
43 rue de Seine
46. Académie de la Grande Chaumière
14 rue de la Grande-Chaumière
47. Hôtel de l'Abbaye
10 rue Cassette
48. Hôtel Luxembourg Parc
42 rue de Vaugirard
49. Hôtel La Louisiane
60 rue de Seine
50. Relais Hôtel du Vieux Paris
9 rue Gît-le-Cœur

JARDIN DU LUXEMBOURG

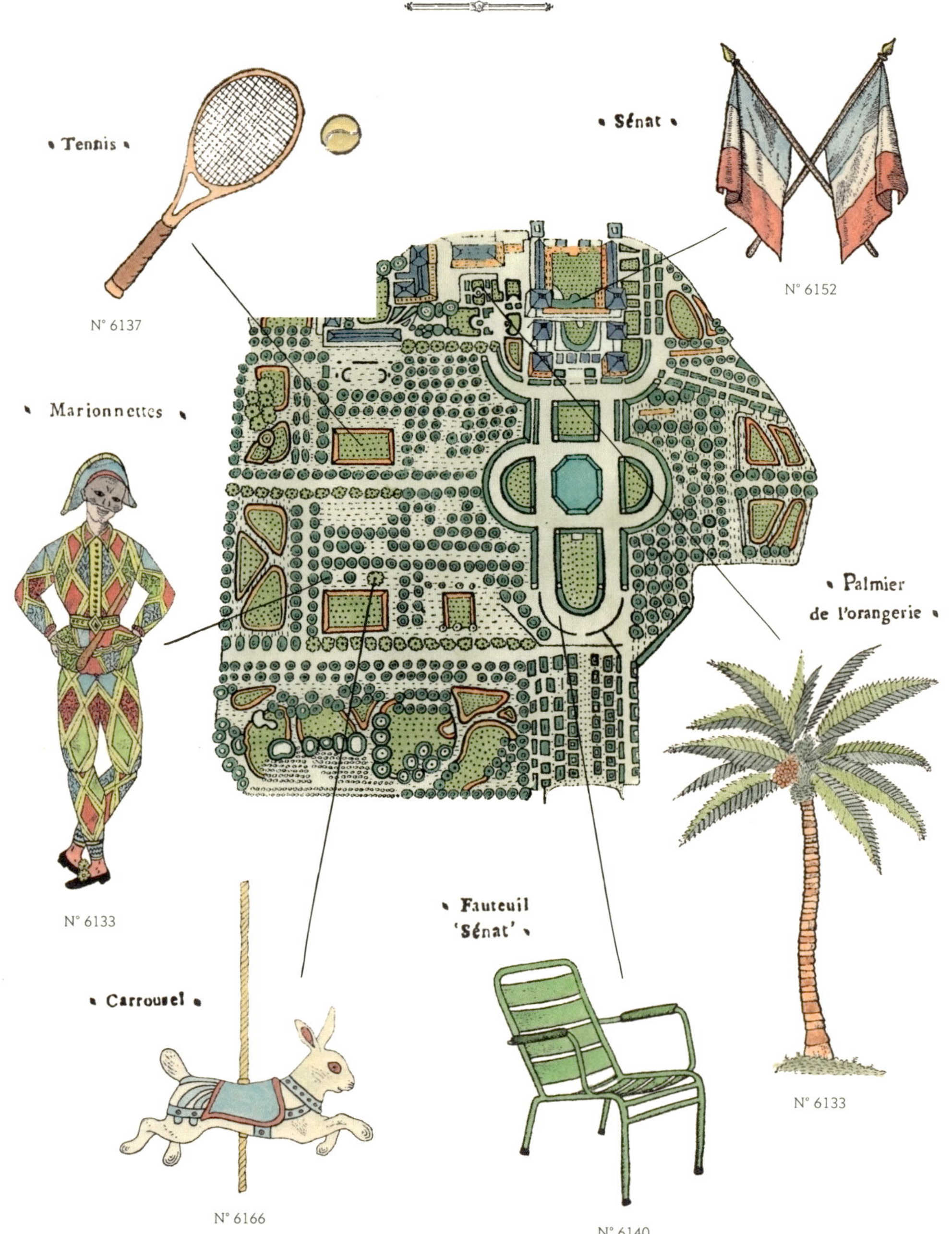

◈ JARDIN DU LUXEMBOURG ◈

1

Entrances rue de Vaugirard, rue de Médicis,
boulevard Saint-Michel, rue Guynemer
M° Notre-Dame-des-Champs / Odéon;
RER Luxembourg
01 42 34 20 00
*jardin.senat.fr/en • @jardinduluxembourg_*

The Luxembourg Garden—tucked between Saint-Germain-des-Prés, Montparnasse, and the Latin Quarter—has always been close to my heart. My mom used to read me a picture book about the park when I was little, and perhaps this explains why I feel such a strong connection to it and just had to open my boutique a stone's throw away. Commissioned by the newly widowed Marie de Medici in 1612, the park was created as a refuge for the homesick regent and her dauphin son, along with an Italianate grotto and a palace, which today houses the Senate. It remains a haven in the center of the capital for Parisians of all stripes, from energetic joggers and tennis players to strolling lovers, leisurely picnickers, and kids having fun in the playground.

N°6762

N°6763

N°6764

TOY SAILBOATS

Entrance porte Gay-Lussac
lesvoiliersduluxembourg.fr

These old-fashioned miniature wooden sailboats, available for rent since 1927, make for a charming sight, taking visitors back in time as tots prod their boat along with a wooden pole until the breeze catches in the sails. Eric, the owner, pampers his fleet of some thirty toy vessels, sewing torn sails, repairing broken masts, and replacing the flags himself in his little workshop hidden away in the park.

N°6071

THÉÂTRE DES MARIONNETTES

Entrance porte Fleurus
M° Notre-Dame-des-Champs
Programs: 01 43 26 46 47 / Information: 06 09 77 28 75
marionnettesduluxembourg.fr

On Sunday mornings, I often bring my niece and nephew here to watch Guignol, France's star puppet, and his battalion of hand-carved marionettes perform their antics. Opened in 1933, this 275-seat puppet theater—the largest of its kind in France—is run by the founder's son, who passionately perpetuates the family tradition and presents his own adaptations of beloved fairy tales and fables, to the delight of youngsters from 3 years and up.

N° 6004 N° 6005 N° 6006 N° 6007 N° 6008

GARNIER MERRY-GO-ROUND

Entrance porte Fleurus

The city's oldest *manège*, nestled in the shade of the park's horse chestnut trees, is a frequent after-school stop when I collect my niece and nephew. Designed by Charles Garnier and opened in 1879, it features a menagerie of hand-carved animals—horses, stags, giraffes, an elephant—and a couple of chariots. The ride also offers kids the possibility to play the *jeu de bagues*, in which they try to collect brass rings on a wand as the carrousel spins—occasionally with help from the friendly staff.

N° 6414 N° 6361

N° 6301 N° 6345 N° 6385

N° 6369

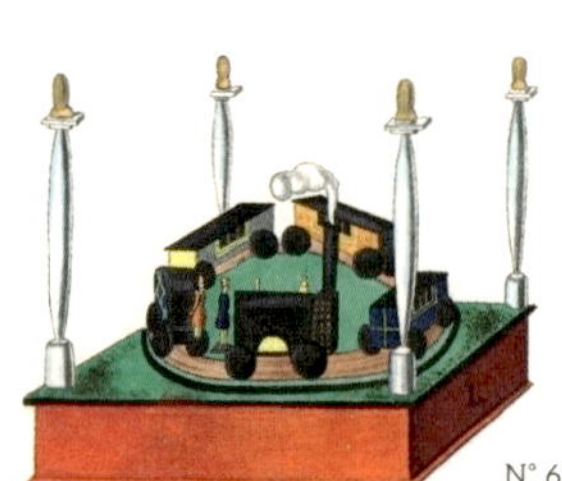

N° 6362

SÉNAT CHAIRS

These steel chairs, so emblematic of the garden, first appeared in 1923 and come in three models: chair, armchair, and the highly prized recliner. Throughout the seasons, visitors will find them strewn around the park, available for use free of charge. An endless source of inspiration for my watercolors, they appear on my collections of porcelain, glasses, scarves, and more.

BEEHIVES

Entrance porte Croquet

The capital's oldest apiary was created in the garden's nursery in 1856, where a beekeeping school has operated ever since. The current apiary, entirely renovated in 1991, perpetuates the unusual tradition of cultivating honey in the heart of Paris. The beehives' production is sold at the annual honey festival, held here in late September, and I never miss the opportunity to stock up for the year!

LA TERRASSE DE MADAME

138 rue de Médicis, Jardin du Luxembourg,
entrance porte Médicis
RER Luxembourg
01 42 01 17 96
@laterrassedemadame

On sunny days, this restaurant housed in a charming kiosk within the park is the perfect spot for lunch. I come here to enjoy the *oeufs mimosa* and a Caesar salad on the terrace and take in the magical surroundings, far from the bustle of the city. And to top it all, the interior is decorated with wallpaper that I illustrated for Pierre Frey—such an honor!

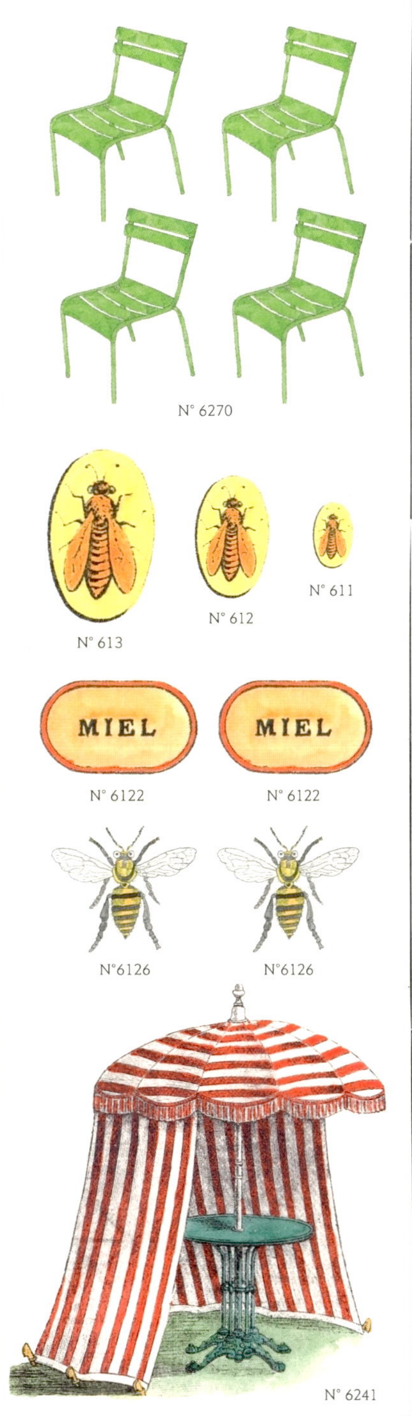

N° 6270
N° 613 N° 612 N° 611
N° 6122 N° 6122
N°6126 N°6126
N° 6241

◈ MUSÉE D'HISTOIRE DE LA MÉDECINE ◈

(2)

12 rue de l'École-de-Médecine
M° Odéon
01 76 53 16 93
u-paris.fr/musee-de-lhistoire-de-la-medecine/

Since 1955, one of the oldest collections of medical instruments in Europe has been on display in this superb gallery, built between 1905 and 1907. Some of the period tools are quite intimidating! This panorama of portraits of famous surgeons, curiosities, and surgical objects from the past is a reminder that time can indeed work wonders.

N°6348

◈ BEAUX-ARTS DE PARIS – COUR DU MÛRIER ◈

(3)

14 rue Bonaparte
M° Saint-Germain-des-Prés

Behind the facade of the École Nationale des Beaux-Arts de Paris lies a hidden garden of which I'm particularly fond: La Cour du Mûrier. Sometimes I settle in here to draw across from the fountain, between the two large trees. Students work diligently, their sketches strewn all over the place, and statues arranged around the cloister wait patiently to be admired. And they're in luck—you'll want to spend hours here.

N°6229

N°6197

N°6231

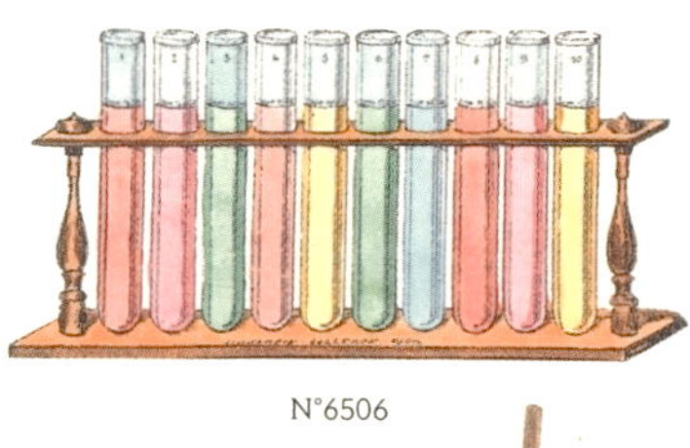

N°6506

N°6364

N°6365

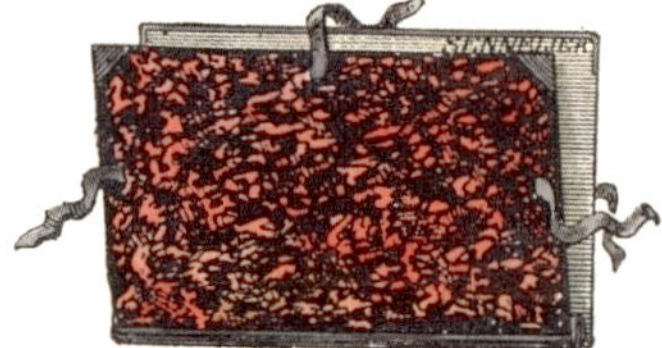

N°6262

◈ MUSÉE D'HISTOIRE DE LA
MÉDECINE

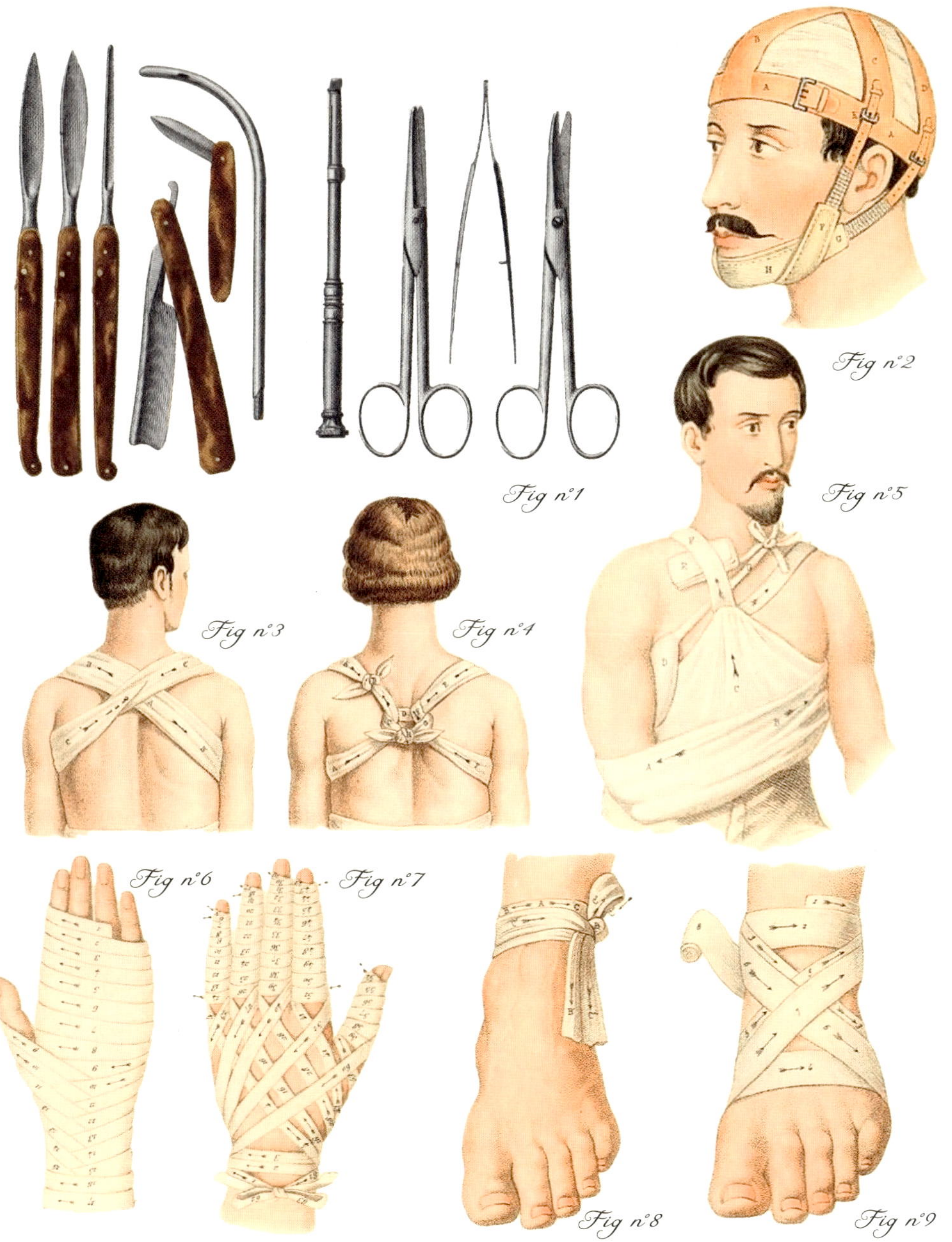

12, RUE DE L'ÉCOLE-DE-MÉDECINE — PARIS 6E

MUSÉE DE MINÉRALOGIE

CURIOSITÉS MINÉRALES

60, BOULEVARD SAINT-MICHEL — PARIS 6^{E}

◈ MUSÉE DE MINÉRALOGIE DE L'ÉCOLE DES MINES ◈

60 boulevard Saint-Michel
RER Luxembourg
01 40 51 91 39
musee.minesparis.psl.eu • @mineralotech

Inside the magnificent Hôtel de Vendôme, home to the elite École des Mines engineering school, this mineralogy museum is a hidden gem. Established in 1794, it boasts an impressive collection of 100,000 mineral specimens (5,000 are on display). Time stands still within the series of old-fashioned galleries featuring antique vitrines, creaking parquet floors, and views over the Jardin du Luxembourg.

N° 6670

◈ MUSÉE ZADKINE ◈

5

100 bis rue d'Assas
M° Notre-Dame-des-Champs; RER Port Royal
01 55 42 77 20
zadkine.paris.fr/en • @museezadkine

This museum offers a haven from the bustle of Montparnasse. For most of his life, artist Ossip Zadkine lived and worked in this building, inaugurated in 1982 and renovated in 2012. After crossing a small courtyard, enter the home-museum where the artist's drawings are exhibited. Then, enjoy a breath of fresh air in the garden dotted with sculptures, before finishing your visit in Zadkine's light-filled studio.

N° 6170

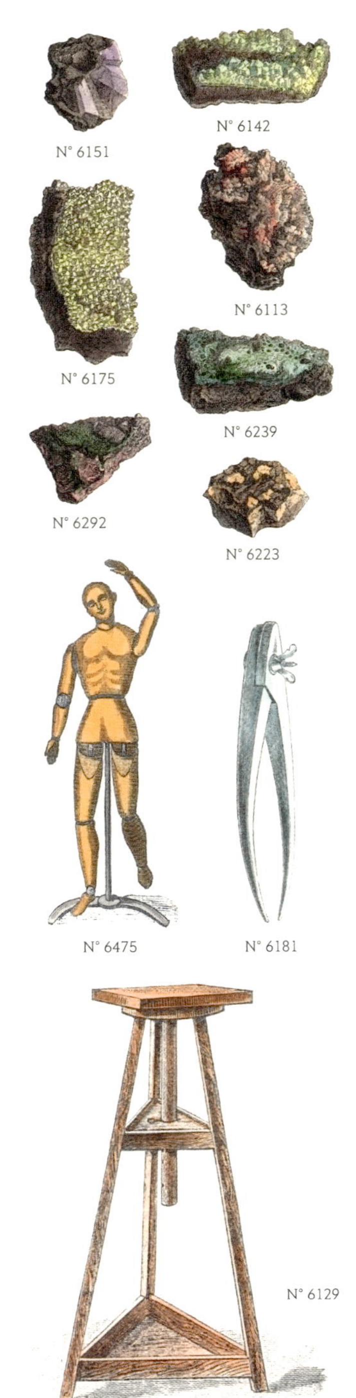

N° 6151 · N° 6142 · N° 6175 · N° 6113 · N° 6239 · N° 6292 · N° 6223 · N° 6475 · N° 6181 · N° 6129

MUSÉE NATIONAL EUGÈNE DELACROIX

6

6 rue de Furstemberg
M° Saint-Germain-des-Prés / Mabillon
01 44 41 86 50
musee-delacroix.fr/en • @museedelacroix

"The sight of my little garden and the cheerful aspect of my studio always fill me with delight." Devoted to artist Eugène Delacroix, this museum is a well-kept secret on one of the most charming squares in Paris. I could sit for hours on the little sun-drenched bench in the garden hidden behind the museum, near the studio, where paint-crusted palettes seem to patiently await the master's return.

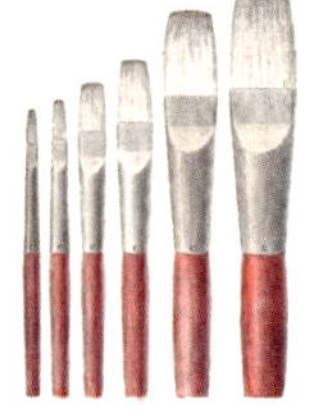

N° 6261

N° 6262

N° 6263

GALERIE JEAN-CLAUDE MARTINEZ

7

21 rue Saint-Sulpice
M° Odéon / Mabillon
09 82 37 08 06

Welcome to the temple of antique prints. This gallery, founded in 1976, occupies a prime spot between the Jardin du Luxembourg and Saint-Sulpice church. Behind its burgundy storefront lie hundreds of prints, engravings, and lithographs from the 16th to 19th centuries, spanning cartography, art, botany, and more. A journey into the Paris of old and a tribute to the decorative tastes of our forebears.

N° 6269

N° 6390

N° 6350

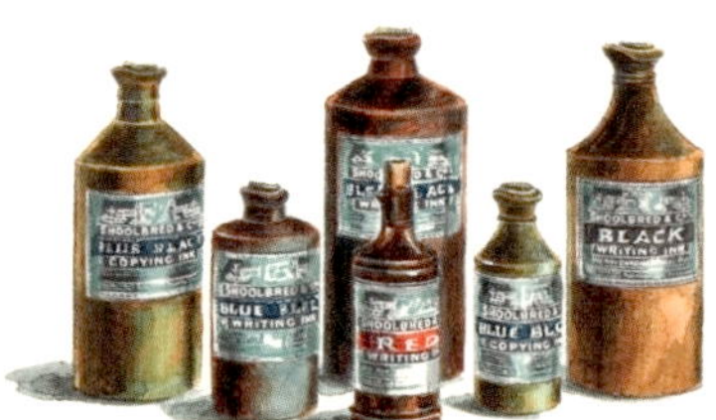

N° 6443

N° 6245

◈ YVELINE ANTIQUES ◈

8

4 rue de Furstemberg
M° Saint-Germain-des-Prés
01 43 26 56 91
yveline-antiquites.com/en/ • @yvelineantiques

Located on Paris's most charming square, this antiques shop has delighted bargain hunters and chance passersby alike since 1954. Agathe Derieux took over from her grandmother in 2013, and she perpetuates Yveline's passion for articulated artists' mannequins—the carefully posed wooden figures have pride of place in this fairytale setting, complete with crystal chandeliers, silvered mirrors, and mesmerizing portraits.

◈ AU BAIN MARIE ◈

9

59 boulevard Raspail
M° Sèvres – Babylone
01 42 71 08 69
aubainmarie.com/en/ • @aubainmarieparis

Reminiscent of a cabinet of curiosities, this store has been dedicated to the art of entertaining since 1977. Founder Aude Clément, today joined by her son César, proposes rare, original, beautiful tableware. This is where I got my favorite plates, from the Forest collection of dinnerware hand-painted with charming animals and plants. A veritable lesson in how to create elegant yet whimsical table settings!

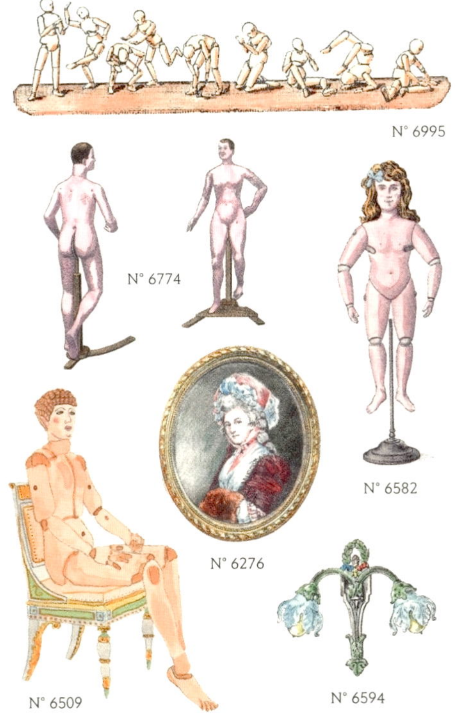

N° 6995
N° 6774
N° 6582
N° 6276
N° 6509
N° 6594

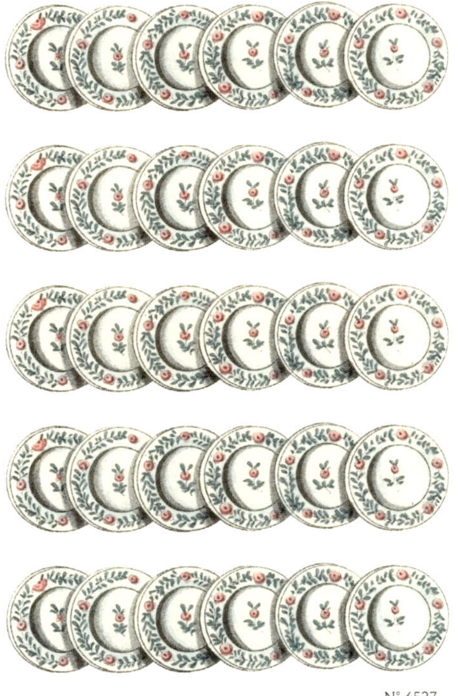

N° 6527

◈ HORLOGES & PENDULES – FRANÇOIS HUBERT ◈

10

43 rue Madame
M° Saint-Sulpice / Rennes
01 45 44 22 00
francois-hubert.fr/en/

A few doors down from my boutique, much-loved local artisan François Hubert has perpetuated the fine, often forgotten, art of clock repairs since 1994. I love the joyful sound of the ticking and chiming of the hundreds of clocks in his workshop, and watching as François examines a faulty mechanism through his loupe, deep in concentration. Antique clocks from his collection are also available to admire or buy.

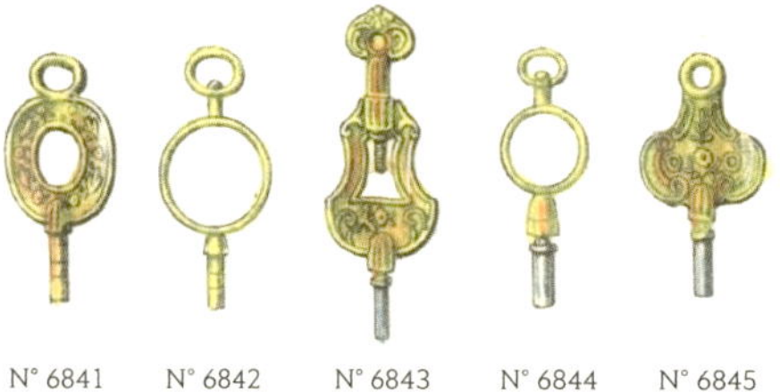

N° 6841 N° 6842 N° 6843 N° 6844 N° 6845

◈ ANTIQ PHOTO ◈

11

11 & 16 rue de Vaugirard
M° Odéon; RER Luxembourg
09 81 92 92 90
antiq-photo.com/en/ • @antiqphotogallery

Antiq Photo is an unclassifiable place. Amid the scent of a studio from a bygone era, daguerreotypes stand behind a 1933 Leica, and weathered camera bodies pose next to optical toys and devices that predate cinema. I love discovering the treasures hidden in this hushed boutique-gallery—a trip here always makes me want to trade my smartphone for a bellows camera.

N° 6439 N° 6503 N° 6607 N° 6149 N° 6132 N° 6745 N° 6224 N° 6238

ZUBER

12

36 rue Bonaparte
M° Saint-Germain-des-Prés
01 42 77 95 91
zuber.fr/en • @zuberofficial

Since 1797, Zuber has provided wall coverings for the world's most beautiful locations. I came here to find wallpaper for my boutique and for other interior design projects. They make everything—from friezes to panoramic scenes—by hand, mainly using woodblock printing techniques on brushed grounds. Run your hand over one of these papers (or look up at the ceiling) to fully appreciate the artistry of the oldest wall covering manufactory still in operation.

N° 6172

ATELIERS LISON DE CAUNES

13

20–22 rue Mayet
M° Duroc
01 40 56 02 10
lisondecaunes.com/en/ • @ateliersLisondecaunes

The somewhat ordinary carriage door at 20 rue Mayet has concealed a place of wonder since 1978. At the end of the small courtyard protected by a climbing vine, you'll find the workshops of Lison de Caunes. This specialist in straw marquetry works with absolute mastery and infinite delicacy. Each piece is a tribute to this exceptional fine craft.

N° 6607 N° 6608 N° 6607

N° 6198

N° 6386

N° 6296

N° 6467

MARIN MONTAGUT

N° 6808

14

48 rue Madame
M° Saint-Placide / Rennes
09 81 22 53 44
marinmontagut.com/en • @marinmontagut

N° 6803

Step through the doorway at 48 rue Madame to embark on a voyage into my bygone Paris. The bell tinkles as you enter, the freshly waxed parquet creaks beneath your feet, and the large pigeonhole display beckons, its many cubbies discretely harboring a thousand stories yet to be written.

I've dreamed of having my own shop since I was a child. Finding this boutique, tucked away in the heart of the 6th arrondissement, was like discovering a forgotten jewel box designed to hold my treasures. Each item on display has a soul, a past, and each detail gives a subtle nod to Paris. Visitors will find bespoke creations artisanally-made in our Parisian workshops: porcelain objects, hand-blown glasses, books with secret compartments, and miniature "showcases of wonders"—all painted by hand. But there are also scarves, pencils, watercolor palettes, curiosities, along with my Tarot cards and my fragrance, L'Eau Douce, to extend your stay in my marvelous world. It gives me so much pleasure to imagine that these little delights will become your own memory-filled souvenirs.

Take the time to browse—here, the visit itself is a chance to get away from it all. In the background, Charles Trenet croons "Revoir Paris," while Glenn Miller makes the stars dance.

AU 48 RUE MADAME À PARIS

MARIN MONTAGUT

MARCHAND D'OBJETS EN TOUS GENRES
SOUVENIRS DE PARIS FAITS À LA MAIN

N° 6300

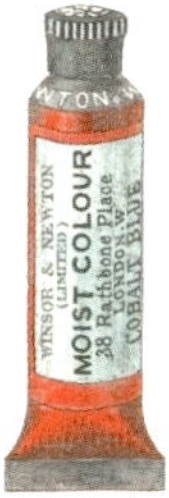

N° 6301

N° 6302

N° 6303

N° 6304

N° 6305

N° 6295

N° 6295

N° 6306

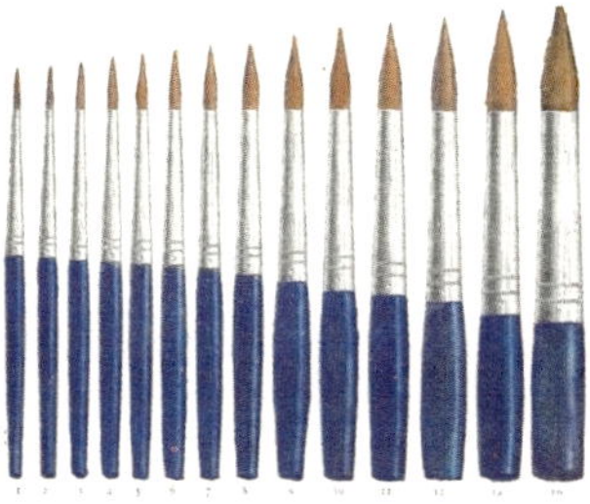

N° 6307

N° 6308

N° 6309

N° 6310

N° 6311

N° 6312

N° 6313

N° 6314

N° 6315

CHERCHE MIDI COULEURS

15

58 rue du Cherche-Midi
M° Rennes / Sèvres – Babylone / Saint-Placide
01 45 48 64 41
cherchemidicouleurs.com • @cherchemidicouleurs

Just steps from my boutique on rue Madame, this perfectly assembled bric-a-brac shop, created in 2012, overflows with just about everything. Usually, I come here for screws or a lightbulb and leave with a few extra candles or even a pretty basket. It's the kind of local hardware store that makes you want to move house to be nearer to it. You are sure to find whatever you need for your home here.

N° 6065 N° 6066 N° 6067 N° 6068

CHARVIN

16

57 quai des Grands-Augustins
M° Pont Neuf / Saint-Michel;
RER Saint-Michel – Notre-Dame
01 43 54 98 97
charvin-arts.com/gb/ • @charvinarts

Walking into Charvin is like stepping into the studio of an artisan-magician. This color alchemist always suggests just the right shade of blue, the perfect varnish, or a rare selection of fine, durable pigments. I worked with this family business, established in 1830, to develop my travel watercolor set—available with a pink or green case—that I take with me everywhere. This is elegance of the highest standard, made on the Côte d'Azur.

N° 6153

N° 6823

N° 6643

N° 6175

N° 6811

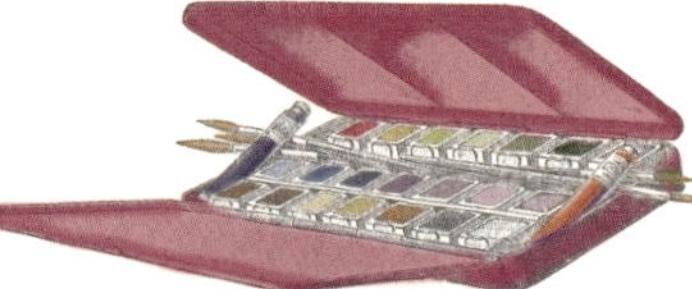

N° 6812

N° 6217

N° 6255

◈ RELMA ◈

3 rue des Poitevins
M° Odéon
01 43 25 40 52
relma.fr • @relmaparis

Many Parisians are unfamiliar with this shop, a must-visit for bookbinding and paper enthusiasts. It's where I get my favorite marbled paper. Tucked away on the narrow rue des Poitevins, this almost century-old boutique is also a bastion of exceptional leathers. Conversation here revolves around bone folders, foil stamping, invisible stitching, and shagreen bindings. A secret address that is hard to share.

N° 6851

◈ TYPODÉON ◈

6 rue Monsieur-le-Prince
M° Odéon
01 43 26 03 31
typodeon.fr

Founded in 1888, this old Parisian workshop, with its lustrous green facade highlighted in gold lettering, is one of the last letterpress printers in Paris. It will always remain special to me as it's where I had my first business card made, when I was 20. Patrick makes elegant custom cards and announcements, bookplates, stationery, and embossed business cards, in English type on Van den Velde paper.

N° 6393

N° 6457

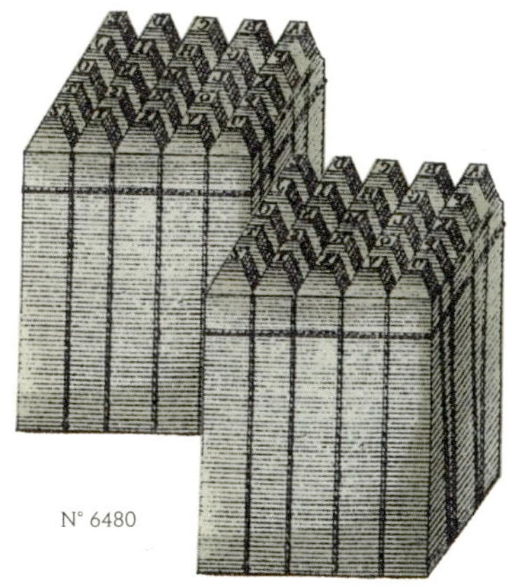

N° 6480

ATELIER LAMBERT BARNETT

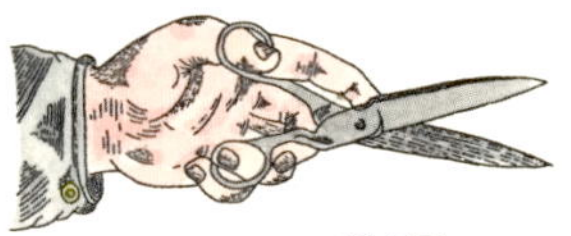
N° 6171

4 rue Monsieur-le-Prince
M° Odéon
01 46 33 08 84
reliure-lb.fr

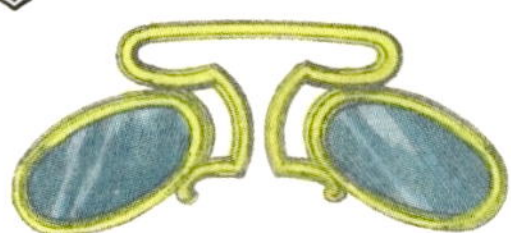
N° 6119

N° 6538

N° 6629

N° 6181

Atelier Lambert Barnett is located on rue Monsieur-le-Prince, in the heart of the printers' district. Its savoir faire is a family affair, handed down from father to son since 1830. The workshop produces exquisite leather-bound volumes, restores all kinds of books from the 16th to 19th centuries, and, in short, keeps the art of fine bookmaking alive.

N° 6596

N° 6086

N° 6870

SAN FRANCISCO BOOK COMPANY

17 rue Monsieur-le-Prince
M° Odéon
01 43 29 15 70
sfparis.com • @sfbooksparis

With a cute red facade that looks straight out of a Harry Potter novel, this landmark secondhand English-language bookstore—open since 1997—is a bright portal connecting Paris to the generous literary spirit of its namesake city. The shelves are stacked with everything from fiction and science fiction to history, art, philosophy, theater, music, film, and food. Open seven days a week!

LIBRAIRIE RIEFFEL

15 rue de l'Odéon
M° Odéon
01 43 54 92 23
@librairie_rieffel

Open since 1870, Librairie Rieffel is my favorite cabinet of literary curiosities. Visitors are greeted by the distinctive scent of aged paper. I enjoy spending time among the beautiful old books with their gilded covers. Rummage around in the bins outside the entrance and never leave without asking for a recommendation. A book lover's paradise, run by true enthusiasts.

❖ LIBRAIRIE FRANÇOIS CHANUT ❖

41 rue Mazarine
M° Mabillon / Odéon
01 43 54 04 70
@librairie_chanut

For me, this antiquarian bookshop is the most charming in all of Paris. Behind the storefront of this converted butcher's shop, shelves are packed with old books, precious manuscripts, and rare editions reserved for the lucky few. Valérie, François Chanut's daughter, is your guide to this postage stamp of a shop that feels like a chest full of treasure.

N° 6288

❖ LIBRAIRIE ALAIN BRIEUX ❖

48 rue Jacob
M° Saint-Germain-des-Prés
01 42 60 21 98
alainbrieux.com • @alainbrieux

This bookstore-cum-laboratory offers a colorful ramble through the scientific knowledge of yesteryear. Browse 17th-century medical texts, anatomical plates, mannequins, and globes settled comfortably in their displays, under the impervious gaze of the crocodile hanging from the ceiling. Both unsettling and fascinating, this shop always leaves me with the desire to start a new collection.

N° 6103

N° 6104

N° 6185

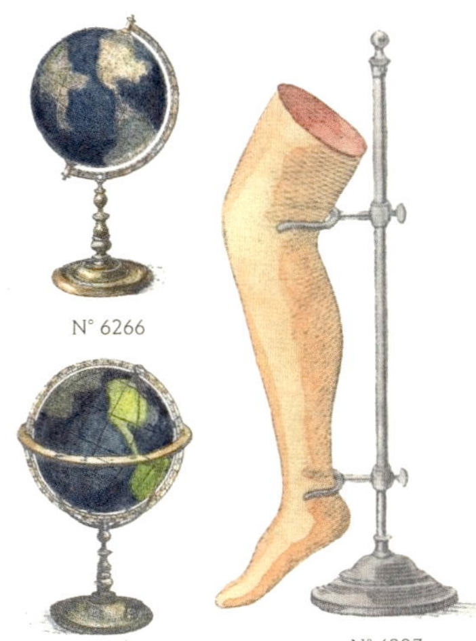

N° 6266

N° 6267

N° 6287

◈ AU PLAT D'ÉTAIN ◈

24

16 rue Guisarde
M° Mabillon / Saint-Sulpice
01 43 54 32 06
soldats-plomb-au-plat-etain.fr

Established in 1775, this little shop overflows with toy soldiers and figurines, many from the historic French manufacturer CBG Mignot. Napoleon, Caesar, Louis XV—the fantasy battalion of colorful figures I once paraded along my grandparents' living room floor now stand to attention on shelves in my nephew's room. Each collectible is entirely crafted and painted by hand.

N° 6490

N° 6648

N° 6417

N° 6120

N° 6385

◈ GALERIE DU JOUET ANCIEN ◈

25

8 rue des Grands-Augustins
M° Saint-Michel; RER Saint-Michel – Notre-Dame
01 43 26 36 75
@galeriedujouetancien

Michel, with his childlike enthusiasm and expert eye for treasures, has been collecting antique toys since the 1960s. Here, miniature cars like the Renault Carambar and the speedsters of the 24 Hours of Le Mans steal the limelight. This shop is the perfect place to find a birthday gift or finally buy your dream car—in 1:43 scale.

N° 6665

N° 6666

N° 6667

N° 6151

N° 6180

N° 6122

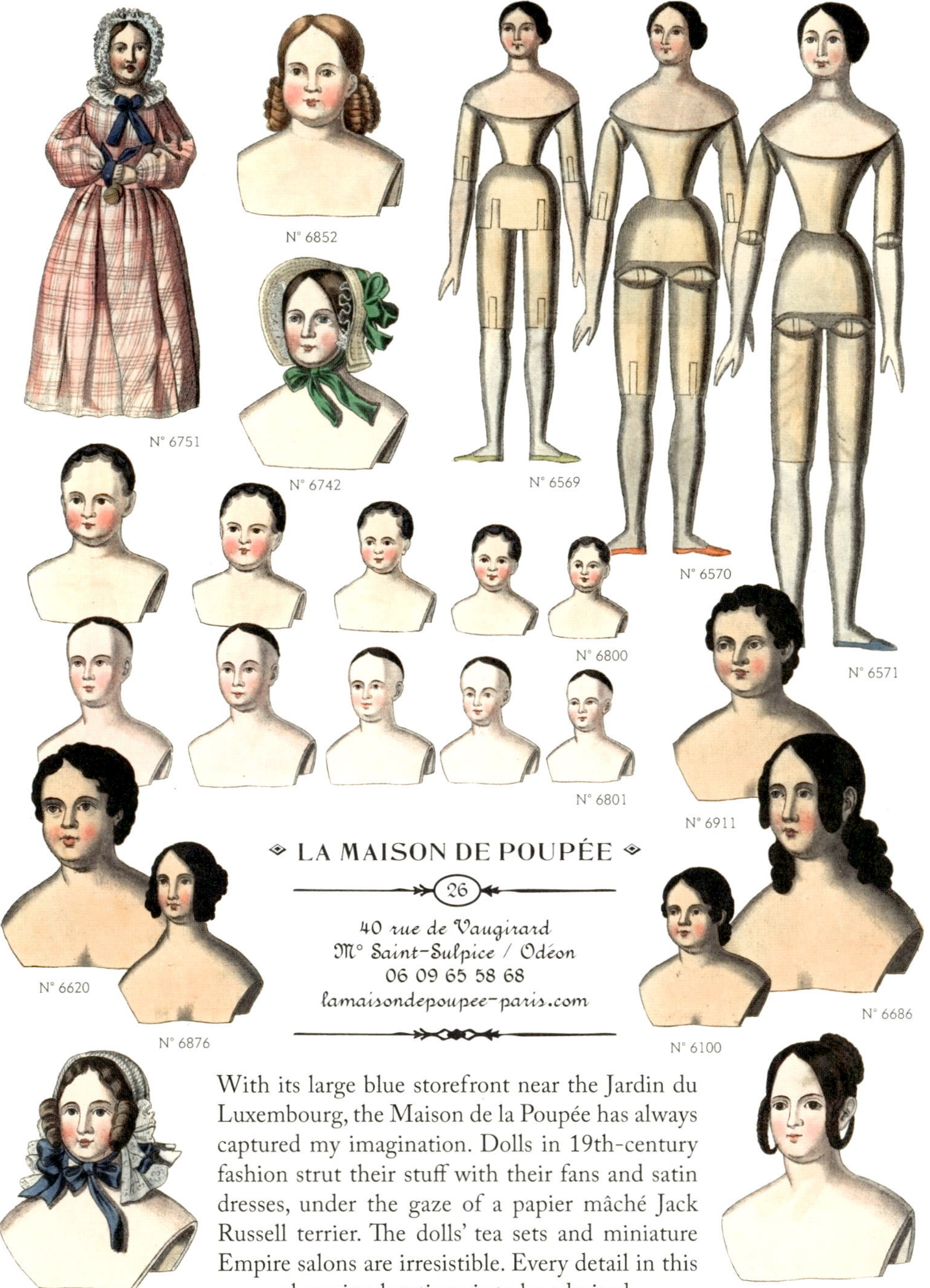

LA MAISON DE POUPÉE

26

40 rue de Vaugirard
M° Saint-Sulpice / Odéon
06 09 65 58 68
lamaisondepoupee-paris.com

With its large blue storefront near the Jardin du Luxembourg, the Maison de la Poupée has always captured my imagination. Dolls in 19th-century fashion strut their stuff with their fans and satin dresses, under the gaze of a papier mâché Jack Russell terrier. The dolls' tea sets and miniature Empire salons are irresistible. Every detail in this charming boutique is to be admired.

AU COR DE CHASSE

25 rue de Condé
M° Odéon
01 43 26 51 89
lagonda.fr/le-cor-de-chasse/ • @lagonda_paris

One day I received an invitation to a charity gala with "Attire: Black Tie" marked at the bottom. Luckily, a good friend of mine recommended this historic store—open for more than 150 years, no less!—where you can rent a tux at the last minute, along with every other elegant accessory you might require to dress the part, and slip into the role of someone else for an evening.

N° 6862

KERSTIN ADOLPHSON

157 boulevard Saint-Germain
M° Saint-Germain-des-Prés
01 45 48 00 14
kerstinadolphson.com/en/ • @kerstinadolphson

This tiny Swedish outpost in the heart of Paris is an ode to cozy comfort. For 30 years, the piles of sweaters and blankets at the entrance have been making folks hope winter will linger. I love exploring the selection of clothing, objects, and accessories, and I especially adore the clogs. Simple, well-made beauty—in a word, Scandinavian elegance.

N° 6247 N° 6248 N° 6249

N° 6250 N° 6251 N° 6252

N° 6197 N° 6197

N° 6222 N° 6223

N° 6360

N° 6289

GEORGES THUILLIER

29

10 place Saint-Sulpice
M° Saint-Sulpice
01 43 26 00 57
thuillier-art-religieux.com

Facing Saint-Sulpice church, this little store, open since 1948, is bursting with all sorts of religious trinkets, including a huge range of colorful Provençal nativity figurines known as *santons*. I came here to choose baptism medals for my five godchildren. I love the beautiful church candles, and on my way out I grab a few saint prayer cards to slip into my wallet.

N° 6076

TRUDON

30

78 rue de Seine
M° Odéon / Mabillon
01 43 26 46 50
trudon.com/us_en/ • @trudon

Claude Trudon established his candle-making business in Paris in 1643. Several years later, he became the Royal Wax Manufacture, supplying candles to the French court. Nothing has changed since: the wax is still made in France, and the fragrances continue to perfume our interiors. The candles are little jewels in themselves. I like coming here to shop for gifts or to stock up on pretty candlesticks.

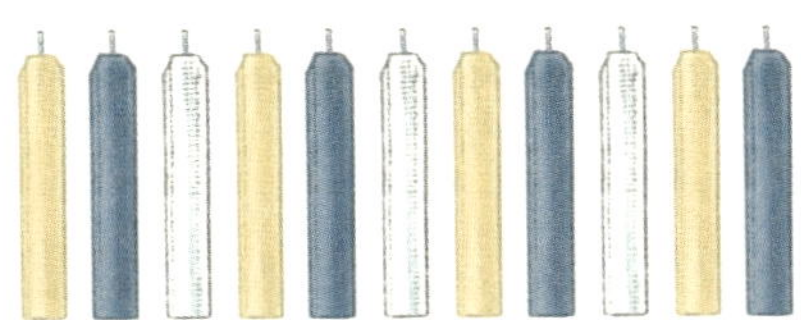

N° 6065

N° 6292

N° 6292

N° 6293

N° 6294

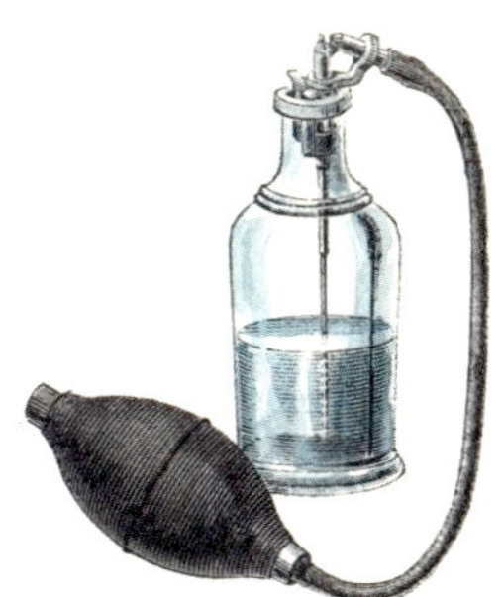

N° 6313

N° 6252

◈ MAISON VEROT ◈

31

3 rue Notre-Dame-des-Champs
M° Saint-Placide / Rennes
01 45 48 83 32
maisonverot.fr • @maison_verot

This award-winning delicatessen-charcuterie changed my mind about *pâté en croute*. The duck, fig, and foie gras version is my favorite, but everything here is as beautiful to the eye as it is to the palate. Dedicated to excellence for four generations, Maison Verot was founded by Jean in 1930 in Saint-Étienne. Parisian pâté aficionados rejoiced when grandson Gilles and his family relocated the business to the French capital in 1997.

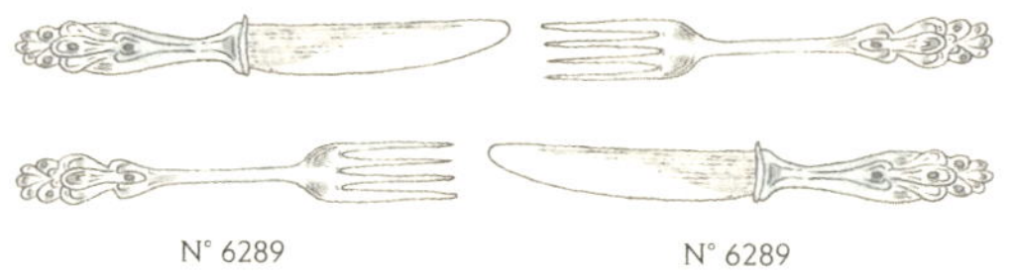

N° 6289 N° 6289

◈ LE SELECT MONTPARNASSE ◈

32

99 boulevard du Montparnasse
M° Vavin
01 45 48 38 24
leselectmontparnasse.fr/en/ • @leselectmontparnasse

Le Select hasn't changed a bit since it opened in 1923. Like a freeze-frame of 1920s Paris, it still offers guests the ambience of a quintessential old-fashioned brasserie. For lunch, enjoy a Niçoise salad made with Ortiz tuna. In the evening, the hand-cut steak tartare made with Aubrac beef takes center stage, followed by the signature lemon tart. And for those in need of a midnight snack, not to worry—the restaurant is open until 3 a.m.

N° 6706

N° 6206

N° 6303

N° 6234

N° 6164

N° 6140

N° 6170

N° 6333

LADURÉE

33

21 rue Bonaparte
M° Saint-Germain-des-Prés
01 44 07 64 87
laduree.fr/en/ • @maisonladuree

I love biting into a delicate macaron surrounded by Ladurée's opulent baroque decor. Madeleine Castaing, an interior designer from the early 20th century, opened her boutique here in 1947; devoted to luxury pastries today, the pâtisserie pays tribute to this artist and her maximalist style. Climb the stairs to the tea room, and you'll immediately feel as though you've walked into a boudoir from another era.

N° 6087

N° 6088

N° 6089

CAFÉ DE LA MAIRIE

34

8 place Saint-Sulpice
M° Saint-Sulpice
01 43 26 67 82
@cafedelamairieparis6

This authentic all-day Parisian café, open for over a century, is as much a monument as the iconic Saint-Sulpice church opposite. I love to sit on the terrace here, soak up the sun and the view, and watch the world go by. I order the *croque monsieur*, just like my idol Jane Birkin used to do, and remember all the great writers, from Georges Perec to André Breton, who have found inspiration here.

N° 6256

N° 6280

N° 6310

Simone de Beauvoir
L'invitée

N° 6541

N° 6288

N° 6350

N° 6253

N° 6201

BRASSERIE LIPP

35

151 boulevard Saint-Germain
M° Saint-Germain-des-Prés
01 45 48 53 91
brasserielipp.fr/en/ • @lippbrasserie

N° 6219

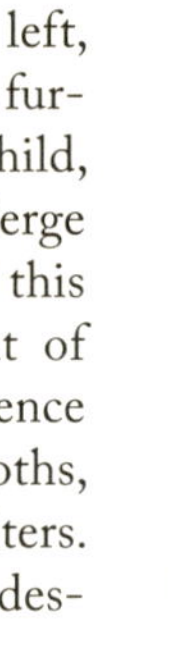

N° 6292

Through the revolving door, on the left, you'll see Yves Saint Laurent's table and, further on, writer Françoise Sagan's. As a child, I lunched next to Jane Birkin and Serge Gainsbourg here. The ground floor of this landmark brasserie has been the haunt of Tout-Paris for 130 years, and the ambience has remained unchanged, with its booths, white tablecloths, and apron-clad waiters. Lipp is the essence of Saint-Germain-des-Prés served on a platter.

LE FLEURUS

36

2 rue de Fleurus
M° Saint-Placide / Rennes
01 45 44 79 79
@lefleurus6

Located a short walk from my boutique, this café-restaurant bedecked in Formica whisks me straight back to the 1960s. I like to observe the neighborhood goings-on and watch people strolling through the Jardin du Luxembourg. The menu is always a sure bet at this cozy spot, where the Duralex drinking glasses conjure up tender childhood memories.

N° 6292

CAFÉ DE FLORE

37

172 boulevard Saint-Germain
M° Saint-Germain-des-Prés / Mabillon
01 45 48 55 26
cafedeflore.fr/en/ • @lecafedeflore

In this legendary café, opened in 1887, you can still feel the beating heart of the Paris literati who came here to pen their greatest masterpieces. I like to head upstairs, where it's calm, to enjoy a cheesy onion soup or a *salade niçoise*. Or, when I want to feel like I'm on vacation in my home city, I mingle with the tourists on the terrace that gives onto rue Saint-Benoît.

N° 6113

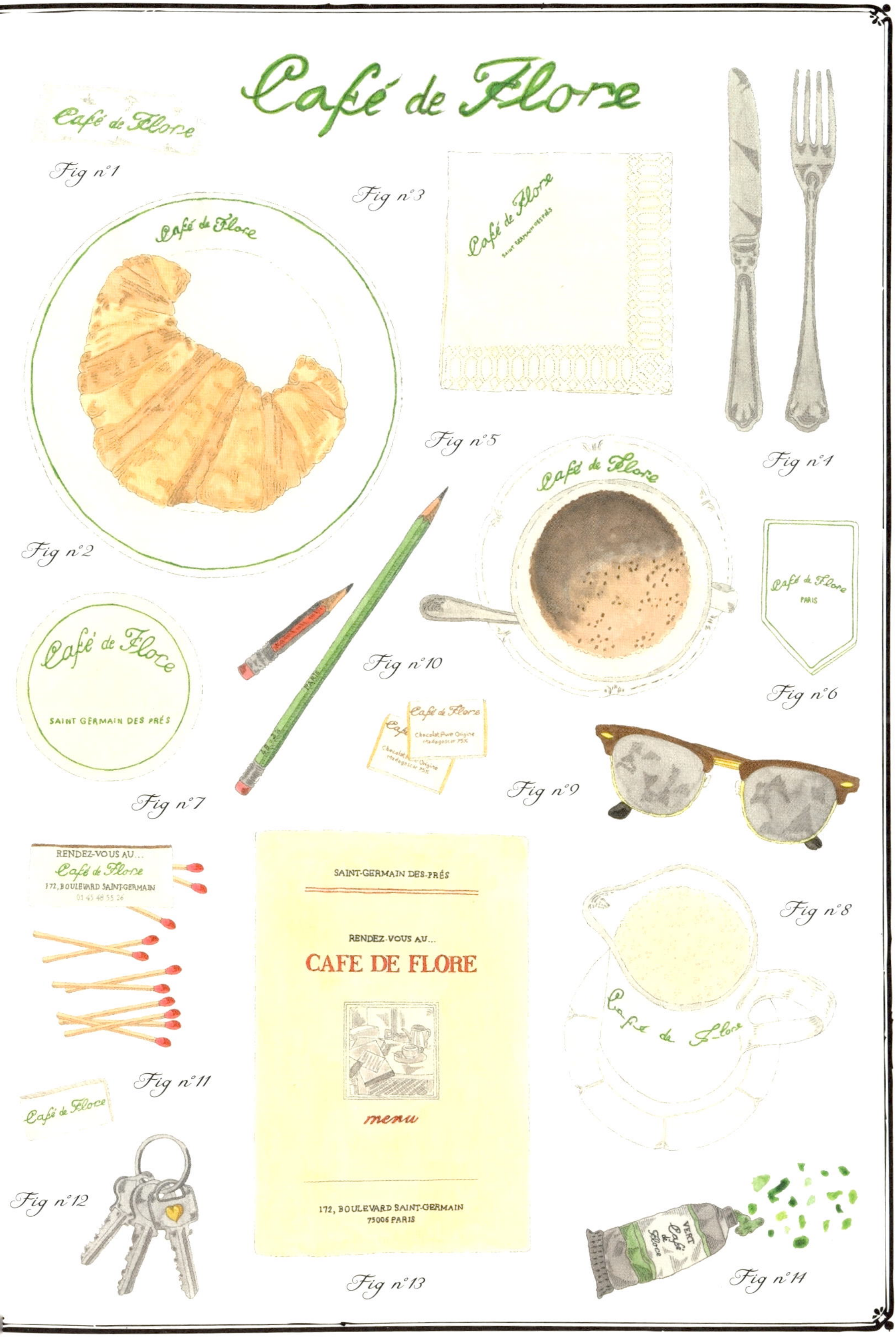
Café de Flore
Café de Flore
Fig n°1
Café de Flore
Fig n°2
Café de Flore
Saint Germain des Prés
Fig n°3
Fig n°4
Fig n°5
Café de Flore
Café de Flore
Paris
Fig n°6
Café de Flore
SAINT GERMAIN DES PRÉS
Fig n°7
Fig n°8
Café de Flore
Café de Flore
Chocolat Pure Origine Madagascar 75%
Fig n°9
Fig n°10
RENDEZ-VOUS AU...
Café de Flore
172, BOULEVARD SAINT-GERMAIN
01 45 48 55 26
Fig n°11
Café de Flore
Fig n°12
SAINT-GERMAIN DES-PRÉS
RENDEZ-VOUS AU...
CAFE DE FLORE
menu
172, BOULEVARD SAINT-GERMAIN
75006 PARIS
Fig n°13
VERT Café de Flore
Fig n°14

GUENMAÏ

38

6 rue Cardinale
M° Mabillon / Saint-Germain-des-Prés
01 43 25 13 02
@guenmai

This cute canteen dedicated to the macrobiotic diet proudly displays its motto in large letters on its green-and-white storefront: *La santé par l'alimentation* (health through food). Since 1979, chef-owner Sophie has been working to improve Parisians' eating habits. In summer, tables are set up outside to take advantage of the sunny corner in this charming warren of streets behind the Saint-Germain-des-Prés church.

TSUKIZI

2 bis rue des Ciseaux
M° Mabillon
01 43 54 65 19
tsukizi.fr • @tsukiziparis

This tiny sushi bar is the oldest of its kind in Paris. Opened in 1981, it brought a small slice of Tokyo to a pretty little street in Paris. Inside, diners watch as the chef and his assistant, true masters of the art of sushi, engage in a nimble dance. I'm always amazed by the delicacy of the dishes, and the very sight of them makes my mouth water.

N° 6381

POLIDOR

40

N° 6480

41 rue Monsieur-le-Prince
M° Odéon
01 43 26 96 34
polidor.com/en/ • @polidor_restaurant

N° 6462

N° 6608

At Polidor, you'll find checkered napkins, a short menu, and top-notch service. This institution in the Odéon neighborhood is considered one of the oldest bistros in Paris. It's perfect for a quick lunch on the terrace in spring, or a dinner of beef bourguignon and generously buttered mashed potatoes. Hemingway, Verlaine, and Rimbaud all raised a glass here—and rightly so.

N° 6609

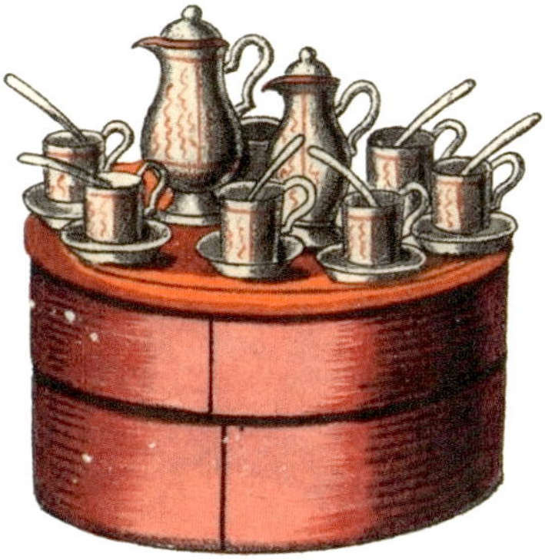

N° 6495

N° 6297

N° 6562

LE PROCOPE

41

13 rue de l'Ancienne-Comédie
M° Odéon
01 40 46 79 00
procope.com/en/ • @restaurantprocope1686

The city's first and oldest café has been a gathering place for great minds—from Voltaire to Rousseau to Diderot—since 1686. Plunging diners into the Age of the Enlightenment, this historic café-restaurant serves a classic French menu, as well as coffee and cake, in a series of elegant salons. I always order the French onion soup or parsnip and foie gras velouté. And its hidden terrasse in the rear courtyard is perfect for a tête-à-tête.

LA CRÈMERIE

42

9 rue des Quatre-Vents
M° Odéon
01 43 54 99 30
@la_cremerie

Likely dating back to 1880, this old dairy shop with its bright blue facade is one of my favorite wine bars in Saint Germain. The original period decor, with its intricately painted ceiling, makes the ideal setting to savor the carefully curated list of natural wines, along with the delicious seasonal menu, prepared in the little open kitchen at the back.

BOUILLON RACINE

43

3 rue Racine
M° Odéon
01 44 32 15 60
bouillonracine.fr • @bouillon_racine

Opened in 1906 by the Chartier brothers, Bouillon Racine is less touristy than its Grands Boulevards counterpart. The art nouveau decor is truly sumptuous, and this ancestor to Parisian brasseries has retained all of its Belle Époque charm, from the stained glass and beveled mirrors to the ceramic tiles and scrolled woodwork. Over a *plat du jour* and a glass of wine, I savor, above all, the experience of traveling back in time.

N° 6304

N° 6292

LAPÉROUSE

44

51 quai des Grands-Augustins
M° Pont Neuf / Saint-Michel;
RER Saint-Michel – Notre-Dame
01 43 26 68 04
laperouse-paris.fr/en/ • @laperouse_paris

Since 1766, this restaurant-boudoir has seen it all. I love exploring the splendid baroque interiors, meandering from one private salon to the next, where traces of the past spark my imagination. I think of Victor Hugo, who brought his grandson here for hot chocolate, and all the authors who came to meet up and enjoy the exceptional cuisine.

N° 6247

N° 6111

N° 6359

N° 6145

N° 6146

N° 6147

LA PALETTE

45

43 rue de Seine
M° Saint-Germain-des-Prés
01 43 26 68 15
la-palette.res-menu.com • @lapalette.officiel

La Palette still exudes a bohemian spirit. Once frequented by Cézanne, Braque, and Picasso, today it is a haunt for local gallery owners. I love the ceramics in the back room and the wonderful collection of painter's palettes (which I have been collecting for 15 years). Admire them over a tin of delicious sardines in olive oil, followed by tarte Tatin with fresh cream.

N° 6321 N° 6247 N° 6321

ACADÉMIE DE LA GRANDE CHAUMIÈRE

46

14 rue de la Grande-Chaumière
M° Vavin
01 43 26 13 72
academiegrandechaumiere.com •
@grandechaumiere_officiel

Since 1904, this legendary Montparnasse art school has perpetuated the tradition of life drawing. Still furnished with original easels, stools, and potbelly stove, the historic studio, with its crumbling walls, is haunted by the ghosts of famous sculptors and painters, from Antoine Bourdelle and Ossip Zadkine, who taught here, to Marc Chagall, Louise Bourgeois, and Joan Miró, to name but a few of the school's alumni.

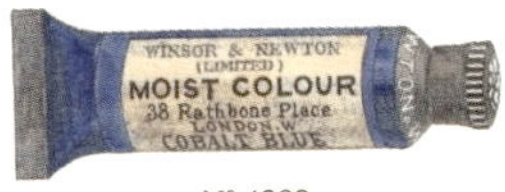

N° 6292

N° 6210

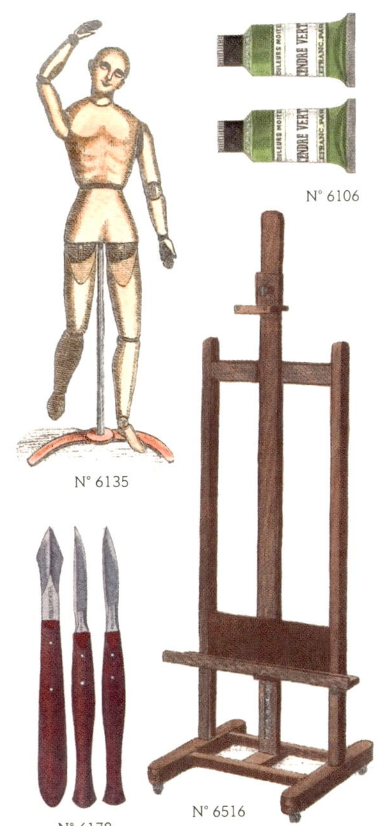

N° 6106

N° 6135

N° 6178

N° 6516

N° 6391  N° 6391  N° 6391

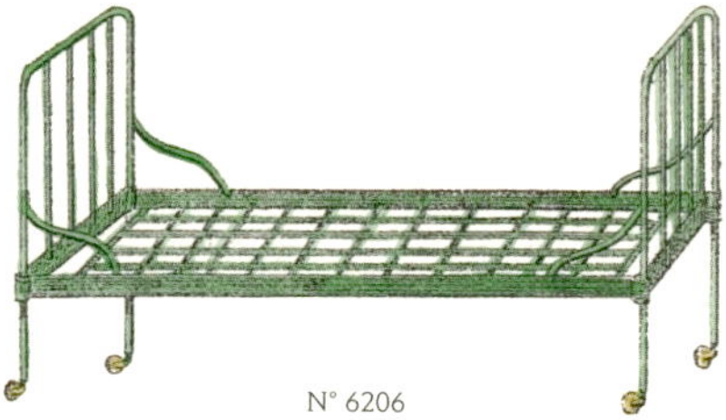

N° 6206

N° 6330

N° 6194

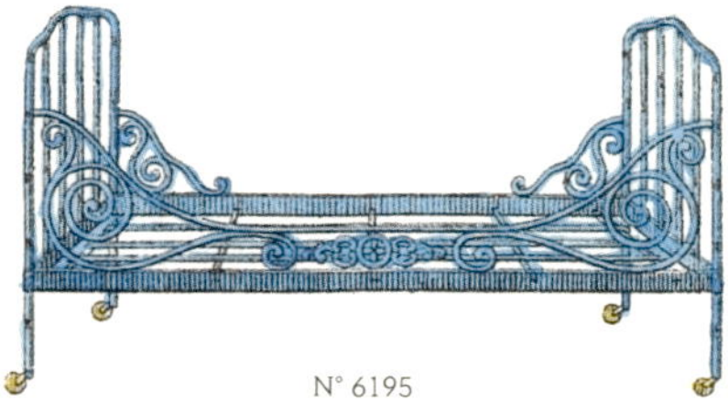

N° 6195

HÔTEL DE L'ABBAYE

47

10 rue Cassette
M° Saint-Sulpice
01 45 44 38 11
hotelabbayeparis.com/en • @hoteldelabbayeparis

I book all my meetings in this beautiful hotel just steps away from my boutique. With its ivy-covered passageway, this peaceful haven feels like a slice of the country in the heart of Saint Germain, so I also like coming here to play tourist! You'll find me huddled by the fire in winter, or sipping a cool drink in the secluded garden in finer weather, to the gentle tinkle of the fountain.

N° 6800

HÔTEL LUXEMBOURG PARC

48

42 rue de Vaugirard
M° Saint-Sulpice / Mabillon; RER Luxembourg
01 53 10 36 50
luxembourg-paris-hotel.com/en/

As the name suggests, sleeping at this hotel means waking up to a garden view. It is tucked away on the corner of rue Servandoni, one of my favorite streets in Saint-Germain-des-Prés. William Faulkner stayed here in 1925, just as his first novel was about to be published. The hotel's charmingly old-fashioned decor gives it incredible charm.

N° 6549

◈ HÔTEL LA LOUISIANE ◈

60 rue de Seine
M° Mabillon / Saint-Germain-des-Prés
01 44 32 17 17
hotel-lalouisiane.com/en • @hotellouisiane

For decades, this legendary hotel was a haven for musicians, poets, and artists who laid down their hats and their troubles here. In 1949, Juliette Gréco and Miles Davis lived their wild yet brief romance in room 10, the only one with a bathtub at the time. Much like at the Hotel Chelsea in New York, guests at La Louisiane almost hope to bump into ghosts roaming the halls.

N° 6230

◈ RELAIS HÔTEL DU VIEUX PARIS ◈

9 rue Gît-le-Cœur
M° Saint-Michel; RER Saint-Michel – Notre-Dame
01 44 32 15 90
vieuxparis.com/en/

This hotel brimming with old-fashioned charm has a long yet literary past. Built in 1480, it was first home to nobles, before becoming known as the "Beat Hotel" in the 1950s, when American Beat Generation writers, including Allen Ginsberg, William S. Burroughs, and Gregory Corso, lodged there. Today, it offers a more luxurious service, with cozy rooms decorated in Toile de Jouy.

N° 6490

N° 6267

N° 6146

N° 6364

N° 6501

N° 6273

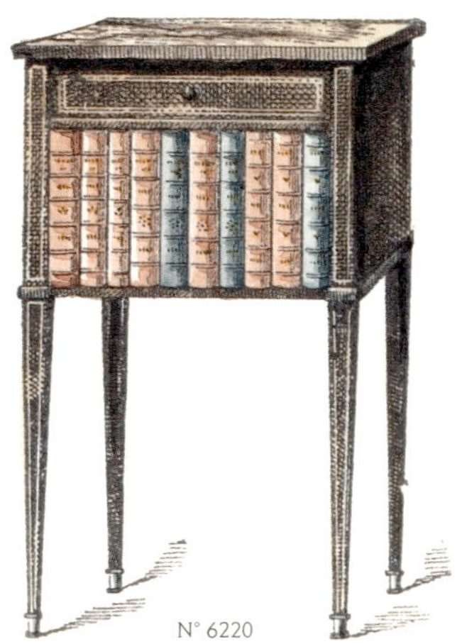

N° 6220

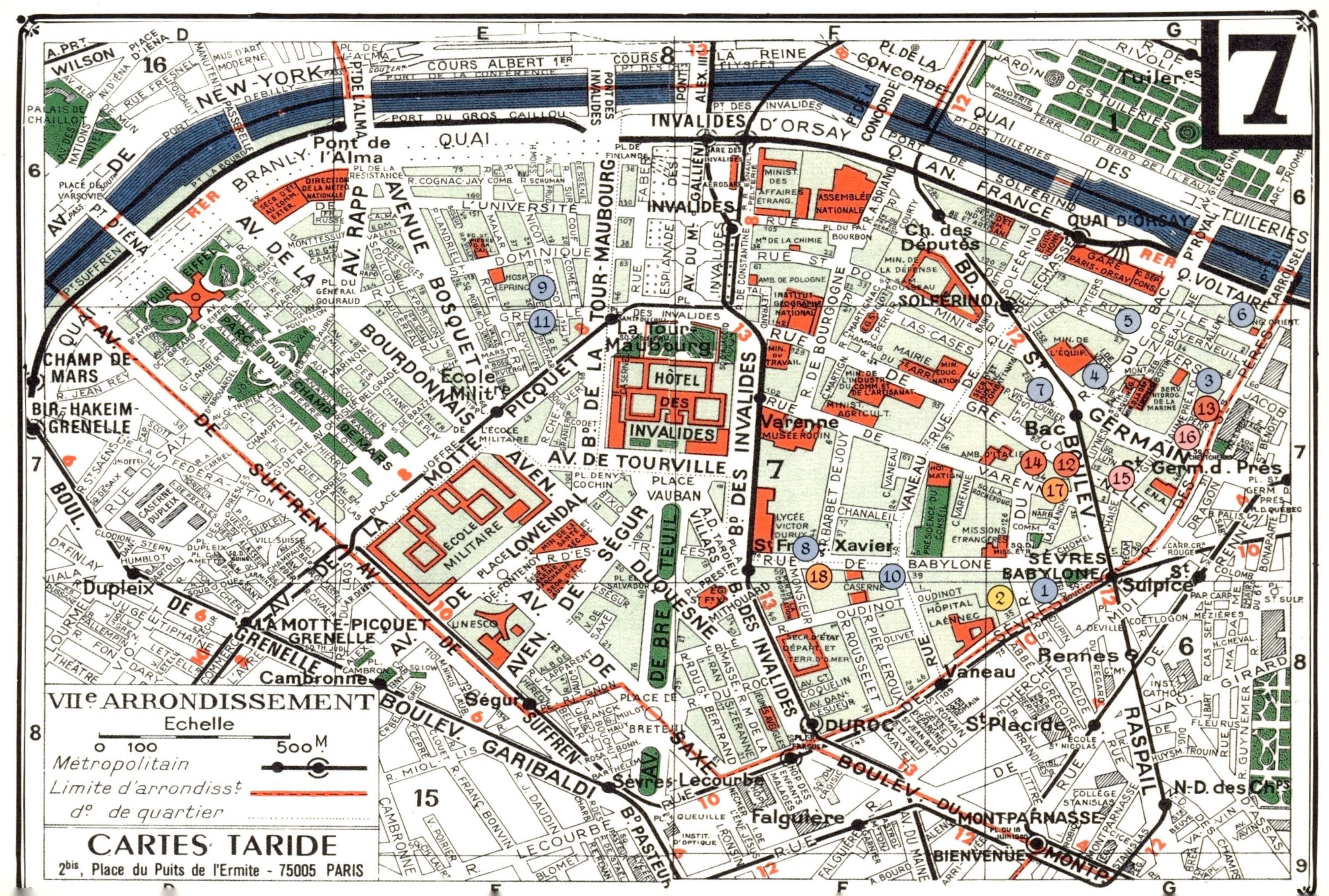
7
VIIe ARRONDISSEMENT
Echelle
0 100 500 M
Métropolitain
Limite d'arrondisst
do de quartier
CARTES TARIDE
2bis, Place du Puits de l'Ermite - 75005 PARIS
QUAI D'ORSAY
Pont de l'Alma
Tour Eiffel
Champ de Mars
Ecole Militaire
Hôtel des Invalides
Invalides
La Tour Maubourg
Ch. des Députés
Solférino
Varenne
Musée Rodin
St François Xavier
Sèvres Babylone
St Sulpice
Bac
St Germ. d. Prés
Rennes
Vaneau
Duroc
St Placide
Falguière
Ségur
Sèvres-Lecourbe
Cambronne
La Motte-Picquet Grenelle
Dupleix
Bir-Hakeim-Grenelle
Bienvenüe
N.D. des Chps
Assemblée Nationale
Gare Paris-Orsay
UNESCO
Hôpital Laënnec
Av. de Suffren
Av. de la Bourdonnais
Av. Bosquet
Av. Rapp
Bd des Invalides
Bd St Germain
Boulev. Raspail
Boulev. Garibaldi
Boulev. du Montparnasse
Av. de Tourville
Av. de Ségur
Av. de Saxe
Av. de Breteuil
Av. Duquesne
Rue de Babylone
Rue de Grenelle
Rue de Sèvres
Rue de Rennes
Rue du Bac
Quai Voltaire
Quai Branly
Cours Albert 1er
Concorde
Tuileries

7^E ARRONDISSEMENT

1. Le Bon Marché
24 rue de Sèvres
2. Chapelle Notre-Dame-de-la-Médaille-Miraculeuse
140 rue du Bac
3. Stéphane Olivier
3 rue de l'Université
4. Deyrolle
46 rue du Bac
5. Le Cabinet de Porcelaine
37 rue de Verneuil
6. Sennelier
3 quai Voltaire
7. Librairie Elbé
213 bis boulevard Saint-Germain
8. Ciné-Images
68 rue de Babylone
9. Duvelleroy
17 rue Amélie
10. Cordonnerie Vaneau
44 rue Vaneau
11. Cotinat
151 rue de Grenelle
12. Roland Barthélemy
51 rue de Grenelle
13. Debauve & Gallais
30 rue des Saints-Pères
14. Boissier Paris
77 rue du Bac
15. La Petite Chaise
36 rue de Grenelle
16. Le Rouquet
188 boulevard Saint-Germain
17. École de Danse Georges & Rosy
20 rue de Varenne
18. La Pagode
57 rue de Babylone

◈ LE BON MARCHÉ ◈

(1)

24 rue de Sèvres
M° Sèvres – Babylone
01 44 39 80 00
lebonmarche.com • @lebonmarcherivegauche

This legendary Parisian shopping destination is the world's oldest department store still in operation. Since opening in 1852, Le Bon Marché has continually innovated in every area, as can be witnessed in its architecture: its metallic structure was designed by none other than Gustave Eiffel. Under the store's magnificent glass ceiling, you'll find leading designers and brands, as well as my own creations, which have their own space in the Homeware department.

N° 7120

◈ CHAPELLE NOTRE-DAME-DE-LA-MÉDAILLE-MIRACULEUSE ◈

(2)

140 rue du Bac
M° Vaneau / Sèvres – Babylone / Saint-François-Xavier
01 49 54 78 88
chapellenotredamedelamedaillemiraculeuse.com

This pretty, light-filled chapel is dedicated to the Virgin Mary. And for good reason: she is said to have appeared to Saint Catherine Labouré here three times, in 1830. The Madonna supposedly commanded Catherine to have a medal struck bearing her image; it would protect anyone who wore it. And so, the "miraculous medal" came to be. I buy them as gifts for my religious friends.

N° 7351

N° 7132 N° 7133

N° 7229

N° 7478

STÉPHANE OLIVIER

3 rue de l'Université
M° Rue du Bac / Saint-Germain-des-Prés
01 42 96 10 00
stephaneolivier.fr/en/ • @galerie_stephane_olivier

Stéphane Olivier, a one-time florist and antiques dealer, is now a decorator and gallery owner. In his Saint-Germain-des-Prés showroom, he has created a wondrous world in which timeless antique pieces, whose worn surfaces reveal a fascinating past, mingle with works by contemporary makers. I love his Swedish Gustavian furniture with its incredible patinas, as well as his painted Italian furniture.

N° 7202

DEYROLLE

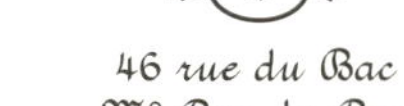

46 rue du Bac
M° Rue du Bac
01 42 22 30 07
deyrolle.com/en • @deyrolle.officiel

Created in 1831, this cabinet of curiosities housed in a former hôtel particulier is home to a donkey courting a lioness, golden sculpture-like crabs, and scarab beetles, among other creatures. Specialized in taxidermy and natural history teaching materials, this fascinating boutique-cum-museum was rebuilt after a devastating fire in 2008, and today it offers educational wall panels, entomology frames, stuffed specimens, and artwork.

N° 7566

N° 7641

N° 7642

N° 7619

N° 7262

LE CABINET DE PORCELAINE

37 rue de Verneuil
M° Solférino; RER Musée d'Orsay
01 42 60 25 40
lecabinetdeporcelaine.com • @lecabinetdeporcelaine

For flowers that never fade, visit this incredible garden created by Samuel Mazy, a porcelain floral artist. Worthy heir to a craft that emerged in the 1740s and sparked a collecting frenzy *chez* Madame de Pompadour at Versailles, Samuel creates porcelain plants that are even more exquisite than nature's own work. My favorites are the tulips and olive trees—symbols of eternal life and prosperity, respectively.

N° 7117 N° 7118 N° 7119

N° 7153

N° 7291

SENNELIER

3 quai Voltaire
M° Saint-Germain-des-Prés; RER Musée d'Orsay
01 42 60 72 15
magasinsennelier.art/en/ • @sennelier1887

Sennelier has belonged to the same family since it was created in 1887, when Gustave Sennelier began manufacturing artists' colors. Cézanne, Degas, Picasso, Hockney—generations of painters have frequented this charming boutique located across from the Louvre. Everything here will make you want to start painting—which is why I collaborated with Sennelier on a collection of watercolor notebooks.

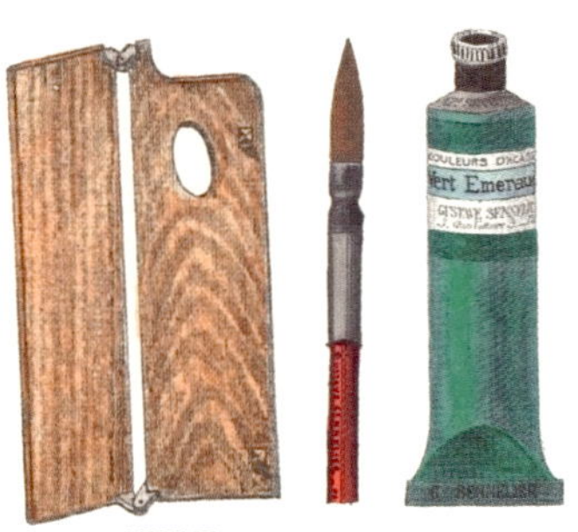

N° 7103 N° 7441

N° 7718

N° 7126

N° 7168 · N° 7548 · N° 7718 · N° 7718 · N° 7549 · N° 7329 · N° 7544 · N° 7149

◈ LIBRAIRIE ELBÉ ◈

(7)

213 bis boulevard Saint-Germain
M° Rue du Bac
01 45 48 77 97
elbe.paris/en/ • @elbeparis

The vintage posters in this gallery founded in 1976 feature advertising with the charm of yesteryear. There are ads for Air France and the SNCF rail company, film posters, and announcements for exhibitions, most of which were produced between 1920 and 1960. And the lithographs, with their high-quality paper and characteristic odor, are even more desirable.

◈ CINÉ-IMAGES ◈

(8)

68 rue de Babylone
M° Saint-François-Xavier
01 43 06 12 00
cine-images.com • @cineimages

How would you like to own the original 1966 poster for *A Man and a Woman*? Or perhaps you'd prefer the 1984 poster for *Paris, Texas*? Either way, Ciné-Images has what you're looking for. This store stocks original posters for French and international movies, and is a goldmine for collectors, fans, and those who wax nostalgic about cult film artwork.

DUVELLEROY

17 rue Amélie
M° La Tour-Maubourg
01 42 84 07 52
eventail-duvelleroy.fr • @duvelleroy

Duvelleroy has been making fans for 200 years. They produce both unique, luxury pieces, designed by artists and intended for display, and prêt-à-porter models, made in France and Spain, that are as practical as they are elegant. I have been using them to keep cool in summer for ages, so, naturally, I ended up collaborating with this historic company to create one of my own.

N° 7305

N° 7337

N° 7901

N° 7902

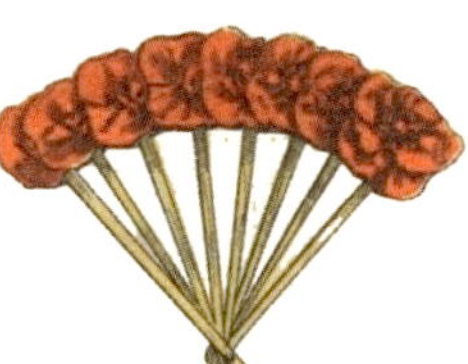

N° 7302

CORDONNERIE VANEAU

44 rue Vaneau
M° Vaneau / Saint-François-Xavier
01 42 22 06 94

Founded in 1946, the oldest cobbler in Paris made a name for itself satisfying the demands of celebrities known for their elegance and fashion sense. Need proof? Their portraits are displayed in the workshop—rather reassuring when you're waiting for a delicate repair on an expensive pair. And their leather care service applies to all leather goods.

N° 7760

N° 7751

N° 7305

N° 7338

N° 7303

N° 7396

COTINAT

11

151 rue de Grenelle
M° La Tour-Maubourg
01 42 73 00 25
cotinat.com • @pharmacie.cotinat

For medication that is also easy on the eye, I like to go to Cotinat—a drugstore that resembles an early-20th-century apothecary. Here, age-old herbal remedies share the shelves with the most innovative health products on the market. You'll find a comprehensive selection of rare natural products sourced from around the world and, in some cases, unavailable elsewhere in France.

ROLAND BARTHÉLEMY

12

51 rue de Grenelle
M° Rue du Bac
01 42 22 82 24
rolandbarthelemy.com • @roland.barthelemy

Roland Barthélemy opened his first dairy in 1971. Since then, he has been traveling the world sharing his expertise. I visit his cheese shop for his delicious baby Mont d'Or wrapped in a green ribbon; his aged Comté, with its lovely, crystalized texture; his homemade Fontainebleau, presented like soft-serve ice cream; his churned, hand-pressed butter; and his extraordinary storefront.

N° 7003 N° 7986

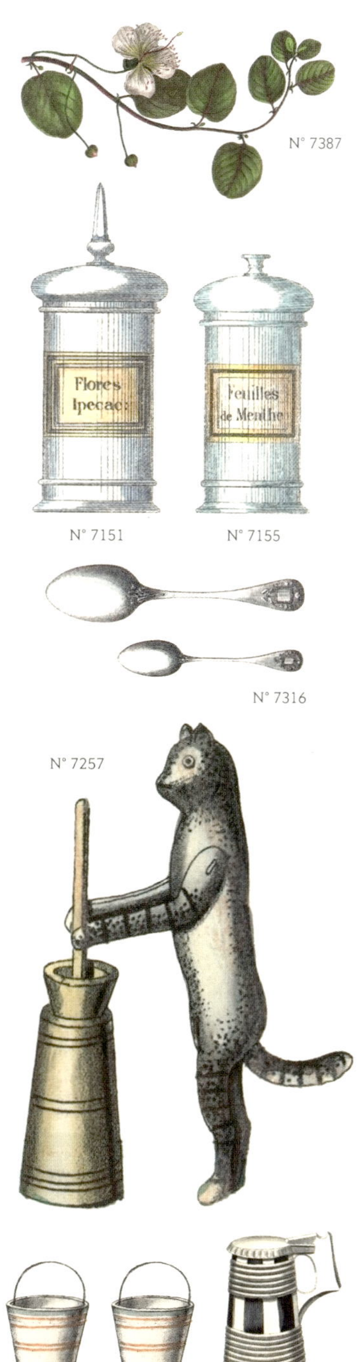

N° 7387

N° 7151 N° 7155

N° 7316

N° 7257

N° 7638 N° 7174

DEBAUVE & GALLAIS

13

30 rue des Saints-Pères
M° Saint-Germain-des-Prés
01 45 48 54 67
debauve-et-gallais.com/en • @debauveetgallais

Debauve & Gallais has been making its chocolate for 225 years. Created in 1800 by Louis XVI's pharmacist, the firm was the first to create "pistoles," a chewable form of chocolate made to soothe Marie Antoinette's headaches by combining medicine with chocolate to improve the former's taste. I come here for the chocolate orange truffles in elegant boxes.

N° 7798

N° 7799

BOISSIER PARIS

14

77 rue du Bac
M° Rue du Bac
01 43 20 41 89
maison-boissier.com • @boissierparis

Founded by Bélisaire Boissier in 1827, this confectioner is a favorite among Parisian gourmets and is said to have been one of Victor Hugo's preferred addresses. I come for the charming boxes of candy that remind me of my childhood: the colorful *perles célestes,* fruit jellies, candied strawberries, and, of course, the Ardechois candied chestnuts and tubes of delicious chestnut cream.

N° 7308

N° 7368

N° 7045

N° 7361

N° 7508

MÉDAILLE D'ARGENT
À L'EXPOSITION DE 1878

MENTIONS HONORABLES
1819-1823

FABRIQUE DE CHOCOLATS ET MAGASINS DE THÉS,

USINE À VAPEUR AU 51 AVENUE DE SÉGUR

DEBAUVE & GALLAIS

FOURNISSEURS DES ANCIENS ROIS DE FRANCE

Fig n°1

Fig n°2

Fig n°3

Fig n°4

Fig n°5

Fig n°6

Fig n°7

Fig n°8

30 Rue des Saints-Pères, PARIS

LA PETITE CHAISE

15

36 rue de Grenelle
M° Rue du Bac / Saint-Germain-des-Prés
01 42 22 13 35
restaurantlapetitechaise.fr/en/ • @lapetitechaiseofficiel

This restaurant has been delighting Parisians since 1680. Racine, Chateaubriand, Colette, Jean-Paul Sartre, and, more recently, Thomas Pesquet have all made an appearance. Inside, the exposed beams, chandeliers, and wallpaper recall a bygone era. As for the food, I always enjoy the escargots, the duck breast confit, and the famous vanilla crème brûlée.

N° 7291

LE ROUQUET

16

188 boulevard Saint-Germain
M° Rue du Bac / Saint-Germain-des-Prés
01 45 48 06 93
@le_rouquet_paris

I love this Formica-filled watering hole, which is much less frequented by tourists than its neighbors, Le Flore and Les Deux Magots. Little has changed in this Parisian café, opened in 1954, and it has managed to preserve the spirit of the neighborhood and its inhabitants, as though frozen in time. I like to come for lunch (the fixed menus are simple and tasty) and order the mackerel or an *entrecôte-frites*.

N° 7232

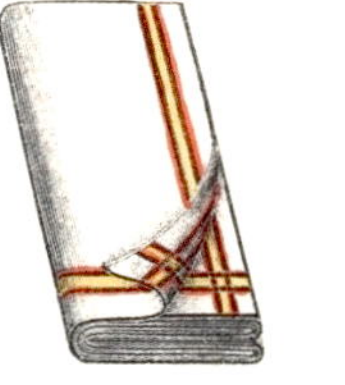

N° 7223 N° 7324

N° 7285

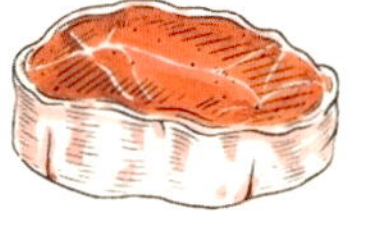

N° 7301 N° 7352

N° 7227

ÉCOLE DE DANSE GEORGES & ROSY

17

20 rue de Varenne
M° Rue du Bac / Sèvres – Babylone
07 49 63 44 95
ecolededansegeorgesetrosy.com • @georgesetrosy

This dance school was founded in 1930 by Georges and Rosy Firdmann, two international ballroom dance champions. Partner dances such as English and Vienna waltzes, Argentine tango, samba, quickstep, paso doble, disco, and the quadrille are all taught here. Famous former students include General de Gaulle, Karl Lagerfeld, Kristin Scott Thomas, and Édith Piaf.

N° 732 N° 733 N° 734 N° 735

LA PAGODE

18

57 rue de Babylone
M° Saint-François-Xavier

In 1896, the director of Le Bon Marché department store had an impressive structure, inspired by a Japanese Shinto shrine, built for his wife, right on rue de Babylone. In 1931, this pagoda became a cinema with specialized programming. Closed in 2015, the space is due to reopen in 2026. I enjoy coming for the arthouse films and the magnificent interiors, covered in Japanese frescos.

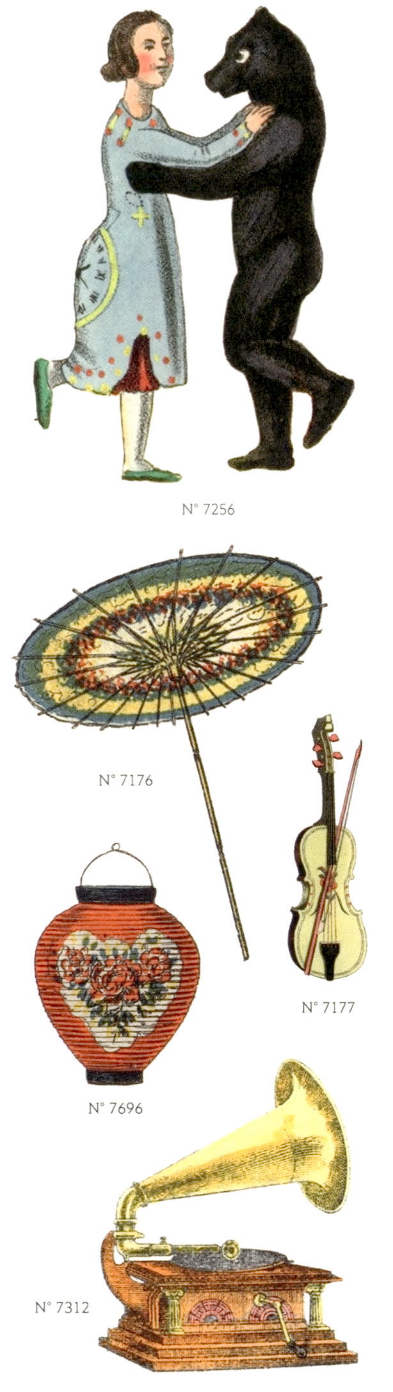

N° 7256

N° 7176

N° 7177

N° 7696

N° 7312

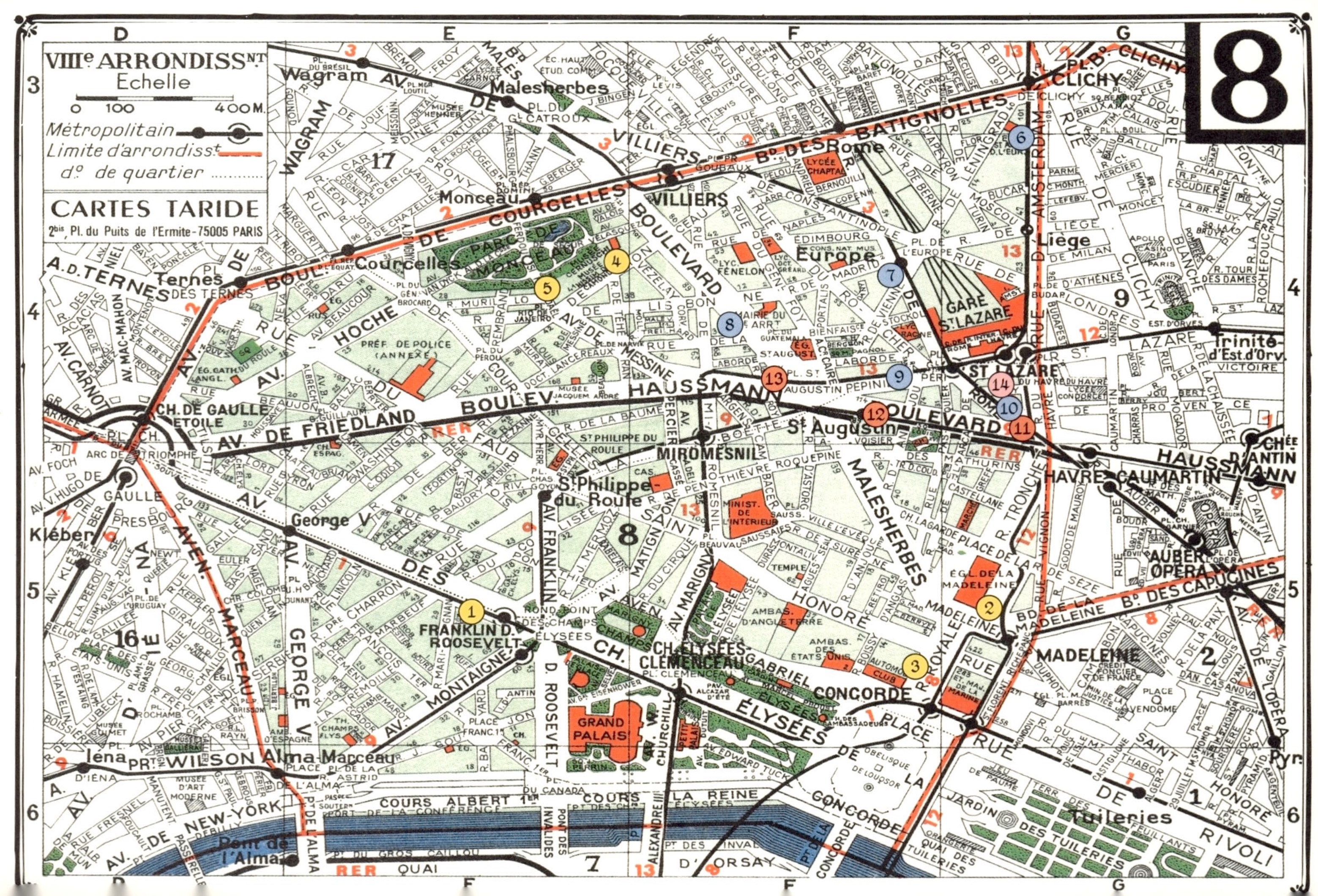
8
VIIIe ARRONDISSNT
Echelle
0 100 400 M.
Métropolitain
Limite d'arrondisst
do de quartier
CARTES TARIDE
2bis Pl. du Puits de l'Ermite - 75005 PARIS
GARE St LAZARE
GRAND PALAIS
PARC DE MONCEAU
BOULEVARD HAUSSMANN
AV. DE FRIEDLAND
AV. DES CHAMPS ÉLYSÉES
PLACE DE LA CONCORDE
MADELEINE
JARDIN DES TUILERIES
RUE DE RIVOLI
AVEN. MARCEAU
AV. GEORGE V
AV. MONTAIGNE
BOULEVARD MALESHERBES
BD DE COURCELLES
BD DES BATIGNOLLES
St Augustin
St Philippe du Roule
Miromesnil
Villiers
Monceau
Courcelles
Ternes
CH. DE GAULLE ÉTOILE
Franklin D. Roosevelt
Alma-Marceau
Iéna
Kléber
Europe
Liège
Trinité d'Est.d'Orv.
Havre Caumartin
Auber
Opéra
Concorde
Tuileries
Pont de l'Alma
MINIST. DE L'INTÉRIEUR
PRÉF. DE POLICE (ANNEXE)
8
9
16e
17
1
2
7

8^E ARRONDISSEMENT

1. Hôtel de la Païva
25 avenue des Champs-Élysées
2. Lavatory Madeleine
Place de la Madeleine
3. Musée Art Nouveau Maxim's
3 rue Royale
4. Musée Nissim de Camondo
63 rue de Monceau
5. Musée de la Pharmacie
4 avenue Ruysdaël
6. Herboristerie de la Place Clichy
87 rue d'Amsterdam
7. Jean Pavie – Luthier
47 rue de Rome
8. Benneton Graveur
75 boulevard Malesherbes
9. Modes & Travaux
10 rue de la Pépinière
10. Coutellerie Laguiole Renaud
128 rue de Provence
11. Les Thés d'Émilie
76 boulevard Haussmann
12. Au Chat Bleu
85 boulevard Haussmann
13. Caves Augé
116 boulevard Haussmann
14. Chez Léon
5 rue de l'Isly

N° 8442

N° 8408 N° 8416 N° 8411

HÔTEL DE LA PAÏVA

25 avenue des Champs-Élysées
M° Franklin D. Roosevelt
01 43 59 75 00

The Hôtel de la Païva—an hôtel particulier full of mystery—was built in the 19th century and has been miraculously well preserved. I never tire of admiring the onyx staircase, the chandeliers in the grand salon, and the bas-reliefs on the dining room ceiling. The Marquessa of Païva, a famous Second Empire courtesan, threw memorable parties here. It's easy to understand why, given just how gorgeous it is.

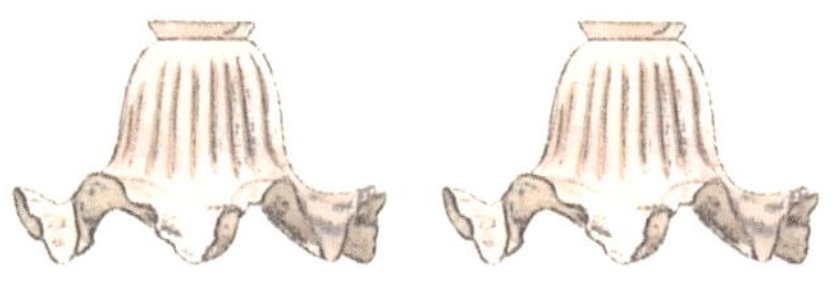

N° 8519 N° 8519

N° 8251

N° 8367 N° 8339 N° 8317

LAVATORY MADELEINE

Place de la Madeleine
M° Madeleine

Under place de la Madeleine lies an art nouveau secret. These public bathrooms, opened in 1905 and renovated in 2023, are an architectural gem. With varnished mahogany paneling, mosaic tiling, and floral stained glass, this space is as astonishing as it is unsuspected. We almost expect to cross paths with a boot polisher or a newspaper boy. A chic stop-off and a throwback to the Belle Époque.

N° 8487 N° 8401

MUSÉE ART NOUVEAU MAXIM'S

3

3 rue Royale
M° Concorde
01 42 65 30 47
@maxims.de.paris

Maxim's "1900 Collection" is a delightful romp through Belle Époque Paris. I love to admire the artwork by Mucha, Majorelle, and Toulouse-Lautrec that fashion designer Pierre Cardin assembled here over the last 60 years. Each piece is redolent of the wild Parisian nights that took place downstairs. There, there's only order and beauty: abundance, *celebration*, and voluptuousness.

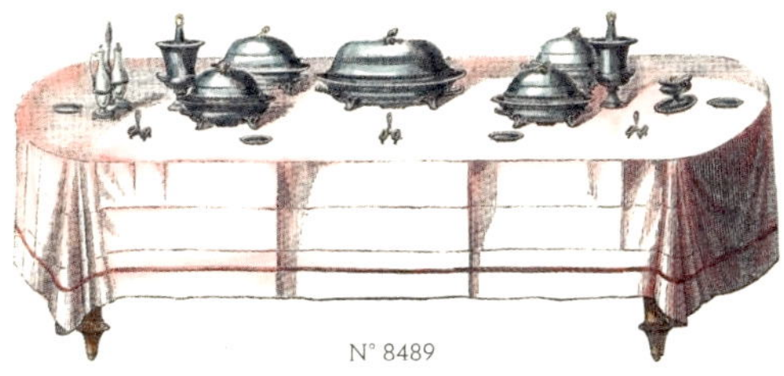

N° 8489

MUSÉE NISSIM DE CAMONDO

4

63 rue de Monceau
M° Monceau
01 53 89 06 50
madparis.fr • @madparis

I visit this museum as I would a friend's home—albeit an extremely beautiful home. Refined furnishings, and rare porcelain and silver pieces are displayed in the 18th-century house's original layout, as though frozen in time. It offers a window onto the destiny of a family enamored of beauty and battered by history. I especially appreciate the blue salon and the small hidden garden.

N° 8201 N° 8202

N° 8381 N° 8341

N° 8579

N° 8229

N° 8183

N° 8186 N° 8704

MUSÉE DE LA PHARMACIE

4 avenue Ruysdaël
M° Monceau
01 56 21 34 67
artetpatrimoinepharmaceutique.fr

The pharmacy museum is home to the French National Chamber of Pharmacists and some very entertaining collections. Surrounded by amber glass apothecary bottles and mysterious 17th-century volumes, I like to pore over the Latin labels, trying to imagine a purpose for each ancient potion. Halfway between medicine and magic, this cabinet of pharmaceutical curiosities occupies a late 19th-century hôtel particulier.

N° 8196

HERBORISTERIE DE LA PLACE CLICHY

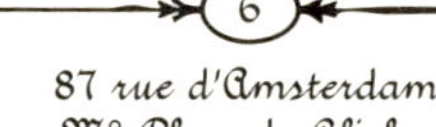

87 rue d'Amsterdam
M° Place de Clichy
01 48 74 83 32

Founded in 1880, this stunning herbalist's store abounds with plants and preparations. Inside, hundreds of carefully hand-labeled concoctions are standing by to treat everyday aches and pains. Digestive and respiratory issues, headaches, insomnia, hangovers, dull skin—for every problem, there is an herbal remedy on offer.

N° 8400

N° 8155

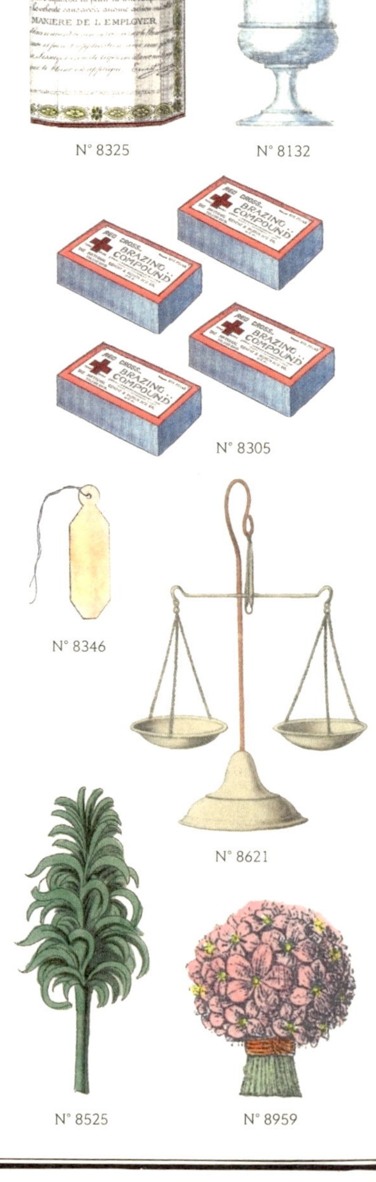

N° 8325

N° 8132

N° 8305

N° 8346

N° 8621

N° 8525

N° 8959

DEPUIS 1880

HERBORISTERIE DE LA PLACE CLICHY

TISANES - PRÉPARATIONS - CONSEILS

Fig n°1 Fig n°2 Fig n°3

Fig n°4

Fig n°5

Fig n°6

Fig n°7

AU 87, RUE D'AMSTERDAM — PARIS VIIIᴱ

JEAN PAVIE – LUTHIER

7

47 rue de Rome
M° Europe / Saint-Lazare
01 43 25 40 40
jean-pavie-luthier.com • @etienne_pavie_luthier

In this discreet workshop, violins are varnished, bows rehaired, and bridges replaced. Since 1987, Jean Pavie and his son Étienne have been making and restoring stringed instruments, first at a location across from Notre-Dame, then on rue de Rome ("luthiers' row"). From the fragrance of woodchips to the sound of pizzicato, everything here is beautiful and touching, even if you don't play an instrument.

N° 8392

BENNETON GRAVEUR

8

75 boulevard Malesherbes
M° Saint-Augustin / Europe / Villiers
01 43 87 57 39
bennetongraveur.com/en/ • @bennetongraveur

Founded in 1880, Benneton specializes in printing and engraving for fine stationery. Printed in relief on beautiful paper, its bespoke designs are exceptionally elegant. The boutique, with its large black storefront, also offers expert heraldic drawings, as well as wax seals and hand-painted pebble paperweights. It takes a lot of willpower to resist the urge to touch everything.

N° 8193

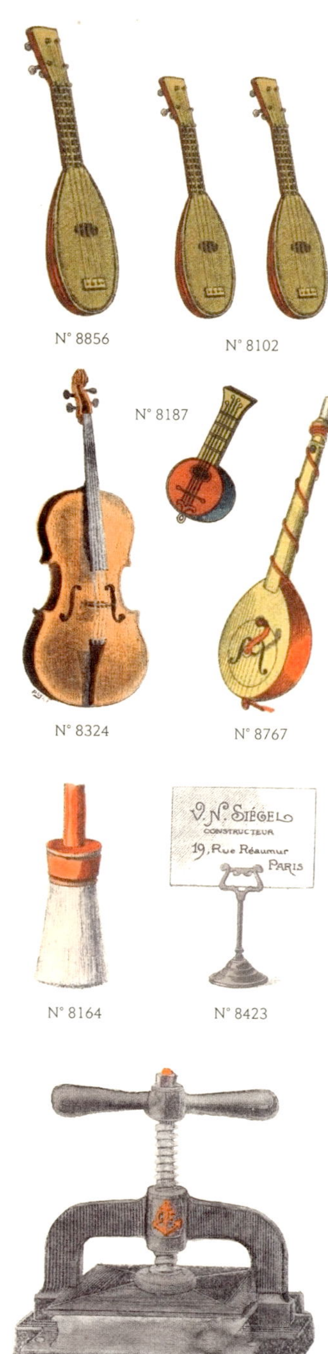

N° 8856 N° 8102

N° 8187

N° 8324 N° 8767

N° 8164 N° 8423

N° 8432

◆ MODES & TRAVAUX ◆

9

10 rue de la Pépinière
M° Saint-Augustin / Saint-Lazare
01 43 87 10 07
boutiquemodesettravaux.fr/en/ • @boutiquemodesettravaux

The oldest notions store in France has delighted fans of needlework and knitting since 1919, and still bears the name of the magazine whose headquarters were once upstairs. You'll find everything you're looking for among the rolls of fabric, embroidery supplies, and vintage thread and buttons. A Singer hums in the background—this is where the true sewists are to be found!

N° 8240

N° 8236

◆ COUTELLERIE LAGUIOLE RENAUD ◆

10

128 rue de Provence
M° Havre – Caumartin / Saint-Lazare; RER Auber
01 43 87 40 65
coutellerie-laguiole-renaud.com •
@laguiole_en_aubrac_renaud

Whether you're looking for a bone-handled knife, an Opinel, shaving supplies, or a Japanese chef's knife, Coutellerie Laguiole Renaud is *the* place to find the right blade. Open since 1908, Renaud is now the oldest knife store in Paris. The scent of leather sheaths mingling with freshly sharpened metal is enough to entice anyone to the kitchen to prepare a nice meal for friends.

N° 8183

N° 8183

N° 8376

N° 8433

N° 8602

N° 8421

N° 8109

N° 8156

N° 8173

N° 8161

N° 8172

N° 8007

◈ LES THÉS D'ÉMILIE ◈

11

76 boulevard Haussmann
M° Havre – Caumartin / Saint-Lazare; RER Auber
01 43 87 39 84
lesthesdemilie.com

This store was founded in 1910 by a descendant of the Twinings family. It took on a new name 30 years ago, but it continues to offer an extensive selection of products imported from England. The scent of bergamot hangs in the air, and I just want to plunge my hands into the large tins of tea and let the leaves sift through my fingers. Oh look! It's tea o'clock.

N° 8189

◈ AU CHAT BLEU ◈

12

85 boulevard Haussmann
M° Saint-Lazare / Saint-Augustin
01 42 65 33 18
@au.chat.bleu

For over a century, the "blue cat" has wandered between Paris and Le Touquet, on France's northern coast, where it was founded in 1912. Jars of jam and honey sit in neat rows on glass shelves in the shop window while inside, chocolate, pralines, candy, and fruit jellies abound. I always give in, but never for the same sweet—that way, I'll have to keep coming back until I've tasted everything.

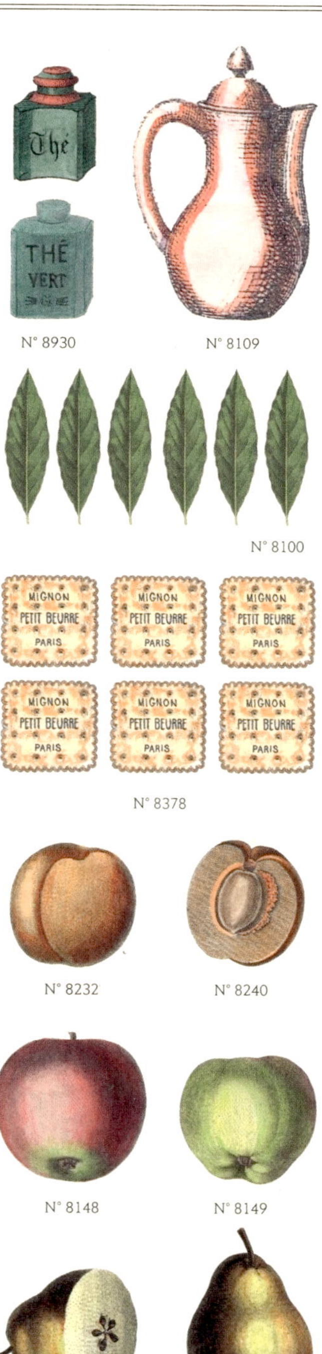

N° 8930 N° 8109

N° 8100

N° 8378

N° 8232 N° 8240

N° 8148 N° 8149

N° 8278 N° 8279

◈ CAVES AUGÉ ◈

13

116 boulevard Haussmann
M° Saint-Augustin / Saint-Lazare
01 45 22 16 97
@cavesauge

The oldest wine shop in Paris, Caves Augé has been jam packed with distinctive vintages since 1850. Each bottle is worthy of the company's reputation; the cellar supplies the finest hotel restaurants. Barrels, ladders, and wooden wine crates complete the lingering Second Empire ambience. I often come here in search of just the right bottle to bring to a dinner party.

N° 8232

◈ CHEZ LÉON ◈

14

5 rue de l'Isly
M° Saint-Lazare / Havre – Caumartin
01 43 87 42 77
FB: Restaurant Léon

This is my sanctuary, close to Saint-Lazare. Opened in 1910, Chez Léon is one of the last *routiers*—restaurants for truck drivers—in Paris. I love its retro ambiance, patinaed wood tables, checkered tablecloths, yellow Formica furniture, and generous dishes that remain true to the restaurant's original spirit. It's such a pleasure when I'm greeted by the aroma of blanquette de veau, or roast chicken and homemade fries.

N° 8214 N° 8238

N° 8061

N° 8771

N° 8772

N° 8231

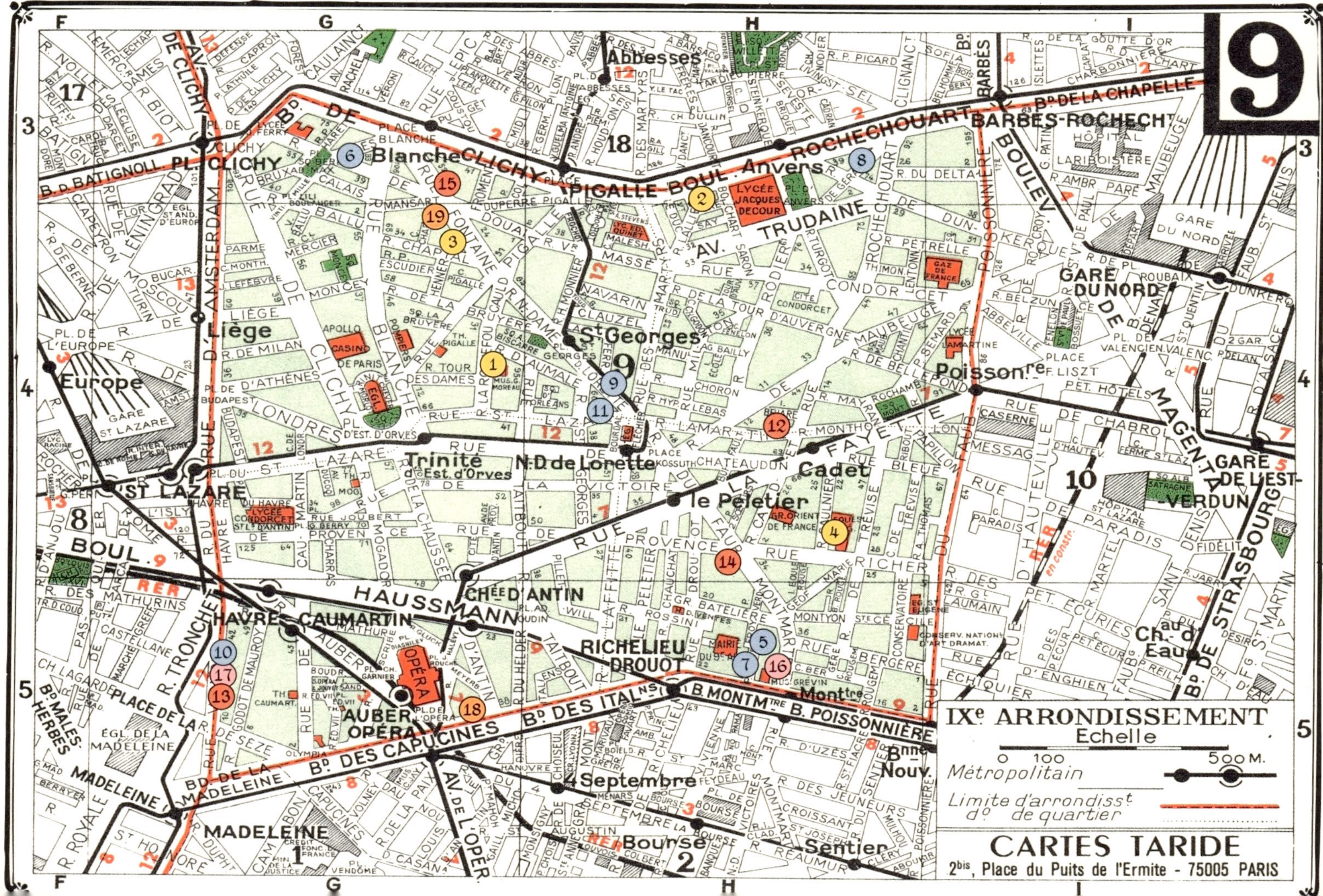
9
IXe ARRONDISSEMENT
Echelle
0 100 500 M.
Métropolitain
Limite d'arrondisst
do de quartier
CARTES TARIDE
2bis, Place du Puits de l'Ermite - 75005 PARIS
Abbesses
Blanche
Pigalle
Anvers
Barbès-Rochecht
Gare du Nord
Poissonre
Gare de l'Est
Magenta
St Georges
N.D. de Lorette
Trinité d'Est. d'Orves
Liège
Europe
Pl. Clichy
St Lazare
Havre-Caumartin
Chée d'Antin
Haussmann
Le Peletier
Cadet
Richelieu Drouot
Montmartre
Opéra
Auber
4 Septembre
Bourse
Sentier
Madeleine
Bd. de Rochechouart
Av. Trudaine
Rue La Fayette
Bd. des Italiens
Bd. des Capucines
Bd. Montmartre
B. Poissonnière
Bd. de Clichy
Bd. de la Chapelle
Bd. de Strasbourg
Bd. Malesherbes
Lycée Jacques Decour
Lycée Condorcet
Casino de Paris
Gare St Lazare
Gare du Nord
Hôpital Lariboisière
Verdun
Ch. d'Eau

9E ARRONDISSEMENT

1. Musée National Gustave Moreau
14 rue Catherine-de-la-Rochefoucauld

2. Phono Museum Paris / Phonogalerie
53 boulevard de Rochechouart / 10 rue Lallier

3. Musée de la Vie Romantique
16 rue Chaptal

4. Atelier Caraco
4 rue Saulnier

5. Librairie du Passage
48 passage Jouffroy

6. Trans-Europ-Trains
48–50 rue de Douai

7. Pain d'Épices
29–33 passage Jouffroy

8. La Blouse de Lyon
21 rue Gérando

9. Pyrofolie's
18 rue Notre-Dame-de-Lorette

10. Oriza L. Legrand
34 bis rue Vignon

11. Detaille
10 rue Saint-Lazare

12. Au Lac de Van – Heratchian
6 rue Lamartine

13. La Maison du Miel
24 rue Vignon

14. À la Mère de Famille
35 rue du Faubourg-Montmartre

15. Le Comptoir à l'Étoile d'Or
30 rue Pierre-Fontaine

16. Bouillon Chartier
7 rue du Faubourg-Montmartre

17. Le Roi du Pot au Feu
34 rue Vignon

18. Pathé Palace
2 boulevard des Capucines

19. La Nouvelle Ève
25 rue Pierre-Fontaine

◈ MUSÉE NATIONAL GUSTAVE MOREAU ◈

14 rue Catherine-de-la-Rochefoucauld
M° Saint-Georges
01 83 62 78 72
musee-moreau.fr/en • @museegustavemoreau

In 1895, Gustave Moreau decided to turn his home into a museum. On the ground floor, hundreds of paintings and drawings are displayed. The floor above is home to his apartment and living room, and his studios occupy the upper floors. This house-museum immerses visitors in both the artist's oeuvre and his life. I always come away with new ideas.

N° 9165

N° 9232

◈ PHONO MUSEUM PARIS / PHONOGALERIE ◈

53 boulevard de Rochechouart / 10 rue Lallier
M° Pigalle / Anvers
01 45 26 45 80 / 06 80 61 59 37
phonomuseum.fr • @phonomuseum.paris
phonogalerie.com • @phonogalerie

Featuring gramophones with grandiose horns, talking machines, and posters from the 1930s, this gallery-museum is dedicated to sound. Collector Jalal Arlo wanted his unique pieces to reach more than just collectors and enthusiasts: in 2004, he created the Phonogalerie, then the Phono Museum. Amid the crackling of spinning records and the fragrance of varnished wood, visitors are treated to a history of sound. I'd gladly trade Spotify for an old 78 record.

N° 9377

N° 9377

N° 9285

N° 9378

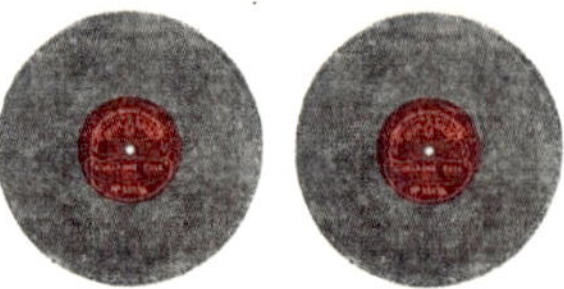

N° 9642

MUSÉE DE LA VIE ROMANTIQUE

3

16 rue Chaptal
M° Pigalle / Saint-Georges
01 55 31 95 67
museevieromantique.paris.fr/en • @museedelavieromantique

In the garden of this charming museum that resembles a home, located at the end of a calm pedestrian street, lies a hidden secret: a wonderful tearoom. After passing through the glass-roofed pavilion to pick up a drink, settle in at one of the tables in the shade of the trees. Savor what feels like a few moments in the country. I love filming in this bucolic haven.

ATELIER CARACO

4 rue Saulnier
M° Cadet
06 87 50 68 56
ateliercaraco.fr • @atelier_caraco
(Open to the public during certain events)

Established in 1988 by Claudine Lachaud, Atelier Caraco has become a reference for tailor-made costumes for live shows and movies. I love looking over the lace, braids, and ribbons that I can expect to see later on stage or on the silver screen. From cutting to sewing to dyeing, everything is done in-house, at the studio, by a hugely talented team. Claudine doesn't just design costumes, she brings them to life.

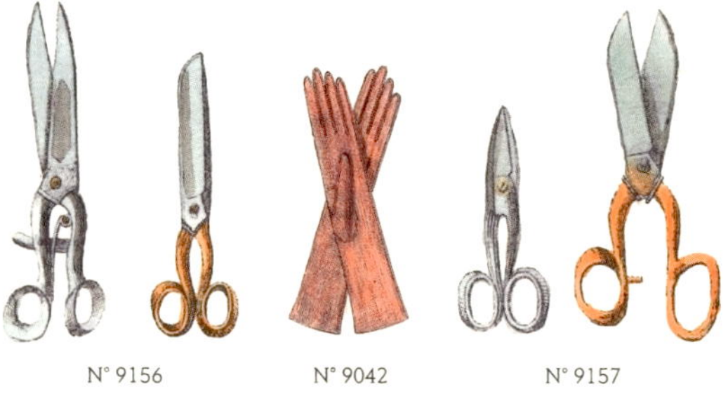

N° 9156 N° 9042 N° 9157

LIBRAIRIE DU PASSAGE

48 passage Jouffroy
M° Grands Boulevards
06 23 62 45 06
librairiedupassage.com • @librairiedupassage

Tucked away in the passage Jouffroy—itself worthy of a detour—the Librairie du Passage has specialized in old books for more than 20 years. I love leafing through centuries-old atlases, unearthing a volume that will inspire my future creations, and imagining the stories behind ancient, signed books. A refuge for book lovers and a haunt for experts with a thousand anecdotes to tell.

N° 9307 N° 9205 N° 9130 N° 9137 N° 9138 N° 9298 N° 9234 N° 9322

◈ TRANS-EUROP-TRAINS ◈

6

48–50 rue de Douai
M° Place de Clichy / Blanche
01 48 74 71 97
transeurop-train.fr

Trans-Europ-Trains is a one-way trip back to childhood. Since 1994, this boutique has captured the hearts of rail fans. Scale models, miniature railroads, station master's whistles—each object invites wanderlust. Found a locomotive in the attic? You can bring it here to be repaired. Who said you have to leave home to journey afar?

N° 9912

◈ PAIN D'ÉPICES ◈

7

29–33 passage Jouffroy
M° Richelieu – Drouot
01 47 70 08 68
paindepices.fr • @paindepicesboutiqueoff

Opened in 1979, this store rekindles my love for old dollhouses. The figurines are collectible treasures, and the distinctive odor of wooden toys takes me back to my childhood. Everything is incredibly elegant and sophisticated, from the tiny furnishings to the little tea sets. Some dollhouses are even wired for electricity. A wonderland in miniature.

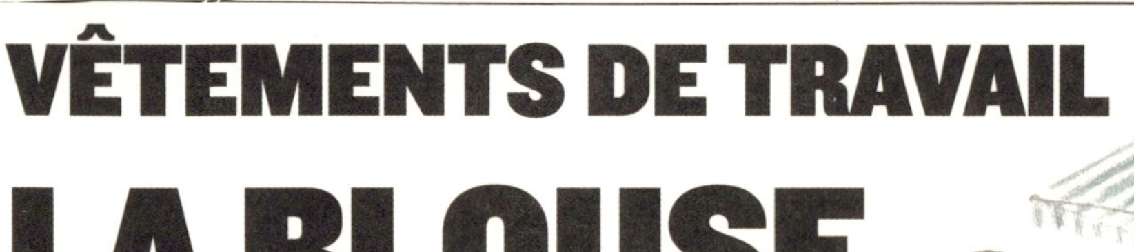

VÊTEMENTS DE TRAVAIL

LA BLOUSE DE LYON

CASQUETTES

1	2	3
Soie noire genre Desfoux, visière cuir ou en pareil . . . 4 50	Soie noire, forme russe, visière cuir. . . 5 » Drap bleu foncé, forme russe 5 50	Forme amiral. Velours marron ou beige. 2 75 Forme amiral, drap bleu foncé. . . . 1 75

BONNETERIE

Demandez le Catalogue spécial de Bonneterie Hommes et Dames

CALEÇONS ou GILETS TRICOT	CHAUSSETTES	CHAUSSETTES	GILET de CHASSE
Beige ou gris 2 50 et 2 95 Écru . . . . 2 95 et 4 95	Coton cachou ou écru. *La paire.* 0 65 0 95 et 1 45	Pure laine, nuance naturelle. *La paire* 1 10 1 45 1 95 et 2 45	Loutre, marine, noir. De 8 90 à 35 »

CHANDAILS. Laine à côtes, col droit, boutonnant sur l'épaule, marine, noir, gris . . . 7 75

CHEMISES, CALEÇONS ET GILETS

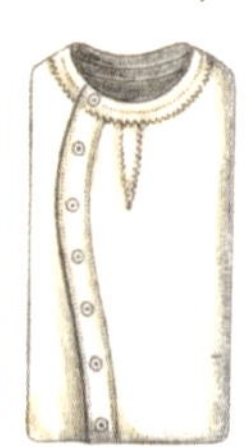

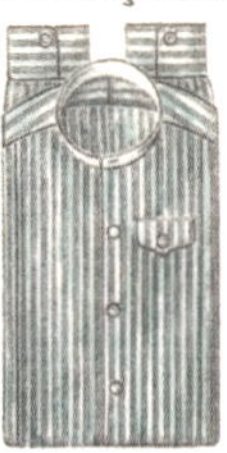

CHEMISES	GILETS FLANELLE	CHEMISES	CALEÇONS	CHEMISES
cretonne tissée, [illegible]ouleur, [illegible] forte, co[illegible] 4 [illegible] Coton écru, qualité forte, col rabattu, petits poignets. 4 »	cretonne pure laine, sans manches. 3 25 à 7 25 Demi-manches. 5 » à 9 » Manches longues. [illegible] » à 10 75 [illegible]le pure laine [illegible] Demi-m[illegible] 5 » à [illegible] Manches longues. 6 » à 10 75	belle flanelle mixte fantaisie, avec ou sans col et poche . 8 75 Flanelle anglaise sans poche. . 6 75 Flanelle extra [illegible] laine, avec ou sans [illegible]75 12 75 [illegible]75	cretonne écrue, qualité forte. 3 25 Croisé blanc, qualité extra. 3 95 Flanelle coton extra. 4 25 Zéphyr fantaisie. 3 95	flanelle coton, belle qualité, avec ou sans col 3 50 et 5 » Avec poche. . 4 25 CHEMISES couleur sans col, devant plis souples. . . . 4 50 5 75 6 75 et 8 75

Nº 1450. — **SACOCHE DE RECETTE.** Façon sellier, en vache grain long, havane ou noire, doublée peau, séparation intérieure, 1 poche extérieure, avec banderole.

TAILLES	PRIX
0m16.	10 25
0m18.	11 50
0m21.	12 75
0m21.	14 25

21 RUE GÉRANDO, PARIS 9E

LA BLOUSE DE LYON

8

21 rue Gérando
M° Anvers / Barbès – Rochechouart
01 48 78 65 16
lablousedelyon.com/en • @lablousedelyon

Tradition, modernity, impeccable cuts, and quality fabrics—since 1937, this institution has been dressing artists, craftspeople, and laborers, as well as Parisians in search of the perfect jacket. The shelves are lined with thick cotton shirts, workwear pants, studio aprons, and more. You'll want to come up with a worksite just to have an excuse to buy everything.

N° 9519

PYROFOLIE'S

9

18 rue Notre-Dame-de-Lorette
M° Saint-Georges
01 55 07 86 00
pyrofolies.com • @pyrofolies

It's true: everything here is faux. Since the early 1970s, Jean-François has been having fun here, as he puts it. He creates all kinds of off-the-wall special effects for the movies. So it's no surprise that in his store you'll find 1001 amusing objects, from fake ice cubes to fireworks to snow canons, to name just a few.

N° 9175 N° 9130 N° 9175

N° 9136
N° 9902 N° 9103
N° 9167 N° 9174 N° 9123 N° 9130 N° 9126
N° 9175 N° 9110 N° 9168

ORIZA L. LEGRAND

34 bis rue Vignon
M° Havre – Caumartin / Madeleine; RER Auber
01 71 93 02 34
orizaparfums.com/en/ • @orizalegrand

Since 1720, this perfumer has been known for its impeccably crafted, innovative fragrances, and has supplied scents to France's most illustrious leaders. The store, which resembles a small boudoir, sells jewel-like perfumes along with the house specialty, "Vinaigre Aciduliné." I use a few drops of this cosmetic vinegar to delicately perfume my bathwater or to soothe my skin after a shave.

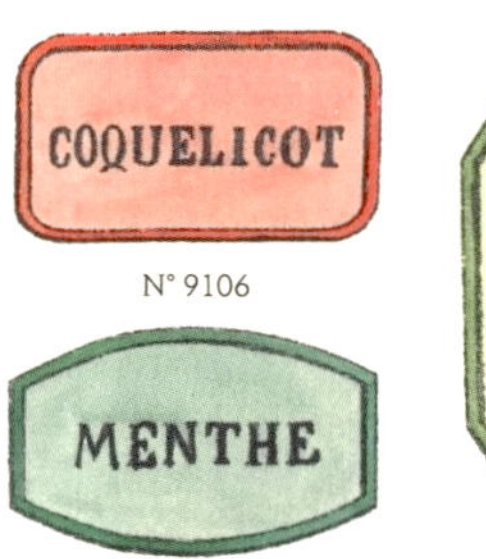

N° 9106

N° 9107

N° 9974

DETAILLE

10 rue Saint-Lazare
M° Notre-Dame-de-Lorette
01 48 78 68 50
detaille.com/en/ • @detaille_1905

I love breathing in the scents of the delicate perfumes at this boutique, founded in 1905 by the Countess of Presle. The bottles lining the floor-to-ceiling wood shelves remind me of Belle Époque Paris. Detaille quickly made a name for itself in the world of fine fragrance with innovative products such as the "Baume Automobile"—one of the first face creams ever created—which the countess used daily.

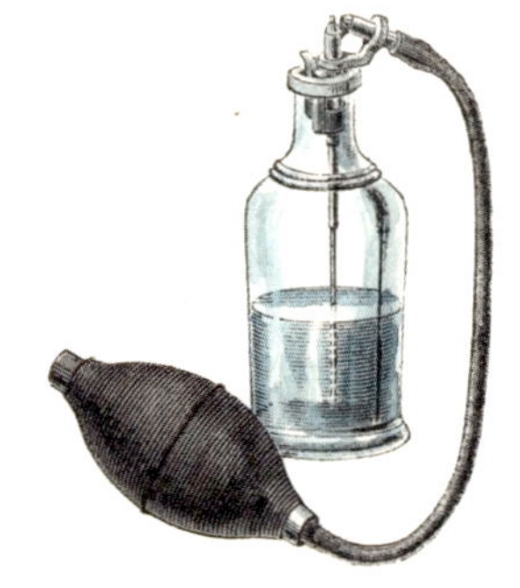

N° 9276

N° 9260

N° 9157

N° 9211

N° 9444

N° 9303

Parfums de sélection tour à tour adoptés
par les favorites des rois de France
et par les cours d'Europe

ORIZA L. LEGRAND

34 BIS RUE VIGNON - PARIS 9^E

◆ AU LAC DE VAN – HERATCHIAN ◆

12

6 rue Lamartine
M° Cadet
01 48 78 43 19

Created in 1925, this pocket-sized bazaar for *fines bouches* is brimming with mouth-watering delights from the Mediterranean and the Levant. Since 1977, Sezar has been regaling customers with his masterful ability to hunt down the tastiest morsels. I go weak in the knees for the huge jars of baba ghanoush and the feta cheese, which I think is among the best in Paris.

◆ LA MAISON DU MIEL ◆

13

24 rue Vignon
M° Madeleine / Havre – Caumartin; RER Auber
01 47 42 26 70
maisondumiel.fr • @lamaisondumiel

Founded in 1898, La Maison du Miel, with its magnificent, perfectly preserved storefront, is one of the oldest boutiques in Paris. Inside, the shelves are filled with many varieties of French honey, along with other bee products. My guilty pleasure is the tree heather (*bruyère blanche*) honey with notes of caramel bordering on chocolate—to be spread generously on a piece of toast.

N° 9331 N° 9557

N° 9894 N° 9895 N° 9896

N° 9266

N° 9214

N° 9284

N° 9975

N° 9444 N° 9443 N° 9445

N° 9168

À LA MÈRE DE FAMILLE

35 rue du Faubourg-Montmartre
M° Le Peletier / Grands Boulevards
01 47 70 83 69
lameredefamille.com/en • @alameredefamille

This superb chocolate shop, the oldest in Paris, dating from 1721, has retained its original splendor. The magical atmosphere conjures the specter of Willy Wonka hiding among all the chocolates and sweets. Carefully preserved savoir faire has been handed down from generation to generation, and everything is made in France, in the company's historic factories.

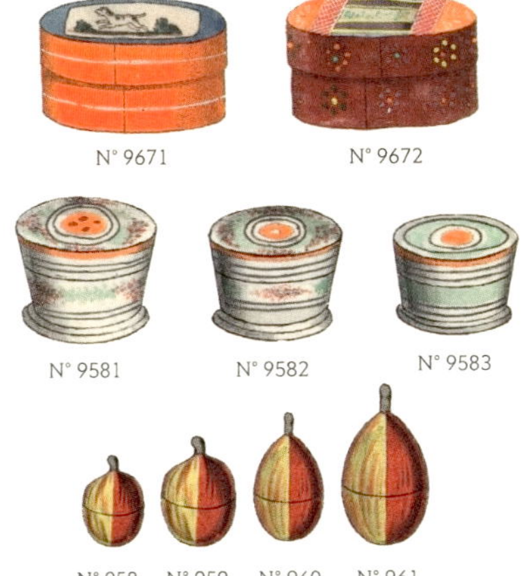
N° 9671 N° 9672

N° 9581 N° 9582 N° 9583

N° 958 N° 959 N° 960 N° 961

N° 9237 N° 9238 N° 9239

LE COMPTOIR À L'ÉTOILE D'OR

30 rue Pierre-Fontaine
M° Blanche / Pigalle
01 81 89 09 98
lechocolat-alainducasse.com/en • @lechocolatalainducasse

In the 1970s, Denise noticed this pretty storefront from 1900 and immediately fell in love. She created a welcoming chocolate shop bursting with delights, and kept up the charming space and its historical Parisian decor. In 2022, Alain Ducasse took over the store and now sells his chocolate creations in this incredible, unchanged setting.

N° 9496 N° 9515

N° 9754 N° 9755 N° 9756

N° 9325 N° 9390 N° 9138 N° 9124

BOUILLON CHARTIER

16

7 rue du Faubourg-Montmartre
M° Grands Boulevards
01 47 70 86 29
bouillon-chartier.com/en/ • @bouillonchartier

This was the first *bouillon* to open in Paris. I come for the gorgeous dining room, the exuberant ambience, and the waiters in white aprons who jot your order down on the table. Since 1896, diners have watched the *garçons* in short jackets nimbly navigate the floor bearing classic French dishes served at modest prices. Come in the afternoon or late at night to avoid the line.

N° 9431

LE ROI DU POT AU FEU

17

34 rue Vignon
M° Madeleine / Havre – Caumartin; RER Auber
01 47 42 37 10
FB: Le Roi Du Pot Au Feu

I come here to savor a classic French dish—pot-au-feu—cooked to perfection. Opened in 1974, this restaurant has maintained its old-fashioned charm: small wooden tables, red-and-white checkered tablecloths, period tiling, and lots of little souvenirs hanging from the walls. And it still serves other hearty home-cooked dishes that never disappoint.

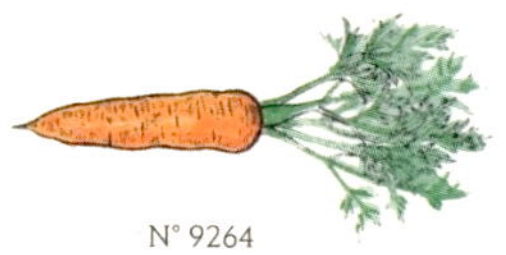
N° 9264

N° 9232 N° 9233

N° 9890

N° 9240

N° 9384

N° 9385

N° 9386

N° 9457

N° 9458

N° 9459

N° 9439 N° 9344

◈ PATHÉ PALACE ◈

18

2 boulevard des Capucines
M° Opéra
08 09 10 31 03
pathe.fr/en/cinemas/cinema-pathe-palace • @pathefrance

This sublime building constructed in 1869 is home to one of the most fabulous cinemas in Paris. The interior, an art deco gem, was renovated in 2024 by Renzo Piano. But hidden inside is another little treat that I particularly love: a premium screening room where you can order a meal with table service and settle into a seat designed for two to watch a movie.

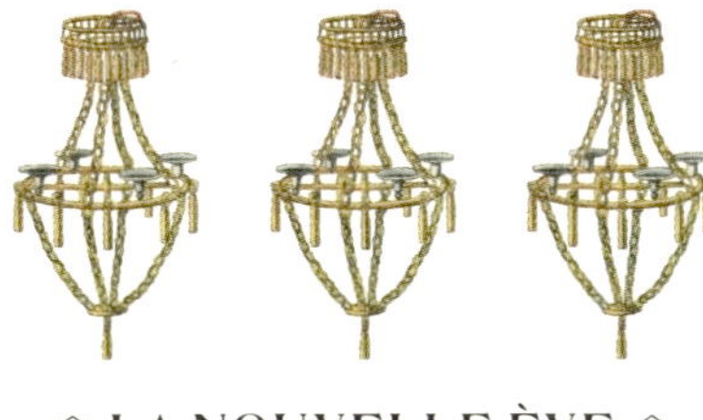

◈ LA NOUVELLE ÈVE ◈

19

25 rue Pierre-Fontaine
M° Blanche / Pigalle
01 48 74 69 25
lanouvelleeveparis.com/en-us • @lanouvelleeveofficiel

Launched in 1898, La Nouvelle Ève was one of the first cabarets to open in Paris. Since then, it has staged spectacular shows and prestigious revues. The Belle Époque style and the starry ceiling make for a magical atmosphere. I particularly like coming to this dreamy little place to watch my friend Fifi Chachnil perform, while I sip a glass of champagne.

N° 9001 N° 9002 N° 9003

N° 9924

N° 9320

N° 9802

N° 9385

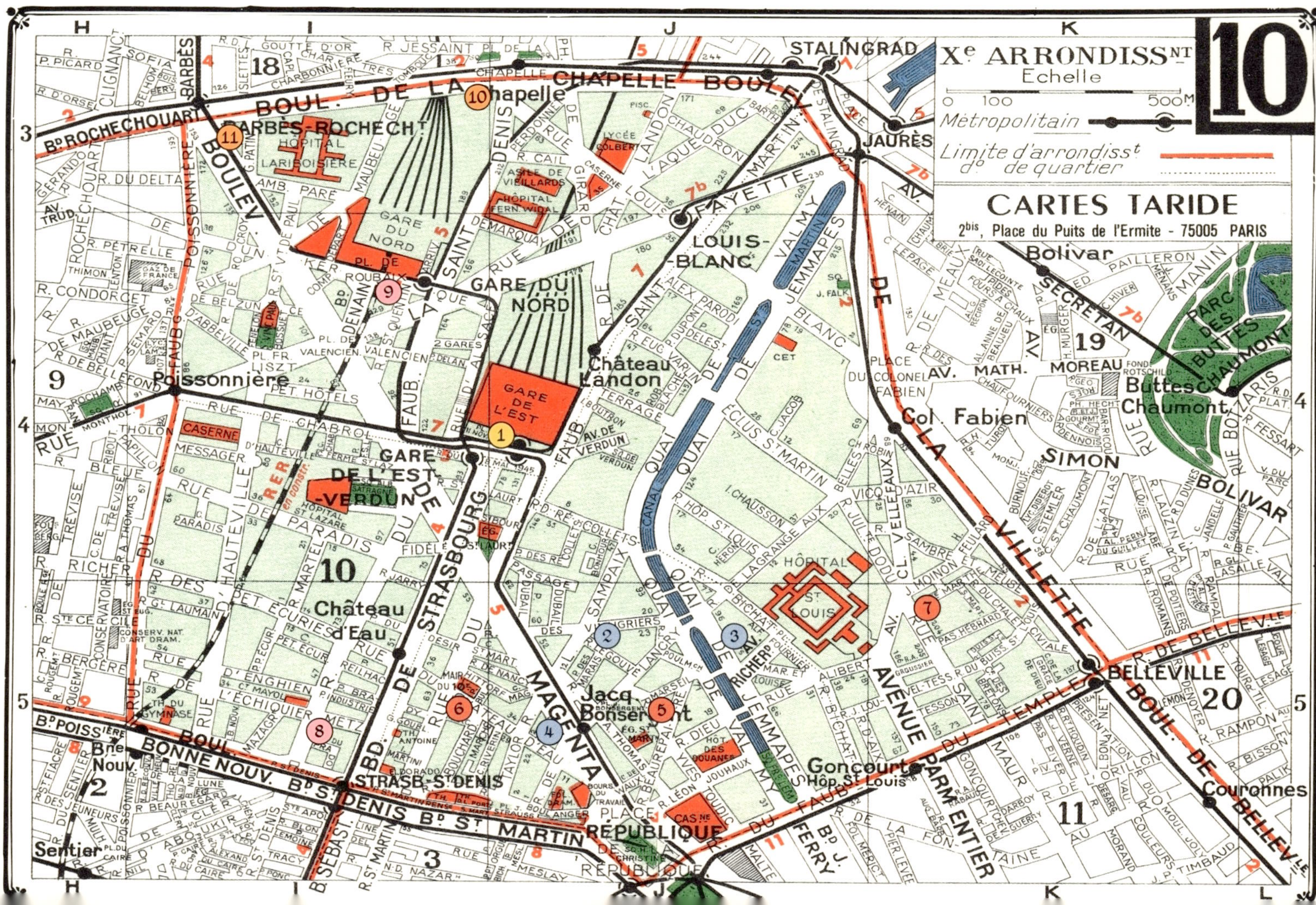

10
Xe ARRONDISSNT
Echelle
0 100 500M
Métropolitain
Limite d'arrondisst
do de quartier
CARTES TARIDE
2bis, Place du Puits de l'Ermite - 75005 PARIS
Stalingrad
Jaurès
Louis-Blanc
Bolivar
Buttes Chaumont
Col. Fabien
Belleville
Goncourt Hôp. St Louis
République
Jacq. Bonsergent
Château Landon
Gare de l'Est
Gare du Nord
Gare de l'Est-Verdun
Château d'Eau
Strasb.-St Denis
Bne Nouv.
Sentier
Poissonnière
Barbès-Rochechouart
La Chapelle
Boul. de la Chapelle
Bd Rochechouart
Boul. de la Villette
Boul. de Belleville
Bd de Strasbourg
Bd de Magenta
Bd St Denis
Bd St Martin
Boul. Bonne Nouv.
Avenue Parmentier
Quai de Valmy
Quai de Jemmapes
Canal St Martin
Hôpital St Louis
Hôpital Lariboisière
Parc des Buttes Chaumont
Secrétan
Simon
Moreau
18
19
20
11
10
9
3
2

10E ARRONDISSEMENT

1. Association Française des Amis des Chemins de Fer
Place du 11-Novembre-1918 (Gare de l'Est)
2. Bouclerie Poursin
35 rue des Vinaigriers
3. Cristalleries Schweitzer
84 quai de Jemmapes
4. À la Pipe du Nord
21 boulevard de Magenta
5. Du Pain et des Idées
34 rue Yves-Toudic
6. Boucherie Denis Chainay
43 rue du Château-d'Eau
7. La Tête dans les Olives
2 rue Sainte-Marthe
8. Bouillon Julien
16 rue du Faubourg-Saint-Denis
9. Terminus Nord
23 rue de Dunkerque
10. Théâtre des Bouffes du Nord
37 bis boulevard de la Chapelle
11. Le Louxor
170 boulevard de Magenta

ASSOCIATION FRANÇAISE DES AMIS DES CHEMINS DE FER

1

Place du 11-Novembre-1918 (Gare de l'Est)
M° Gare de l'Est
01 40 38 20 92
afac.asso.fr

Founded in 1929, this organization exists to champion the French railroad system and educate the public. But most importantly, its offices, tucked away in the Gare de l'Est station, are home to an enormous, ultra-realistic miniature railway that can be viewed every first Saturday of the month, if you book. The painstaking work dazzles me every time.

N° 1060

N° 1069

BOUCLERIE POURSIN

2

35 rue des Vinaigriers
M° Jacques Bonsergent
01 46 07 17 07
poursin.com • @maisonpoursin

Specialized in the manufacture of brass fastenings and closures since 1830, this company opened a location on rue des Vinaigriers in 1890. Who would imagine that behind the pretty blue door lies the workshop of the oldest *bouclerie* in Paris? Initially focused on riding accessories, the brand has since expanded its savoir faire and now supplies luxury fashion brands. Individual customers are also welcome.

N° 1027 N° 1023 N° 1022

N° 1023

N° 1018

TOUTE LA BOUCLERIE et la CUIVRERIE

S. POURSIN

35, Rue des Vinaigriers _ PARIS (xe) _ Nord: 17-07

Plus de cent années
de Technique ...
et de belle fabrication

•CRISTALLERIES SCHWEITZER•

Cristallerie d'art – Gravure sur verre – Réparation d'objets en verre – Restaurateur d'objets en cristal – Taille du cristal – Savoir-faire

MAISON FONDÉE EN 1890

1080 1063 1146 1032 1097 1127 1127a

977a 917a 1295 1205 1216 1070 2051a 1254 1132

1127 1127a 2567 2568 2569 2570 2571

1540

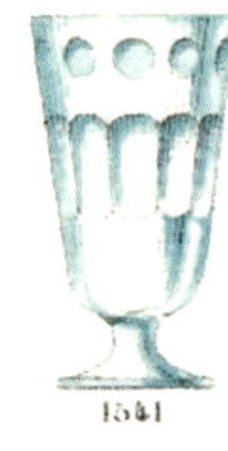

1541

1542

1543

1544

1545

CRISTALLERIES SCHWEITZER

3

84 quai de Jemmapes
M° Jacques Bonsergent
01 42 39 61 63 / 09 74 56 14 93
cristalleries-schweitzer-paris.com •
@cristalleriesschweitzer

In 1890, the Schweitzers founded this workshop on the Canal Saint-Martin, where the water was used to activate the steam-powered machines. The red-brick and metal storefront retains its historic style, as does the interior, with its new machines that will never outshine the charm of the old. Here, artisans still make fabulous crystal objects or fix those that are brought in for repair.

N° 1013

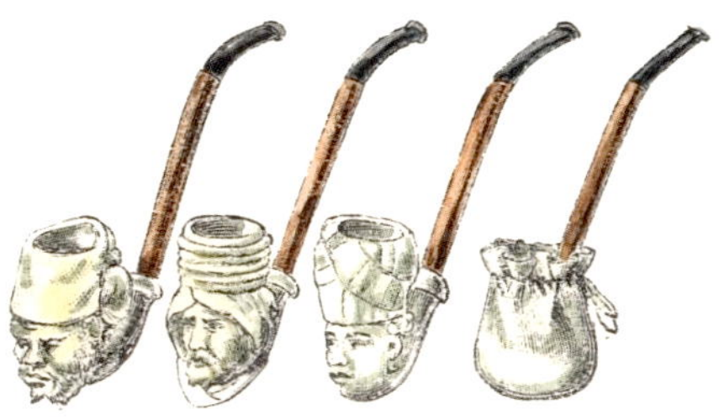

N° 1076

À LA PIPE DU NORD

4

21 boulevard de Magenta
M° Jacques Bonsergent
01 42 08 23 47
alapipedunord.com • @pipedunord

Thanks to skillful expertise and exceptional materials, this fine pipe maker has crafted the most beautiful pipes in Paris since 1867. The thoughtfully decorated store includes a room made to resemble a small apartment, where visitors can test pipes in a pleasant and welcoming ambience. You can also bring pipes here for repair.

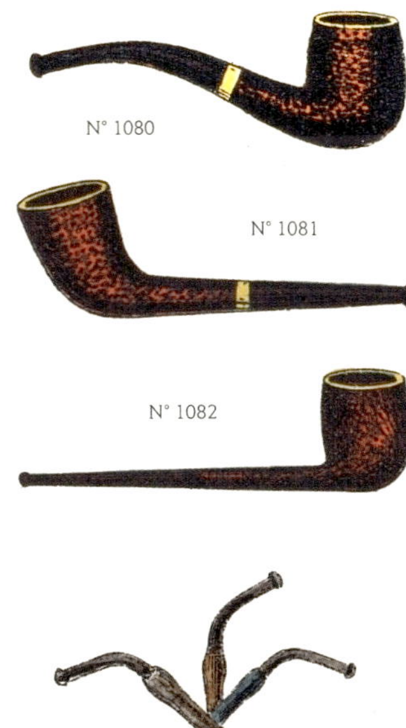

N° 1080

N° 1081

N° 1082

N° 1019

N° 1099

N° 1046 N° 1047

N° 1099

N° 1098

N° 1098

DU PAIN ET DES IDÉES

5

34 rue Yves-Toudic
M° Jacques Bonsergent
01 42 40 44 52
dupainetdesidees.com • @dupainetdesidees

N° 1097

The decor in this French bakery—from the painted glass ceiling or beveled mirrors to the lovely blue storefront—hasn't changed since 1875. Here, loaves and *viennoiseries* await hungry customers in wicker baskets. The smell of freshly baked bread whisks me right back to my childhood, when I would be sent to fetch a baguette. You can even learn to make your own bread here.

N° 1096

N° 1096

N° 1095

N° 1095

N° 1041

N° 1088

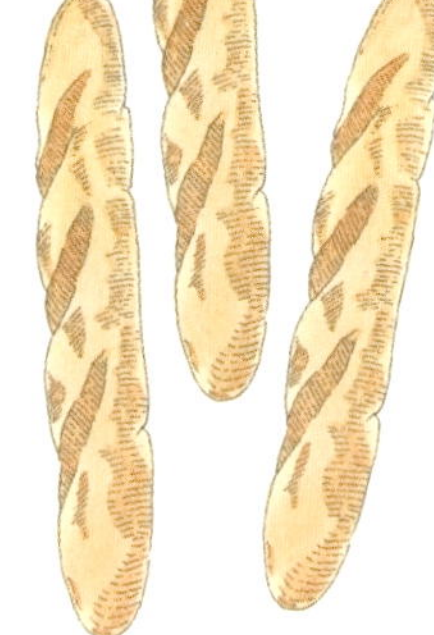

N° 1032

N° 1004

BOUCHERIE DENIS CHAINAY

43 rue du Château-d'Eau
M° Château d'Eau / Jacques Bonsergent
01 42 39 66 40

Built in 1912, this butcher shop has kept most of its original decor, including the marble walls, which at the time helped to keep the meat cool. The pretty wrought-iron storefront also recalls the Paris of old. Since 1982, owner Denis Chainay has kept the spirit of the shop alive with his expertise and selection of high-quality meats.

N° 1089

LA TÊTE DANS LES OLIVES

2 rue Sainte-Marthe
M° Belleville / Colonel Fabien
09 51 31 33 34
@latetedanslesolives

Cédric Casanova left a career in the circus arts to devote himself to his passion—Sicilian cuisine and olives. So, he opened this store, brimming with the island's best products, notably olive oil, which he supplies to the finest hotels. I often come here to refill my oil bottle or to celebrate special occasions around his small *table d'hôte*.

N° 1062

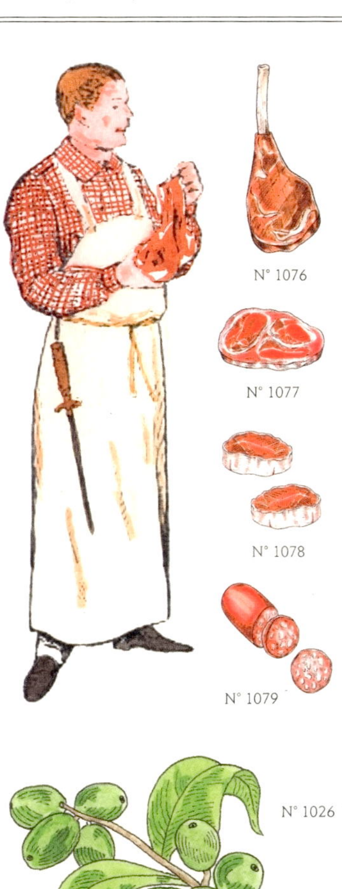

N° 1076

N° 1077

N° 1078

N° 1079

N° 1026

N° 1036

N° 1038

N° 1021

⬥ BOUILLON JULIEN ⬥

16 rue du Faubourg-Saint-Denis
M° Strasbourg – Saint-Denis
01 47 70 12 06
bouillon-julien.com •
@bouillonjulienparis

The greatest masters of the art nouveau style left their mark on this extraordinary restaurant, which opened in 1906. First of all, there's the incredible stained-glass roof, then the fantastic celadon walls, and, finally, the spectacular Cuban mahogany bar lined with tin. The menu is simple: an inventory of the best-loved French classics.

N° 1079

N° 1046

N° 1047

N° 1048

N° 1049

N° 1050

⬥ TERMINUS NORD ⬥

23 rue de Dunkerque
M° / RER Gare du Nord
01 42 85 05 15
terminusnord.com/en/ • @terminusnordbrasserie

Opened in 1925, this brasserie—one of several located across from the Gare du Nord station—stands out for its art deco style. It specializes in seafood, and I like coming here in winter, when I get a craving for good oysters. This restaurant moves to the rhythm of travelers arriving fresh off the trains or waiting for theirs to arrive.

N° 1023

N° 1056

N° 1057

N° 1058

N° 1033 N° 1034

◈ THÉÂTRE DES BOUFFES DU NORD ◈

10

37 bis boulevard de la Chapelle
M° La Chapelle
01 46 07 34 50
bouffesdunord.com/en • @les_bouffes_du_nord

I have a soft spot for this warm, welcoming theater. Built in 1876 on the ruins of a former barracks, it experienced a period of instability until it was renovated a century later, in 1974. Against a sumptuous backdrop in wood, musicians, actors, and artists participate in a rich and varied program of performances.

N° 1045

N° 1099

◈ LE LOUXOR ◈

11

170 boulevard de Magenta
M° Barbès – Rochechouart
01 44 63 96 96
cinemalouxor.fr • @cinema_louxor

Le Louxor opened in 1921. From the sidewalk, the decor, inspired by Egyptian antiquities, immerses visitors in a fascinating mythological world. In the main theater, a modern screen conceals an incredible antique one, set into a gilded frame, which the cinema uses when it shows silent films. It's precisely for this little secret that I love coming here so much.

N° 1046

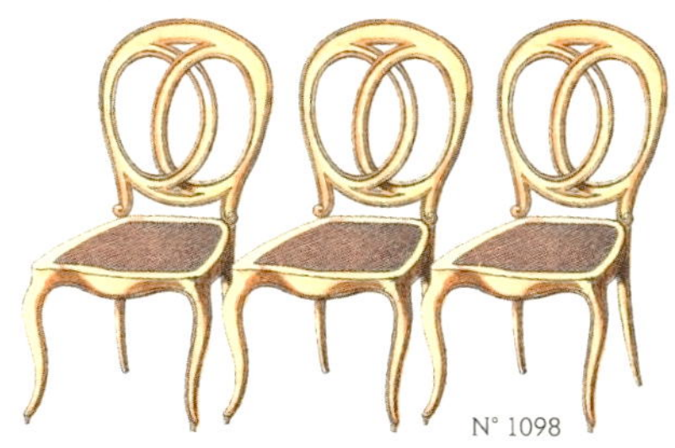

N° 1098

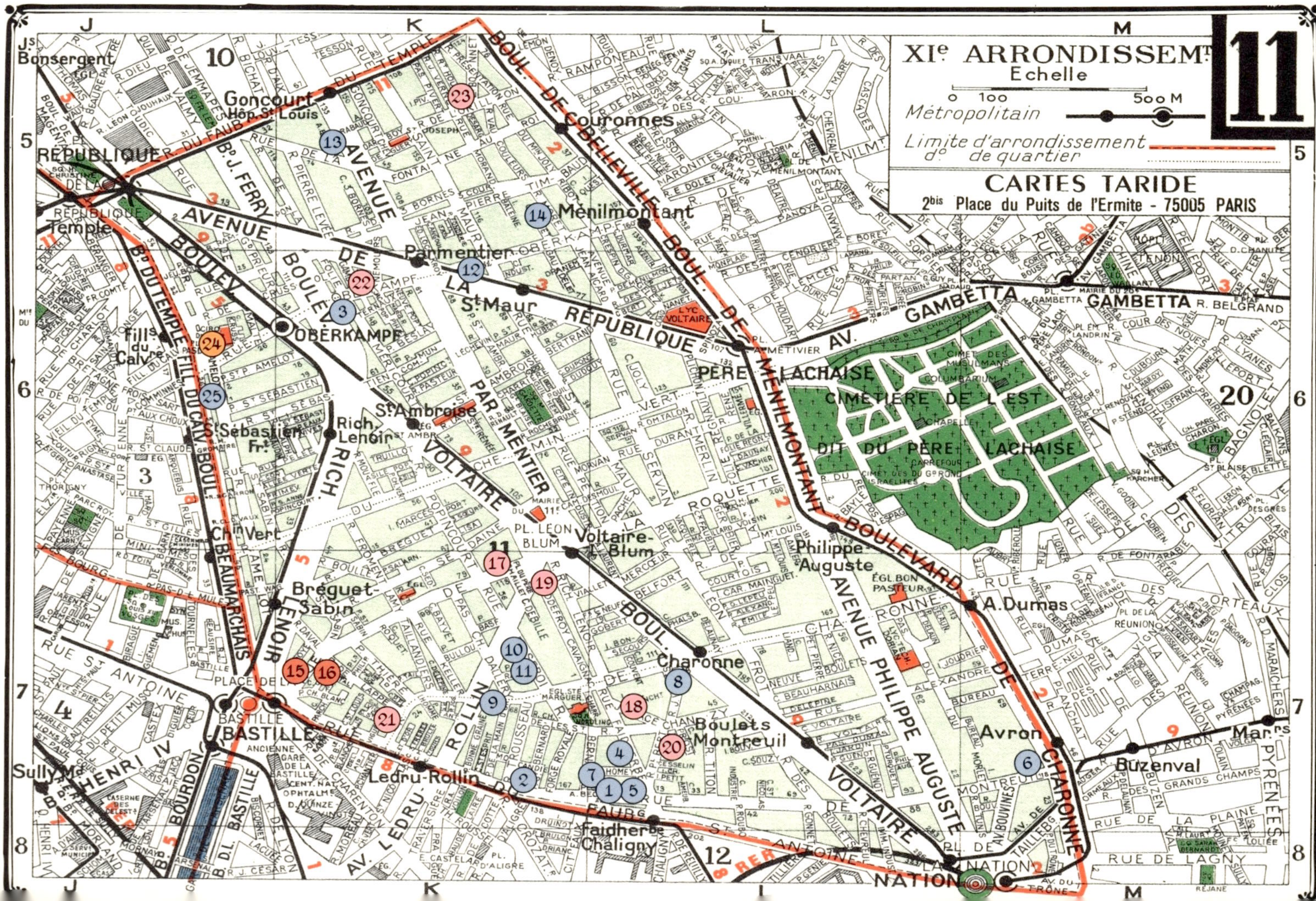

11
XIe ARRONDISSEMENT
Echelle
0 100 500 M
Métropolitain
Limite d'arrondissement
d° de quartier
CARTES TARIDE
2bis Place du Puits de l'Ermite - 75005 PARIS
RÉPUBLIQUE
Temple
Goncourt
Hôp. St Louis
Couronnes
Ménilmontant
Parmentier
St Maur
OBERKAMPF
St Ambroise
Rich. Lenoir
St Sébastien Frt
Filles du Calvre
Chin Vert
Breguet-Sabin
Voltaire-L. Blum
Père Lachaise
Philippe Auguste
A. Dumas
Charonne
Boulets Montreuil
Avron
Buzenval
Marrs
GAMBETTA
BASTILLE
Sully Md
Ledru-Rollin
Faidherbe Chaligny
NATION
CIMETIÈRE DE L'EST DIT DU PÈRE LACHAISE
AVENUE DE LA RÉPUBLIQUE
BOULEVARD DE MÉNILMONTANT
BOUL. DE BELLEVILLE
BOULEVARD DE CHARONNE
AVENUE PHILIPPE AUGUSTE
BOULEV. VOLTAIRE
AVENUE PARMENTIER
BOULEV. RICH. LENOIR
BOULEV. BEAUMARCHAIS
BOULEV. DU TEMPLE
Bd J. FERRY
RUE DU FAUB. ST ANTOINE
AV. LEDRU-ROLLIN
RUE ROQUETTE
RUE OBERKAMPF
RUE DE LA ROQUETTE
RUE DE CHARONNE
LYC. VOLTAIRE
10
20
12
3
4

11E ARRONDISSEMENT

1. Lejeune Frères
209 rue du Faubourg-Saint-Antoine
2. À la Providence
151 rue du Faubourg-Saint-Antoine
3. Reflets d'Antan
110 boulevard Richard-Lenoir
4. Burach Styles Décors
11 rue Faidherbe
5. Les Frères Nordin
215 rue du Faubourg-Saint-Antoine
6. La Maison du Parquet
131 rue de Montreuil
7. Produits d'Antan
10 rue Saint-Bernard
8. Gaignard Millon
24 rue Jules-Vallès
9. Cannage Paillage
58 rue de Charonne
10. Defrise
23 rue Basfroi
11. Gaëtan Lanzani
19–21 rue Basfroi
12. L'Arrosoir
80 rue Oberkampf
13. JM Vidéo
121 avenue Parmentier
14. Imprimerie du Marais
6 cité Griset
15. L'Atelier de Torréfaction
12 place de la Bastille – cour Damoye
16. Produits d'Auvergne
6 rue de Lappe
17. Chez Aline
85 rue de la Roquette
18. Le Pure Café
14 rue Jean-Macé
19. Aux Bons Crus
54 rue Godefroy-Cavaignac
20. Bistrot Paul Bert
18 rue Paul-Bert
21. Chez Paul
13 rue de Charonne
22. Aux Deux Amis
45 rue Oberkampf
23. L'Orillon
35 rue de l'Orillon
24. Cirque d'Hiver Bouglione
110 rue Amelot
25. Zapateria
97 rue Amelot

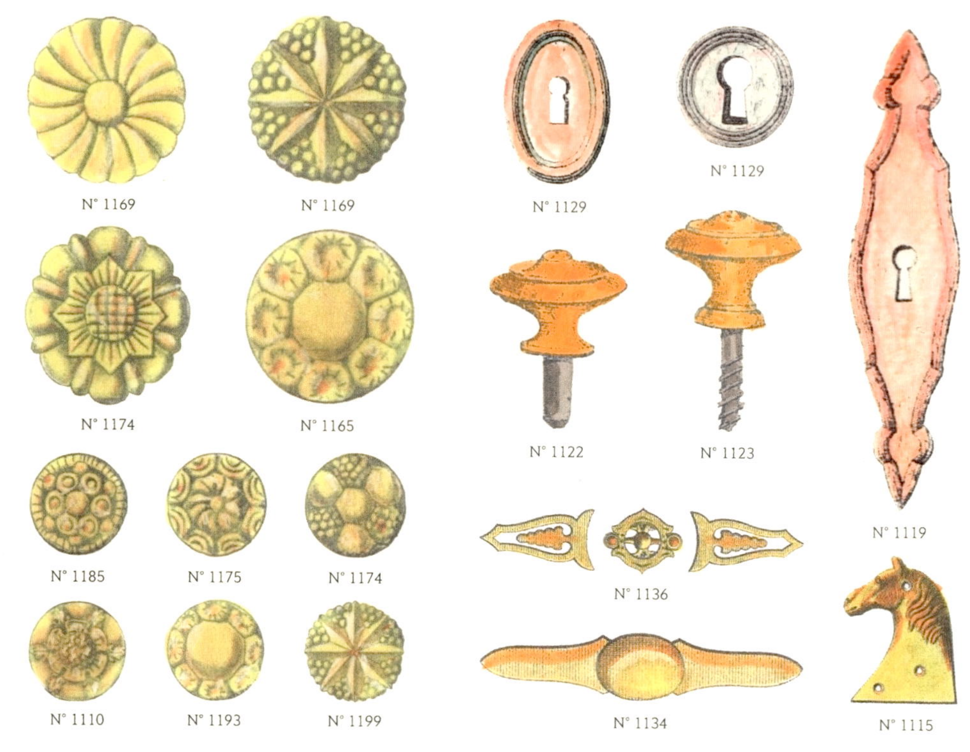

LEJEUNE FRÈRES

1

209 rue du Faubourg-Saint-Antoine
M° Faidherbe – Chaligny
01 43 72 99 26
lejeunefreres.com

This boutique has captured the ambiance of historic, 19th-century Faubourg Saint-Antoine, when the street was lined with artisans of every stripe. Lejeune Frères opened in the early 20th century to supply its neighbors with accessories for woodworking and furniture making. The old shelves are full of bric-a-brac and vintage gems, like the shell furniture handles I add to old workshop cabinets.

À LA PROVIDENCE

2

151 rue du Faubourg-Saint-Antoine
M° Ledru-Rollin
01 43 43 06 41
alaprovidence.com

Dating back to 1830, this hardware boutique perpetuates the soul of the Faubourg Saint-Antoine district, which for centuries was the hub of the furniture trade. Still featuring the original furnishings, including the worn wooden counter, cashier booth, and rows of shelves and drawers containing thousands of items, this highly specialized *quincaillerie* is a treasure trove of antique and vintage doorknobs, lock faceplates, finials, and more.

QUINCAILLERIE LECLERCQ

À LA PROVIDENCE

151 Rue du Faubourg-Saint-Antoine, 75011 Paris

POUR LES DIMENSIONS ET LES QUALITÉS DIVERSES DES ARTICLES FIGURANT À CE CATALOGUE CONSULTEZ LE TARIF CI-JOINT.

◈ REFLETS D'ANTAN ◈

110 boulevard Richard-Lenoir
M° Oberkampf / Parmentier
01 47 00 07 58

This is the kind of artisan anyone would be happy to live near. Since the late 1970s, behind its red storefront, Reflets d'Antan has specialized in restoring seats from every era. You'll even find antique art deco lamps and beautiful armchairs. Whenever I find a chair at a flea market, I bring it here for refurbishing.

N° 1193 N° 1189

◈ BURACH STYLES DÉCORS ◈

11 rue Faidherbe
M° Faidherbe – Chaligny
01 43 72 12 18
moulures-burach.com

I love this kind of old-fashioned store—with its original storefront and extravagant interiors—that opens a window on historic Paris. Since 1936, Burach Styles Décors has specialized in all manner of woodworking, which is becoming increasingly rare in the heart of the capital. I come here to have pedestals turned for the sculptures I find at flea markets.

N° 1121

N° 1190

N° 1191

N° 1192

N° 1195

N° 1126 N° 1127

N° 1128 N° 1129

N° 1130 N° 1131

N° 1110

N° 1129

N° 1110

LES FRÈRES NORDIN

5

215 rue du Faubourg-Saint-Antoine
M° Faidherbe – Chaligny
01 43 72 38 35
freresnordin.fr • @lesfreresnordin

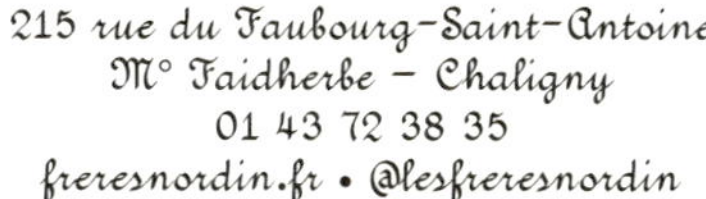

N° 1117

Despite its discreet appearance, this boutique is home to incredible artistry. Since the 1970s, the workshop has restored furniture from every period, as well as reproducing antique patinas. When I first opened my store on rue Madame, I often came here to recreate and preserve the old-fashioned charm of the painted furniture I had bought at flea markets.

N° 1117

N° 1171

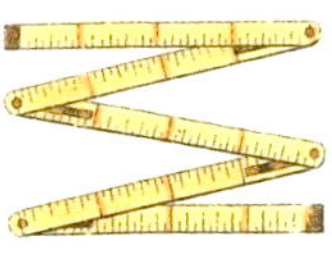
N° 1138

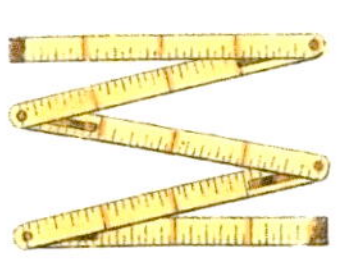
N° 1138

N° 1171

N° 1124

N° 1170

N° 1175

N° 1124

LA MAISON DU PARQUET

6

131 rue de Montreuil
M° Avron / Buzenval
01 43 73 80 80
lamaisonduparquet.com • @lamaisonduparquetparis

This "house" of parquet is a carpenter's paradise. When I first opened my store, it was a frequent destination of mine to create molding by the yard and custom shelves. The store is so full of wood and parquet varieties, it's hard to know where to look. I love places like this, where the volume of choice (talk about a Cornelian dilemma) does not preclude a job well done.

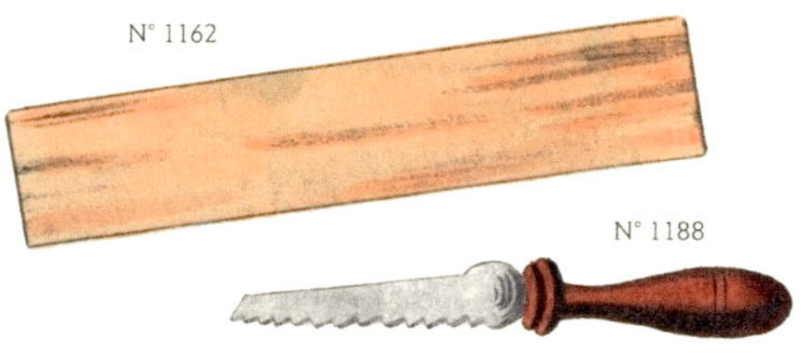

N° 1162

N° 1188

PRODUITS D'ANTAN

7

10 rue Saint-Bernard
M° Faidherbe – Chaligny
01 43 71 82 85
produits-dantan.com • @pmsb_produits_dantan

Preserving the traditions of the artisans of the Faubourg Saint-Antoine quarter, this specialist emporium of household products was created nearly a century ago. Professionals and DIY enthusiasts alike flock here to choose from the thousands of products and tools available for restoring or maintaining every kind of material—from marble or wood to leather or brass—displayed in the store's original decor.

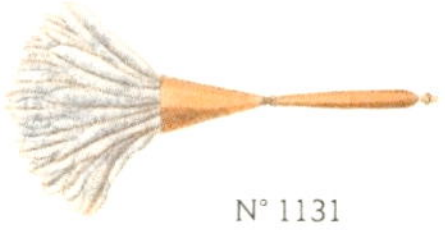

N° 1131

N° 1115

N° 1158

N° 1134

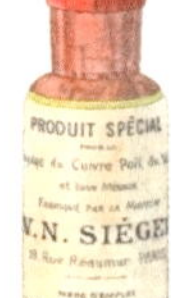

N° 1133

N° 1128

GAIGNARD MILLON

8

24 rue Jules-Vallès
M° Charonne
01 43 71 28 96
gaignard-millon.com • @gaignardmillon1875

In the 19th century, Faubourg Saint-Antoine was home to all the furniture craftsmen in Paris. Gaignard Millon set up shop here in 1875, to supply tools to his fellow artisans. The boutique has stayed the same ever since, including its lovely original storefront, antique furnishings, and perfectly organized bric-a-brac, which I like to admire through the window.

N° 1146

CANNAGE PAILLAGE

9

58 rue de Charonne
M° Ledru-Rollin
01 48 05 29 40
ventedecannageparis.com

I love this kind of store that embodies age-old craftsmanship: it seems to preserve a little slice of history. This is the workshop of an artisan caner who perfectly masters the art of caning and rushing. I bring old chairs here to have the rushing restored, as well as beautiful armchairs with traditional, often fragile caning in need of refurbishment.

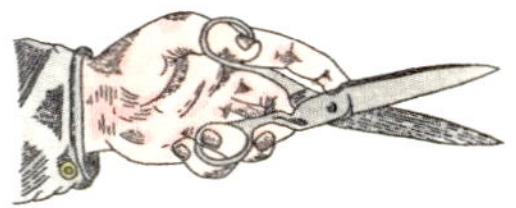

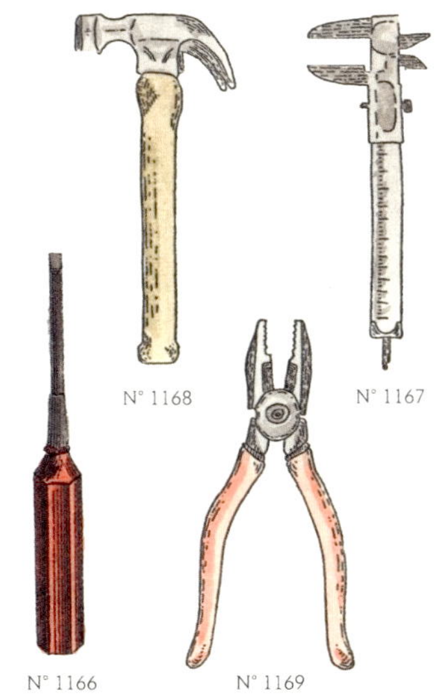
N° 1168 N° 1167 N° 1166 N° 1169

N° 1178

N° 1179

LANZANI

— LOCATION DE MATÉRIEL DÉCORATIF —

19-21 RUE BASFROI **EN TOUS GENRES** PARIS XIE (SEINE)

N° 5457

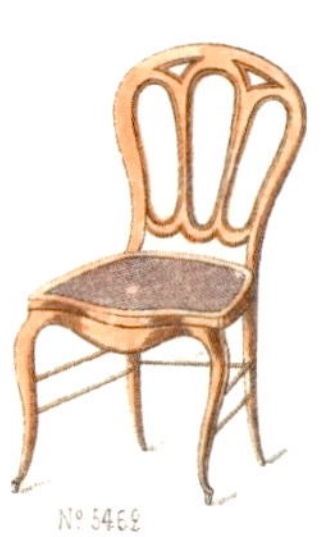

N° 5462

N° 5460

◇ DEFRISE ◇

10

23 rue Basfroi
M° Voltaire
01 43 79 78 29
defrise.paris • @defriseparis

This place is wild! What *don't* they have? Objects, accessories, and knickknacks from every era are carefully organized on shelves as far as the eye can see. I'm fascinated by the huge wall of telephones from the 1900s to 1990s, and another one of dishware, to name just two. Since 1952, the collections have been available to rent for film or photo shoots.

N° 1193 N° 1193

N° 1138 N° 1138

N° 1121

N° 1122

N° 1123

N° 1159

N° 1128

N° 1129

N° 1127

◇ GAËTAN LANZANI ◇

11

19–21 rue Basfrois
M° Voltaire
01 43 79 00 74
gaetanlanzani.com • @gaetanlanzani

This set decor rental house began life in the 1930s, when the eponymous founder opened a workshop that reproduced and restored period furniture. Today, it provides the entertainment industry with props of every kind and from every era. I love to wander the maze of corridors to discover the decorative objects for hire, from stuffed deer heads to Aubusson carpets or Amazonian headdresses.

N° 1124 N° 1125

◈ L'ARROSOIR ◈

12

80 rue Oberkampf
M° Parmentier
01 43 57 15 61
larrosoirparis.com • @larrosoirparis

Walking through the door of this floral oasis is like escaping to the countryside, right in the center of Paris. Opened in the 1920s, this florist shop—bursting with extraordinary flowers presented in a bucolic setting with timeless antique furniture—was recently taken over by an American who came to Paris for love. I buy wildflowers—my favorites—here.

N° 1115

◈ JM VIDÉO ◈

13

121 avenue Parmentier
M° Goncourt / Parmentier
01 43 57 21 49
jmvideo.fr • @jmvideoparis

This is one of the last video rental stores in Paris. When JM Vidéo opened on rue Parmentier in 1993, it was the golden age of video. But by the end of the 2000s, its heyday was over. Now iconic, JM Vidéo has become something of a film museum, presenting thousands of DVDs in a 1990s ambiance that borders on geeky. I love coming here for movies that I can't find anywhere else.

N° 1177

N° 1145

N° 1109

N° 1143

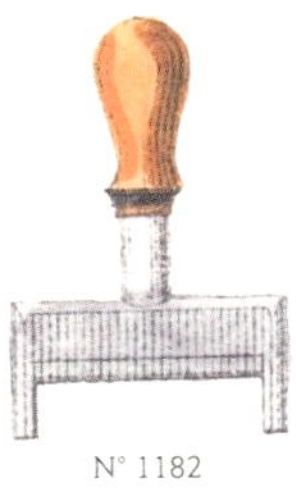
N° 1182

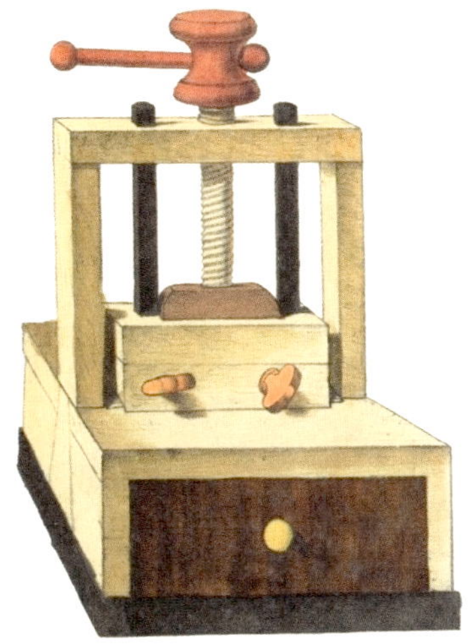

N° 1156

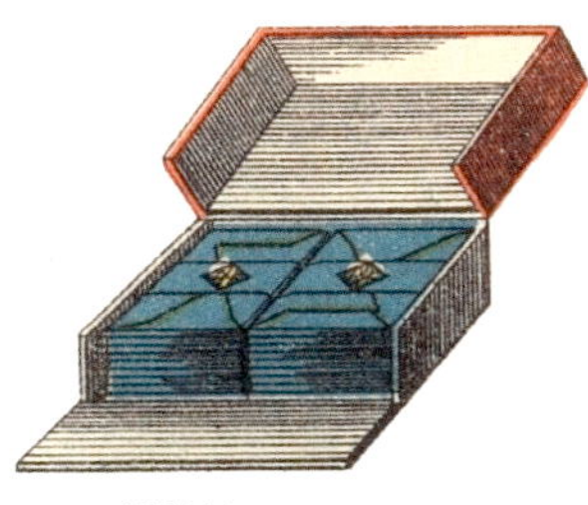
N° 1144

N° 1183

N° 1128

IMPRIMERIE DU MARAIS

14

6 cité Griset
M° Rue Saint-Maur / Ménilmontant / Couronnes
01 42 72 10 56
imprimeriedumarais.com/en • @imprimeriedumarais

This legendary printing works, dating from 1971, relocated in 2021 from rue Chapon to this impressive red-brick building that evokes Paris's working-class history. Endowed with a wealth of expertise, they print all kinds of art-focused projects and books, as well as invitations for luxury fashion shows. I especially appreciate their Heidelberg presses dating from the early 20th century.

N° 1184

N° 1185

N° 1124

N° 1133

N° 1114

L'ATELIER DE TORRÉFACTION

15

12 place de la Bastille – cour Damoye
M° Bastille / Bréguet – Sabin
01 43 14 20 11
@latelierdetorrefaction

I enjoy the calm of cour Damoye, sheltered from the bustle of the Bastille district. At the courtyard's center, this charming café has preserved its industrial, 19th-century exterior dating from a time when the area was full of artisan workshops. It has replaced Daval, a coffee roasting institution since the 1970s. I like the peaceful terrace, especially in summer, when a cool break is more than welcome.

PRODUITS D'AUVERGNE

16

6 rue de Lappe
M° Bréguet – Sabin / Bastille
01 47 00 41 28

Standing out among the many bars lining the street, this charming red boutique has made it a mission to import specialties from the Auvergne region since 1865. Of course, they stock delicious cheese, jam, and charcuterie. But I make a special trip here for their saucissons, which always go over well at an *apéro* with friends or at a family dinner.

N° 1132

CHEZ ALINE

17

85 rue de la Roquette
M° Voltaire
01 43 71 90 75

The art of the sandwich is taken to new heights here. Every lunchtime, the two proprietors write up the day's creations in white marker: sky-high sandwiches and salads sold by weight. I also love the original colorful decor of this former butcher shop from the 1970s. A good local address to have on hand, should your stomach start rumbling.

N° 1199

N° 1198

N° 1106

N° 1105

N° 1195

N° 1109

N° 1189

LE PURE CAFÉ

14 rue Jean-Macé
M° Charonne
01 43 71 47 22
lepurecafe.shop • @lepurecafeparis

Let me set the scene for you: a storefront from 1905, interiors from the 1950s, tiling straight out of my grandmother's kitchen, and—at the heart of the action—a central zinc bar. I always find some reason to come here: a work-related appointment, to get some work done over breakfast, to have an *apéro* with friends, or to enjoy a generous burger at the bar.

N° 1163

AUX BONS CRUS

54 rue Godefroy-Cavaignac
M° Voltaire
01 45 67 21 13
auxbonscrus.fr • @auxbonscrusparis

This is one of Paris's rare *routiers*—restaurants created for truck drivers in need of a break—which flourished in the early 1930s. Since then, Aux Bons Crus has become a neighborhood favorite, especially for fans of hearty classic French dishes. I love the authentic ambience, and the unpretentious bistro decor always puts a smile on my face.

N° 1112

N° 1160

N° 1189

N° 1154

N° 1124

N° 1175

BISTROT PAUL BERT

18 rue Paul-Bert
M° Faidherbe – Chaligny / Charonne
01 43 72 24 01
bistrotpaulbert.fr/404 • @bistrotpaulbert

I hole up in this prewar estaminet whenever I get a craving for comfort food. In 1996, when the new owners bought the place, they made a point of keeping the genuine bistro interiors, including the zinc bar and original tiling, as well as the merry ambiance that continues to delight neighborhood patrons.

N° 1106

CHEZ PAUL

13 rue de Charonne
M° Ledru-Rollin / Bréguet – Sabin
01 47 00 34 57
chezpaul.com/en/ • @restaurantchezpaul

This place was already buzzing back in 1900. When the Paul family inherited the restaurant in 1940, they maintained the festive, energetic bistro ambience. Since then, Chez Paul has become a true neighborhood institution that immerses diners in the quintessential Paris spirit. I love this place for the generous French dishes and *bon vivant* staff.

N° 1182

N° 1142 N° 1143 N° 1144 N° 1145

N° 1137

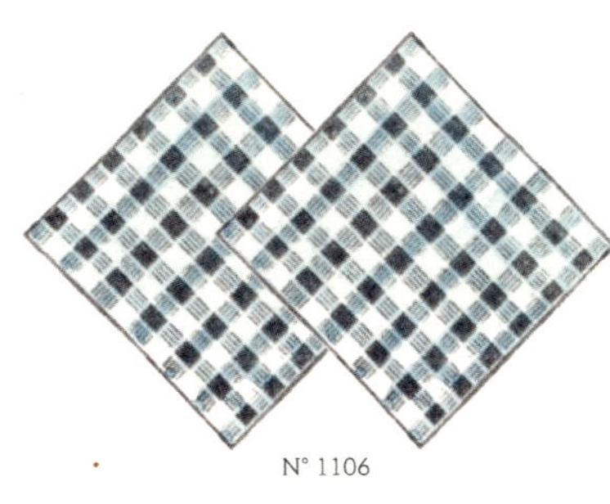

N° 1106

N° 1126

AUX DEUX AMIS

45 rue Oberkampf
M° Oberkampf / Parmentier
01 58 30 38 13
@auxdeuxamis

On Friday nights, you can almost hear the laughter from this small, crowded local bar spilling out onto the sidewalk. Opened in the 1950s, it has since been taken over by new owners who have retained the jovial and friendly atmosphere. I come here quite often for a drink and a plate of Bellota ham, or at lunchtime for their delicious seasonal dishes.

L'ORILLON

23

35 rue de l'Orillon
M° Belleville
01 48 05 68 87
@lorillon_bar_de_quartier

L'Orillon opened in Belleville in the 1960s. For a long time, it was the kind of neighborhood bar where locals would talk for hours at the *comptoir*. It has since been renovated, but the original decor has been retained, including an old telephone booth, as well as the spirit of hospitality. I come for the good food and the *mezcalita*—my favorite cocktail. A bit of advice: show up early to avoid the line.

◈ CIRQUE D'HIVER BOUGLIONE ◈

110 rue Amelot
M° Filles du Calvaire
01 47 00 28 81
cirquedhiver.com/en/ • @cirquedhiverbouglione

Opened in 1852 by Napoleon III, the Cirque d'Hiver can lay claim as the oldest circus in the world. It's a magical experience for the whole family—my niece and nephew love when I bring them here. Their eyes light up as they watch circus artists perform acrobatics and magicians their tricks, in a dreamlike setting that has been perfectly preserved, inside and out.

N° 1186

◈ ZAPATERIA ◈

97 rue Amelot
M° Saint-Sébastien – Froissart
01 49 29 97 71

My niece, nephew, and I always stop here after a show at the Cirque d'Hiver. They love the storefront on this cobbler's workshop that seems as old as the hills, with its dark wood frame and old-fashioned lettering. In the window, dozens of colorful clown shoes from every era and of all shapes and sizes wait for the ringmaster—or intrigued passersby—to make an appearance.

N° 1107

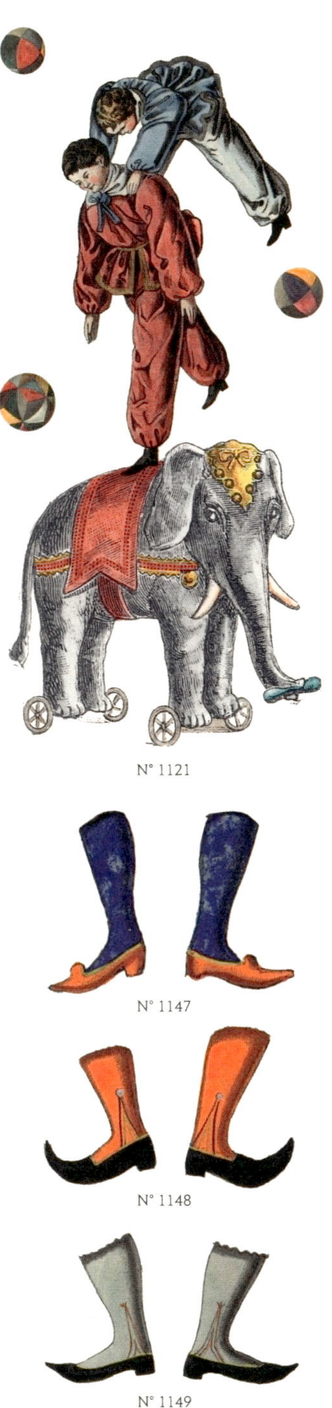

N° 1121

N° 1147

N° 1148

N° 1149

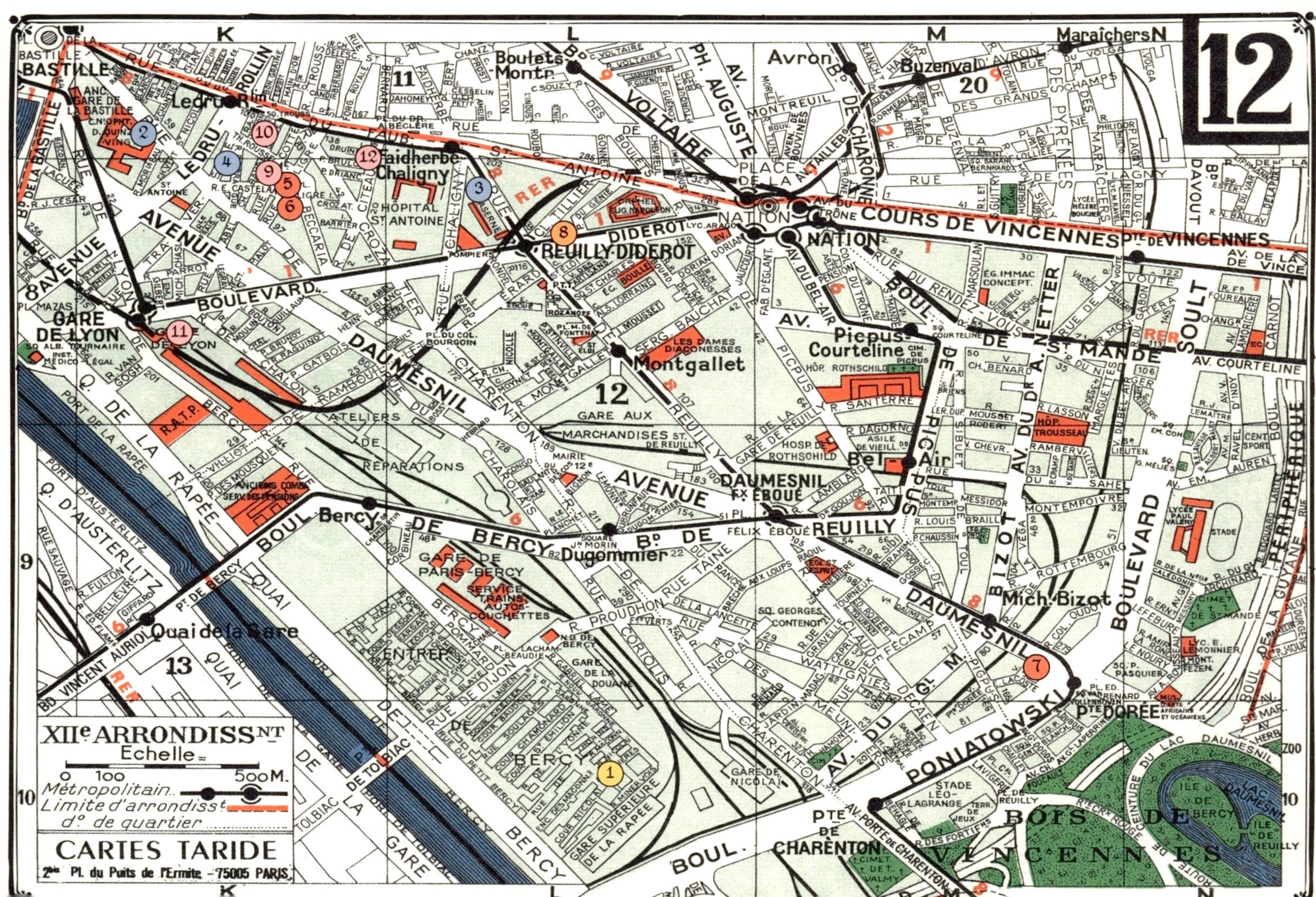

12
XIIe ARRONDISSNT
Echelle
0 100 500M.
Métropolitain
Limite d'arrondisst
do de quartier
CARTES TARIDE
2bis Pl. du Puits de l'Ermite - 75005 PARIS
BASTILLE
Ledru-Rollin
Faidherbe Chaligny
Reuilly-Diderot
Nation
Boulets Montr.
Avron
Buzenval
Maraîchers
Porte de Vincennes
Picpus Courteline
Bel-Air
Montgallet
Daumesnil Fx Éboué
Dugommier
Michel Bizot
Pte Dorée
Pte de Charenton
Bercy
Quai de la Gare
Gare de Lyon
COURS DE VINCENNES
BOULEVARD SOULT
AV. DAUMESNIL
BD DE BERCY
BD DE REUILLY
AV. DU GL M. BIZOT
BD PONIATOWSKI
BD DIDEROT
AV. LEDRU-ROLLIN
BD VOLTAIRE
AV. PH. AUGUSTE
BD DE CHARONNE
RUE DE CHARENTON
QUAI DE LA RAPÉE
QUAI DE BERCY
QUAI D'AUSTERLITZ
QUAI DE LA GARE
PORT DE LA RAPÉE
HÔPITAL ST ANTOINE
HÔP. TROUSSEAU
HÔP. ROTHSCHILD
GARE AUX MARCHANDISES DE REUILLY
ATELIERS DE RÉPARATIONS
GARE DE PARIS-BERCY
SERVICE TRAINS AUTOS COUCHETTES
ENTREPÔT
GARE DE LA DOUANE
GARE DE NICOLAÏ
BOIS DE VINCENNES
LAC DAUMESNIL
ÎLE DE BERCY
ÎLE DE REUILLY
STADE LÉO-LAGRANGE
LYCÉE PAUL VALÉRY
MUS. DES ARTS AFRICAINS ET OCÉANIENS
BD PÉRIPHÉRIQUE
11
12
13
20
K
L
M
N
9
10

12^E^ ARRONDISSEMENT

1. Les Pavillons de Bercy – Musée des Arts Forains
   53 avenue des Terroirs-de-France
2. La Galcante
   38 rue de Charenton
3. Soubrier Antiquités
   14 rue de Reuilly
4. Laverdure
   58 rue Traversière
5. Marché d'Aligre
   Place d'Aligre
6. La Graineterie du Marché
   8 place d'Aligre
7. Vandermeersch
   278 avenue Daumesnil
8. Dominique Léon – Artisan Coiffeur
   89 boulevard Diderot
9. Le Charolais
   15 rue de Cotte
10. Le Square Trousseau
    1 rue Antoine-Vollon
11. Le Train Bleu
    Gare de Lyon
12. L'Ébauchoir
    43 rue de Cîteaux

LES PAVILLONS DE BERCY

Musée des *Arts Forains*

53 AV. DES TERROIRS-DE-FRANCE — PARIS

LES PAVILLONS DE BERCY – MUSÉE DES ARTS FORAINS

1

53 avenue des Terroirs-de-France
M° Cour Saint-Émilion
01 43 40 16 22
arts-forains.com/en • @museedesartsforains

Since 1996, this museum has offered visitors an entertaining journey through the history of funfairs. Step into a waking dream as you enjoy traditional fairground games and rides, as well as numerous shows of all kinds. I love the old-fashioned Magic Mirrors circus tent, and the hot-air balloon with an elephant-shaped basket. Advance booking is essential.

N° 1268

N° 1250

N° 1251

N° 1252

LA GALCANTE

2

38 rue de Charenton
M° Ledru-Rollin / Bastille
01 44 77 87 44
lagalcante.com

Step through the doorway of La Galcante and enter history. In 1975, journalist Christian Bailly began collecting and collating every newspaper published from the French Revolution to the present day. Since then, he has gathered them all here, carefully filed by date and subject. I come here to find newspapers published on my friends' birthdays, to offer them as gifts.

N° 1204

N° 1205

N° 1206

N° 1207

N° 1285

N° 1286  N° 1255  N° 1242  N° 1248

N° 1226  N° 1267  N° 1266  N° 1211  N° 1212

◈ SOUBRIER ANTIQUITÉS ◈

14 rue de Reuilly
M° Faidherbe – Chaligny
01 43 72 93 71
soubrier.com/en • @soubrier

The moment you arrive, you'll feel like you've discovered a hidden treasure chest. Two marble sphinxes will greet you at the entrance, giving you the impression you've stepped back in time. Created in the early 19th century, Soubrier initially made furniture. Since 1960, it has specialized in collecting and renting antique furniture, to the delight of film set designers.

◈ LAVERDURE ◈

4

58 rue Traversière
M° Ledru-Rollin
01 43 43 38 85
laverdure.fr • @laverdureparis

This is the kind of secret spot I love in Paris. Since 1911, Laverdure has been a reference for fine crafts, and cabinetmaking in particular. The boutique stocks all the materials necessary for this beautiful art. But most of all, I appreciate the classic exterior, with its window display of countless pigments, and the pretty antique furniture, for their authenticity and history.

Ameublement
Adresse Télégraphique
SOUBRIER-REUILLY-PARIS
TÉLEPHONE
HANOI 1887
BRUXELLES 1888
MELBOURNE 1888
MÉD. D'OR
MÉDAILLE D'OR
MÉD. D'OR
Soubrier
14, Rue de Reuilly
Fig n°1
Fig n°2
Fig n°3
Fig n°4
Fig n°5
Fig n°6
Fig n°7
Fig n°8
Fig n°9
Fig n°10
Fig n°11

MARCHÉ D'ALIGRE

5

Place d'Aligre
M° Ledru-Rollin
FB: Les amis du Marché Beauvau

Also known as the Marché Beauvau, this is one of the oldest and most iconic markets in Paris. Butchers first gathered here when it was created in 1618, before a covered market was added in 1781. Since then, the market has included fruit and vegetable stalls, second-hand vendors, and florists, including the oldest seed seller in Paris. I live nearby, so I come here regularly, especially for pretty flowers and quality products.

N° 127 N° 1276

N° 1277 N° 1278

N° 1245

N° 1275

LA GRAINETERIE DU MARCHÉ

6

8 place d'Aligre
M° Ledru-Rollin
01 45 84 46 36
@lagraineteriedumarche

I always stop in at this store whenever I go to the Marché d'Aligre. With glass vases full of candy that remind me of my childhood, and a selection of peppers from around the world, the interior has remained practically the same since the boutique opened in the 1930s. A veritable memory box, it is bursting with plants and jars, and you'll find all kinds of seeds here—to eat, plant, or feed the birds.

N° 1214

N° 1238 N° 1244

VANDERMEERSCH

7

278 avenue Daumesnil
M° Porte Dorée
01 43 47 21 66
boulangerie-patisserie-vandermeersch.com •
@stephane.vandermeersch

After working for a time with Pierre Hermé, Stéphane decided to set up shop in this attractive, late-19th-century bakery in 1999. Since then, he has nurtured his enthusiasm for excellent bread and pastries, especially kouglof, his specialty, which he sells by weight. I love the way he wraps it up in pretty paper, *à l'italienne.*

N° 1216

DOMINIQUE LÉON – ARTISAN COIFFEUR

8

89 boulevard Diderot
M° Reuilly – Diderot
01 43 72 00 85

Dominique's clients come to him for more than just a haircut: since 1991, they've also come here to chat or confide their secrets. In his little parlor that resembles an old boat cabin, it's easy to let your hair down and open up. As for Dominique, he isn't a slave to fashion: he creates unique styles for each of his clients. And there's even a documentary featuring conversations that took place in the salon between 2007 and 2012.

N° 1231 N° 1236

N° 1232 N° 1237

N° 1233 N° 1238

N° 1234 N° 1239

N° 1235 N° 1240

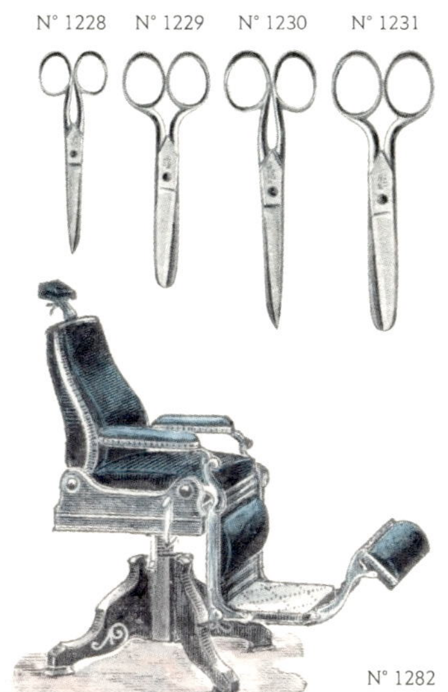

N° 1228 N° 1229 N° 1230 N° 1231

N° 1282

◈ LE CHAROLAIS ◈

15 rue de Cotte
M° Ledru-Rollin
01 43 45 14 72

When a ray of sunlight falls across the Marché d'Aligre, I pull up a seat here. I enjoy the lively view from the terrace: passersby on their way to the market, the server opening oysters on an old wine barrel, and my glass of white wine sparkling in the sun. Opened in 1905, this little bistro is still committed to serving generous, good-quality food.

N° 1280

N° 1223

◈ LE SQUARE TROUSSEAU ◈

1 rue Antoine-Vollon
M° Ledru-Rollin
01 43 43 06 00
squaretrousseau.com/en • @squaretrousseau

Situated here since 1907, between Faubourg Saint-Antoine and the Marché d'Aligre, this restaurant has resisted the vagaries of fashion and maintained its original charm. Diners are first greeted by dessert—a buffet of cakes beckons from the entrance—before being tempted by the delicious hand-cut steak tartare. For me, this is the perfect meeting place for professional appointments.

N° 1219

N° 1220

N° 1274

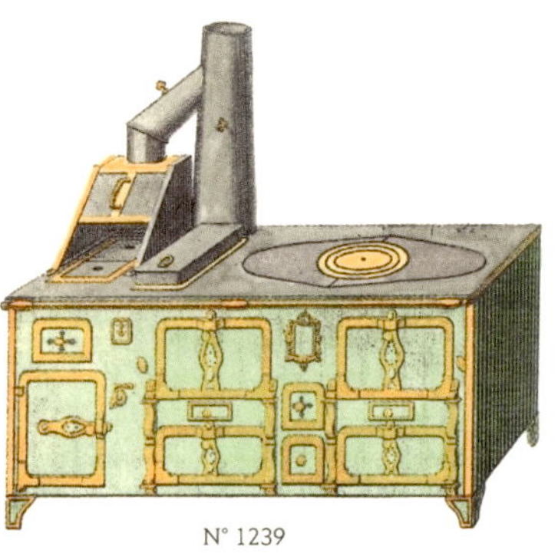

N° 1239

N° 1256

N° 1221

◈ LE TRAIN BLEU ◈

11

Gare de Lyon
M° / RER Gare de Lyon
01 43 43 09 06
le-train-bleu.com/en • @restaurantletrainbleu

This magnificent restaurant overlooks the trains arriving at the Gare de Lyon station. Opened in 1901, this establishment is an icon for travelers heading to the South of France and encapsulates that sweet feeling at the start of a vacation. I like to sit and wait here when I arrive early for my train to Marseille, in a spectacular setting worthy of a movie on the Belle Époque.

N° 1211

◈ L'ÉBAUCHOIR ◈

12

43 rue de Citeaux
M° Faidherbe – Chaligny
01 43 42 49 31
lebauchoir.com • @restaurant_lebauchoir

Created by two brothers, this restaurant is my go-to for a relaxed meal. Since I live nearby, I come here often enough to have my usual table. The small terrace, away from prying eyes, is perfect for summer lunches. On the menu, there's a delicious side of truffle purée, a wonderful pavlova for dessert, and wine served *à la ficelle*, so you only pay for what you drink, just like in the old days.

N° 1253

N° 1274

N° 1225

N° 1213

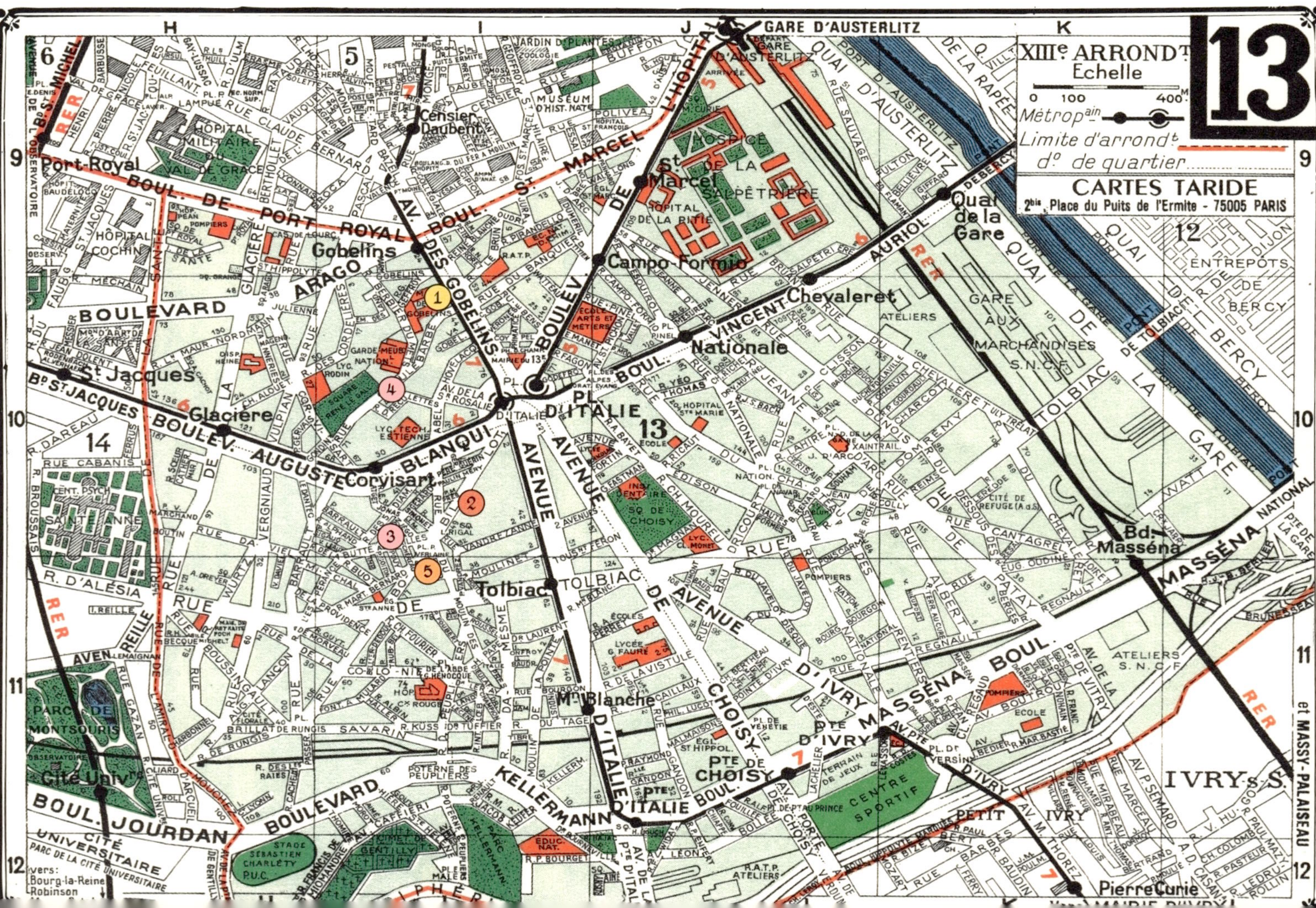
13
XIIIe ARRONDT
Echelle
0 100 400M
Métropain
Limite d'arrondt
do de quartier
CARTES TARIDE
2bis Place du Puits de l'Ermite - 75005 PARIS
et MASSY-PALAISEAU
GARE D'AUSTERLITZ
QUAI D'AUSTERLITZ
QUAI DE LA GARE
Quai de la Gare
GARE AUX MARCHANDISES S.N.C.F.
BOUL. DE L'HOPITAL
HOSPICE DE LA SALPÊTRIÈRE
BOUL. VINCENT AURIOL
Chevaleret
Nationale
Campo-Formio
St Marcel
BOUL. ST MARCEL
PL. D'ITALIE
AVENUE D'ITALIE
AVENUE DE CHOISY
AVENUE D'IVRY
AV. DES GOBELINS
Gobelins
BOULEVARD ARAGO
BOUL. DE PORT ROYAL
Port-Royal
Censier Daubent.
BOULEV. AUGUSTE BLANQUI
Corvisart
Glacière
St Jacques
Bd ST JACQUES
Tolbiac
RUE DE TOLBIAC
Mn Blanche
BOULEVARD KELLERMANN
PARC KELLERMANN
BOUL. MASSÉNA
Bd Masséna
Pte d'Ivry
Pte de Choisy
Pte d'Italie
CENTRE SPORTIF
BOUL. JOURDAN
Cité Univre
CITÉ UNIVERSITAIRE
PARC DE MONTSOURIS
Pierre Curie
IVRY-S-S.
RER
12
13
14
5
6

13E ARRONDISSEMENT

1. Mobilier National & Manufacture des Gobelins
1 rue Berbier-du-Metz / 42 avenue des Gobelins

2. La Cave Bobillot
23 rue Bobillot

3. Le Temps des Cerises
18–20 rue de la Butte-aux-Cailles

4. Auberge Etchegorry
41 rue de Croulebarbe

5. Piscine de la Butte-aux-Cailles
5 place Paul-Verlaine

MOBILIER NATIONAL

MANUFACTURE NATIONALE DES GOBELINS

Se Trouve

AU 1, RUE BERBIER-DU-METS À PARIS

N° 1360 N° 1361

◈ MOBILIER NATIONAL & MANUFACTURE DES GOBELINS ◈

1

MN: 1 rue Berbier-du-Mets
01 44 08 53 59 / 01 44 08 52 00
MG: 42 avenue des Gobelins • 01 44 08 53 49
M° Les Gobelins
mobiliernational.culture.gouv.fr • @mobiliernational

N° 1312

N° 1313

N° 1303

N° 1390

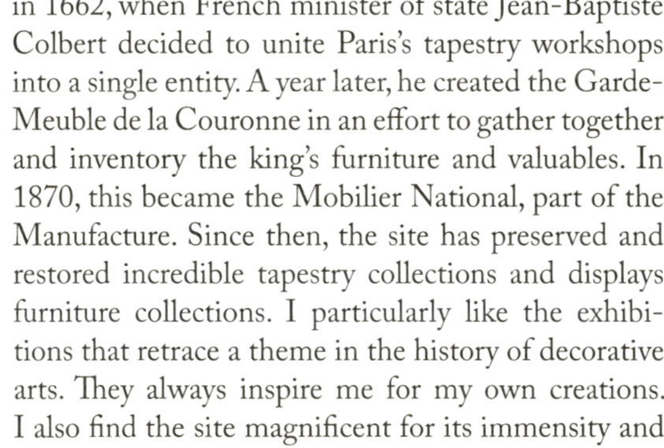

The history of the Manufacture des Gobelins began in 1662, when French minister of state Jean-Baptiste Colbert decided to unite Paris's tapestry workshops into a single entity. A year later, he created the Garde-Meuble de la Couronne in an effort to gather together and inventory the king's furniture and valuables. In 1870, this became the Mobilier National, part of the Manufacture. Since then, the site has preserved and restored incredible tapestry collections and displays furniture collections. I particularly like the exhibitions that retrace a theme in the history of decorative arts. They always inspire me for my own creations. I also find the site magnificent for its immensity and for the history it embodies.

N° 1394

N° 1307

N° 1356

N° 1358

LA CAVE BOBILLOT

23 rue Bobillot
M° Place d'Italie
01 45 80 10 52
@lacavebobillot

There is nothing ordinary about this wine store. Since 1962, it has been offering clients wine, of course, but also liquors from around the world and unusual bottles that attract the eye and titillate the tastebuds. It's the perfect place to find a good bottle to slip under the tree at Christmas, or to share at a dinner party, without compromising on quality.

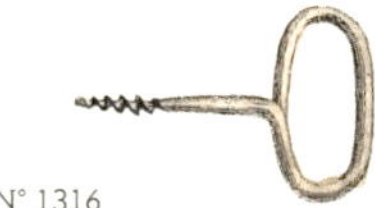

N° 1316

N° 1315

LE TEMPS DES CERISES

18–20 rue de la Butte-aux-Cailles
M° Corvisart
01 45 89 69 48
letempsdescerisescoop.com

Opened in 1976 in the heart of the Butte-aux-Cailles village-neighborhood, Le Temps des Cerises is a cooperative restaurant that divides profits fairly among its employees. The menu changes daily, and the establishment even offers 1€ meals for students. It has retained its working-class charm, serving varied, high-quality food that is accessible to all.

N° 1353

N° 1322 N° 1322

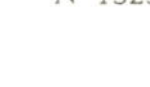

N° 1323 N° 1323

N° 1327

N° 1328

N° 1329

N° 1330

N° 1331

N° 1332

N° 1333

N° 1334

N° 1335

N° 1336

AUBERGE ETCHEGORRY

4

41 rue de Croulebarbe
M° Corvisart / Place d'Italie
01 44 08 83 51
etchegorry.fr/en

This place has seen it all. Built at the dawn of the 19th century, it was initially a cabaret run by Madame Grégoire, an icon of Parisian nights pulsing with folly and excess. In 1930, it was acquired by a Basque family who turned it into a hotel and then, in the 1960s, into the (Basque) restaurant that it is today, taking care to preserve the original exterior.

N° 1399

N° 1318

N° 1301

N° 1310

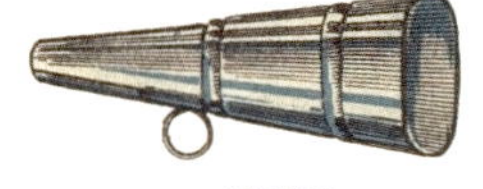

N° 1319

N° 1387

PISCINE DE LA BUTTE-AUX-CAILLES

5

5 place Paul-Verlaine
M° Place d'Italie
01 45 89 60 05
paris.fr/lieux/piscine-de-la-butte-aux-cailles-2927

N° 1342

Built in the 1920s, this swimming pool has retained its old-fashioned charm, complete with immaculate white tiling, blue accents reminiscent of Deauville, and vaulted ceiling that lets the sunlight filter gently through. A far cry from pools of Olympic proportions, its small size makes it a pleasant spot to practice your strokes, in addition to the heated outdoor pool, where you can swim even in winter.

N° 1317

N° 1333

N° 1320

N° 1333

LOUIS BONNIER
ARCHITECTE

VILLE • DE • PARIS

1924

ÉTABLISSEMENT • BALNÉAIRE DE • LA • BUTTE • AUX • CAILLES

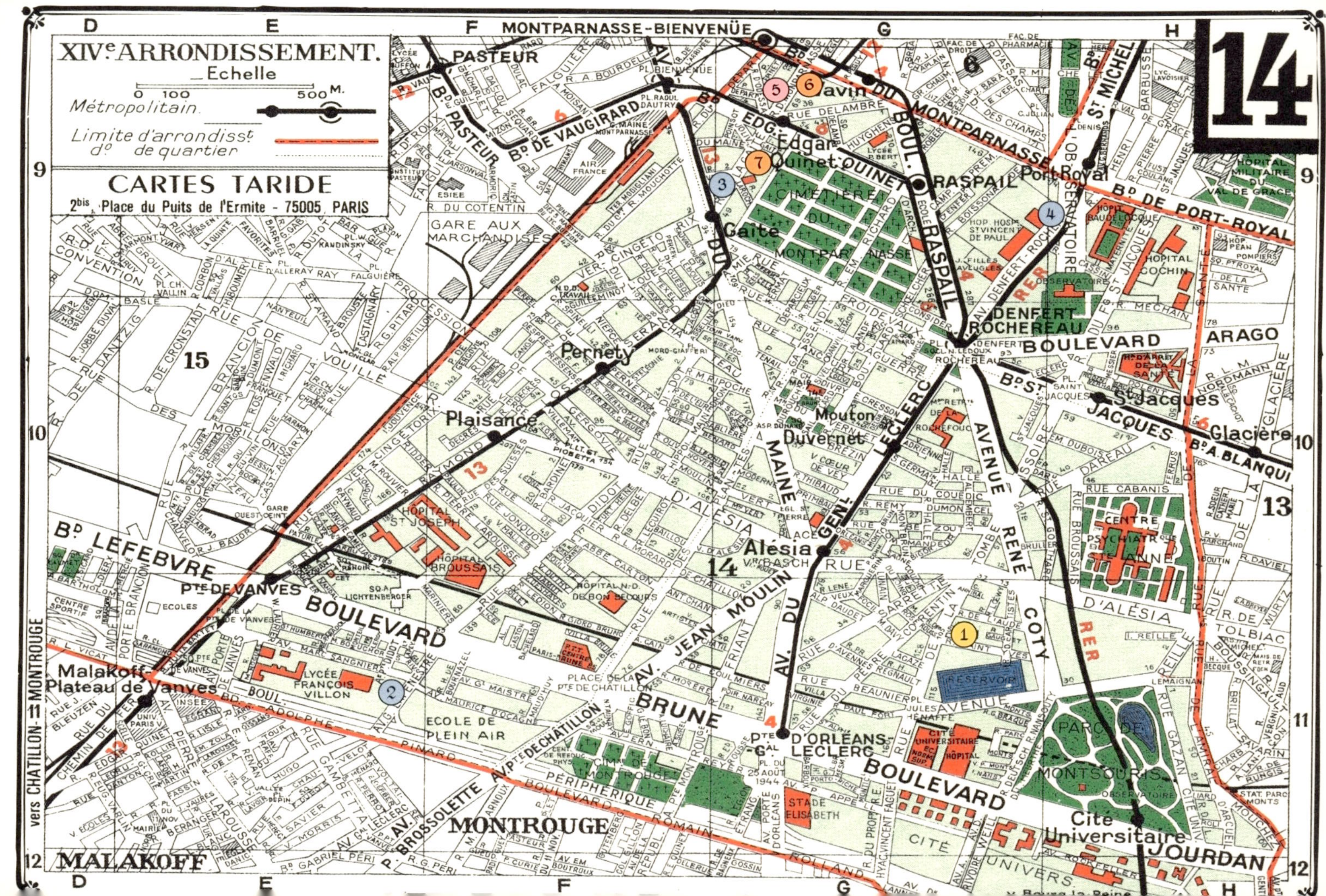

14
XIVe ARRONDISSEMENT.
Echelle
0 100 500 M.
Métropolitain
Limite d'arrondisst
do de quartier
CARTES TARIDE
2bis Place du Puits de l'Ermite - 75005 PARIS
MONTPARNASSE-BIENVENÜE
PASTEUR
Bd DE VAUGIRARD
Bd PASTEUR
GARE AUX MARCHANDISES
Edgar Quinet
Gaîté
RASPAIL
BOUL. DU MONTPARNASSE
Vavin
Port Royal
Bd DE PORT-ROYAL
Bd St MICHEL
DENFERT ROCHEREAU
BOULEVARD
ARAGO
St Jacques
Glacière
Bd A. BLANQUI
Pernety
Plaisance
Mouton Duvernet
MAINE
LECLERC
AVENUE RENÉ COTY
Alésia
AV. DU GÉNl LECLERC
AV. JEAN MOULIN
Bd LEFEBVRE
Pte DE VANVES
BOULEVARD BRUNE
Malakoff Plateau de Vanves
Pte D'ORLÉANS Gal LECLERC
BOULEVARD PÉRIPHÉRIQUE
PARC DE MONTSOURIS
Cité Universitaire
JOURDAN
RÉSERVOIR
CIMETIÈRE DU MONTPARNASSE
RER
MONTROUGE
MALAKOFF
vers CHATILLON-MONTROUGE
15
13
6
14

◈ 14E ARRONDISSEMENT ◈

1. Ateliers-Musée Chana Orloff
7 bis villa Seurat

2. Puces de Vanves
Avenue Georges-Lafenestre & avenue Marc-Sangnier

3. L'Odyssex
28 rue de la Gaîté

4. L'Artisanat Monastique
68 bis avenue Denfert-Rochereau

5. La Crêperie Bretonne
56 rue du Montparnasse

6. IDEM Paris
49 rue du Montparnasse

7. La Comédie Italienne
17–19 rue de la Gaîté

ATELIERS-MUSÉE CHANA ORLOFF

1

7 bis villa Seurat
M° Alésia
06 60 92 22 17
chana-orloff.org/en • @chana_orloff

Chana Orloff arrived in Paris from Ukraine in 1910 to train as a seamstress. She went on to become one of the greatest sculptors of the 20th century. Each visit to her studio, opened in 1926, brings me closer to this exceptional artist, who was an intimate of Soutine, Modigliani, and Anaïs Nin. I love wandering here on weekends, admiring drawings and singular sculptures in the studio's soft light.

N° 1456

N° 1410

N° 1474

N° 1465

PUCES DE VANVES

2

Avenue Georges-Lafenestre & avenue Marc-Sangnier
M° Porte de Vanves
pucesdevanves.com • @lespucesdevanveparis14e

This flea market, established in 1920, is one of my favorite places to stroll on weekends. It's not quite as well known as the Puces de Saint-Ouen, so you can find some good deals and hunt down great pieces among the 380 vendors. Some dealers even come here to buy antique items before selling them on at Saint-Ouen. The open-air format adds to the pleasure.

N° 1490

N° 1491

N° 1452

Avenue Marc-Sangnier

PUCES DE VANVES

Avenue Georges-Lafenestre

CHAQUE SAMEDI ET DIMANCHE DE L'ANNÉE,
FÊTES COMPRISES, AVEC LE SOLEIL OU AVEC LA PLUIE

5043

4712

5043

4714

5043

N° 5351

4715

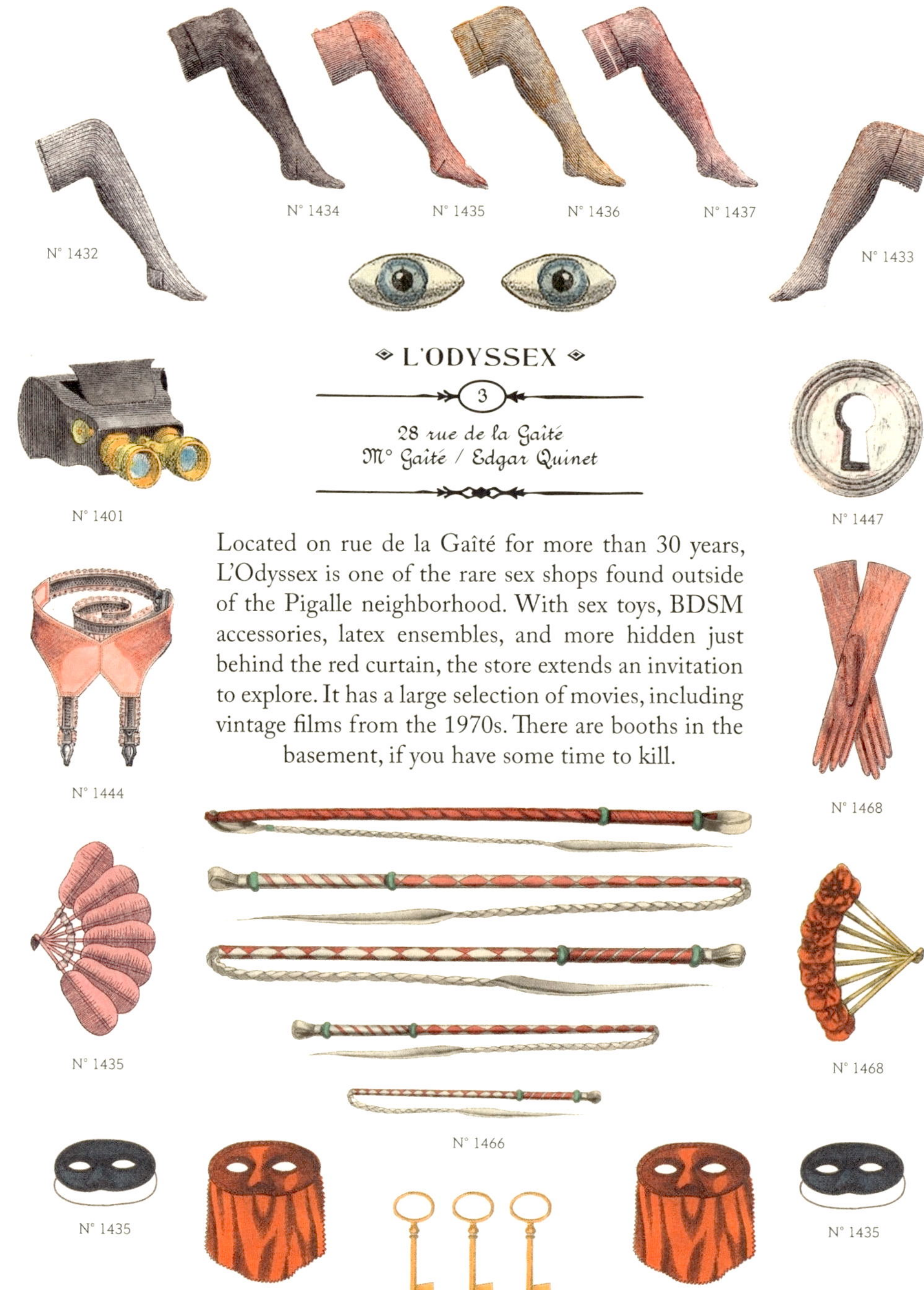

L'ODYSSEX

3

28 rue de la Gaîté
M° Gaîté / Edgar Quinet

Located on rue de la Gaîté for more than 30 years, L'Odyssex is one of the rare sex shops found outside of the Pigalle neighborhood. With sex toys, BDSM accessories, latex ensembles, and more hidden just behind the red curtain, the store extends an invitation to explore. It has a large selection of movies, including vintage films from the 1970s. There are booths in the basement, if you have some time to kill.

L'ARTISANAT MONASTIQUE

4

68 bis avenue Denfert-Rochereau
M° Denfert-Rochereau; RER Port-Royal
01 43 35 15 76
artisanatmonastique.com • @artisanat.monastique

Since 1951, several abbeys and Carmelite convents have collaborated to sell their products, including perfumed candles, jams, and liqueurs that can't be found anywhere else. The store is chock-full of meticulously crafted little wonders. I'm a huge fan of their hand cream. There's something soulful about each product, and the proceeds from sales go to people in need.

N° 1413

LA CRÊPERIE BRETONNE

5

56 rue du Montparnasse
M° Edgar Quinet / Montparnasse – Bienvenüe
01 43 20 89 58
la-creperie-bretonne.com • @la_creperie_bretonne

Whenever I get a sudden longing for Brittany, I head to La Crêperie Bretonne at Montparnasse, where the recipe for buckwheat galettes has been handed down from generation to generation since 1937. The pretty blue storefront reminds me of a little village in the Finistère region. And, of course, there's the friendly, welcoming service that will have you ordering another *bolée* of cider in no time.

N° 1461

N° 1491 N° 1411

N° 1439

N° 1401 N° 1401

N° 1429

N° 1450

N° 1433

IMPRIMEUR - LITHOGRAPHE

IDEM

ANCIEN ÉTABLISS^T MOURLOT

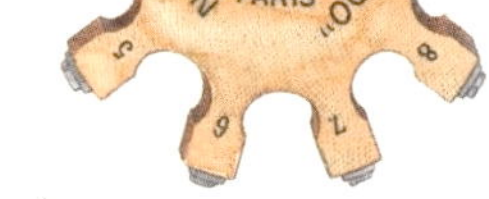

RÉF : 001

RÉF : 002

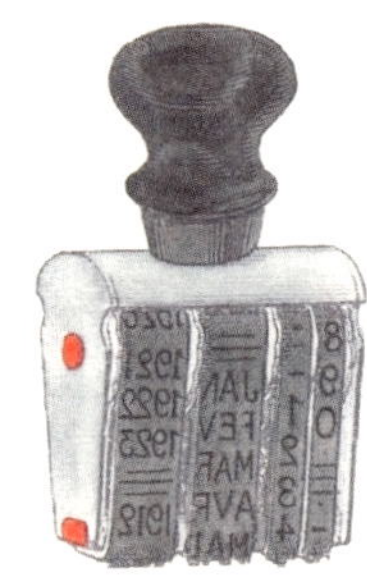

RÉF : 003

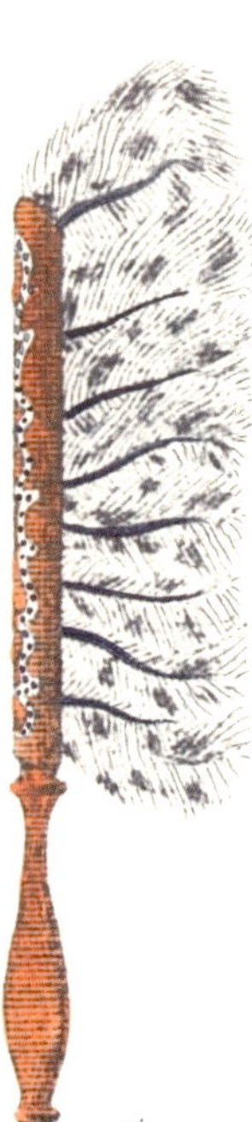

RÉF : 004

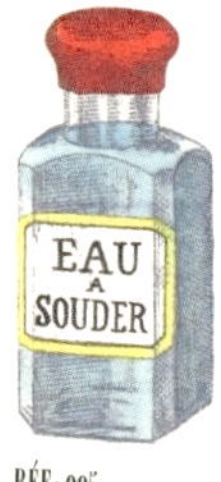

RÉF : 005

RÉF : 006

RÉF : 007

RÉF : 008

RÉF : 009

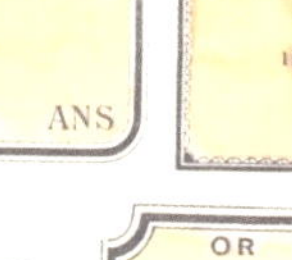

RÉF : 010

RÉF : 011

49 RUE DU MONTPARNASSE, PARIS XIVE

IDEM PARIS

6

49 rue du Montparnasse
M° Vavin / Edgar Quinet
01 43 35 35 35
idemparis.com/en • @idemparis

Tucked away in a beautiful white and red-brick building lies this printing works created in 1881. It originally printed geographical maps before specializing in art prints. It has conserved the lithographic plates of works by some of the greatest 20th-century artists, like a sublime history book. Today, it works with contemporary creators to perpetuate its savoir faire.

LA COMÉDIE ITALIENNE

17–19 rue de la Gaîté
M° Edgar Quinet / Gaîté
01 43 21 22 22
comedie-italienne.fr

The Comédie Italienne roamed the streets of Paris from the 17th century to 1980, when it finally found a home on rue de la Gaîté, in a former police station well known to artists in the neighborhood. Today, it is the only Italian theater in France. The charm of the *commedia dell'arte* is still alive and well, and, in my opinion, the incredible baroque exterior alone is worth the detour.

N° 1487

N° 1470

N° 1488

N° 1476

N° 1477

N° 1478

N° 1479

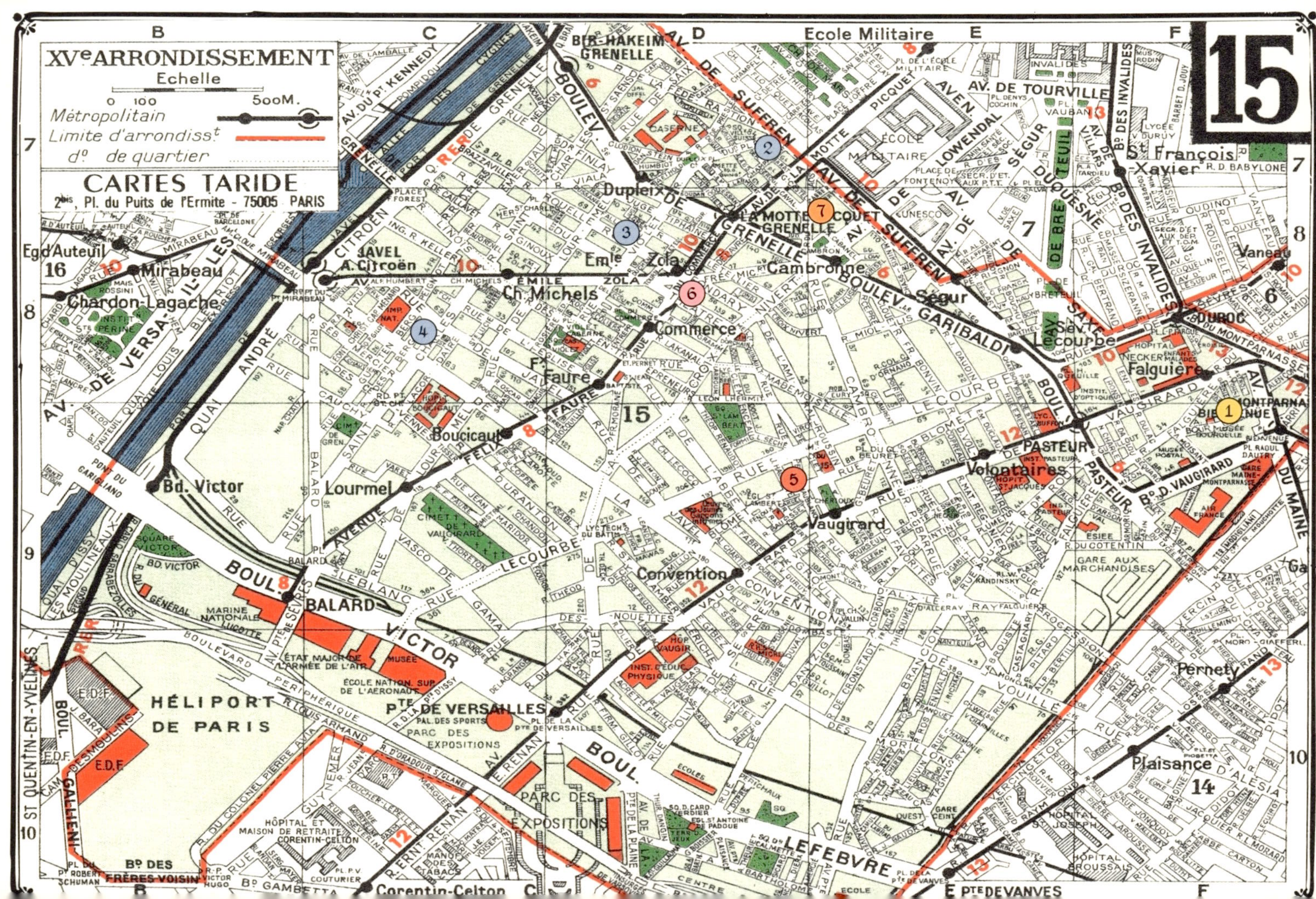

15
XVe ARRONDISSEMENT
Echelle
0 100 500M.
Métropolitain
Limite d'arrondisst
do de quartier
CARTES TARIDE
2bis, Pl. du Puits de l'Ermite - 75005 PARIS
Ecole Militaire
Bir-Hakeim Grenelle
Dupleix
La Motte Picquet Grenelle
Cambronne
Sèvres Lecourbe
Pasteur
Volontaires
Vaugirard
Convention
Commerce
Emile Zola
Ch. Michels
Javel A. Citroën
Mirabeau
Chardon-Lagache
Egd Auteuil
Bd. Victor
Lourmel
Boucicaut
Félix Faure
Balard
Pte de Versailles
Falguière
Montparnasse Bienvenüe
Duroc
Vaneau
St François-Xavier
Ségur
Pernety
Plaisance
Corentin-Celton
Pte de Vanves
Héliport de Paris
Parc des Expositions
Av. de Suffren
Bd Garibaldi
Bd de Grenelle
Bd des Invalides
Bd Victor
Bd Lefebvre
Rue de Vaugirard
Rue Lecourbe
Ecole Militaire
St Quentin-en-Yvelines

15E ARRONDISSEMENT

1. Musée Bourdelle
18 rue Antoine-Bourdelle
2. Galerie Jabert
78 avenue de Suffren
3. La Boîte de Soldats
28 rue Violet
4. Au Facteur Cheval
124 rue Saint-Charles
5. L'Équilibre
108 rue Blomet
6. Le Café du Commerce
51 rue du Commerce
7. Tennis de la Cavalerie – Association Tennis Suffren
6–8 rue de la Cavalerie

MUSÉE BOURDELLE

18 rue Antoine-Bourdelle
M° Falguière / Montparnasse – Bienvenüe
01 49 54 73 73
bourdelle.paris.fr/en • @museebourdelle

Since 1949, this museum has preserved the spirit of Montparnasse's 19th-century *cités*—collective spaces where artists lived and worked. Rooms dedicated to sculptor Antoine Bourdelle are connected by three charming gardens filled with imposing sculptures. My favorite is the studio, where I can step into the artist's private world. Immensely inspiring and moving.

N° 1591

N° 1517

N° 1514

N° 1517

GALERIE JABERT

78 avenue de Suffren
M° La Motte-Picquet – Grenelle
01 43 06 45 55
galeriejabert.com/en-gb • @galerie_jabert

Established in 1937, Galerie Jabert is my favorite place to admire Aubusson tapestries and fine textiles, which I have a fondness for. The gallery specializes in antique and modern tapestries. You'll also find magnificent cushions handcrafted by artisans using fragments of tapestries dating from the 16th to 19th centuries.

N° 1502

MUSÉE
BOURDELLE

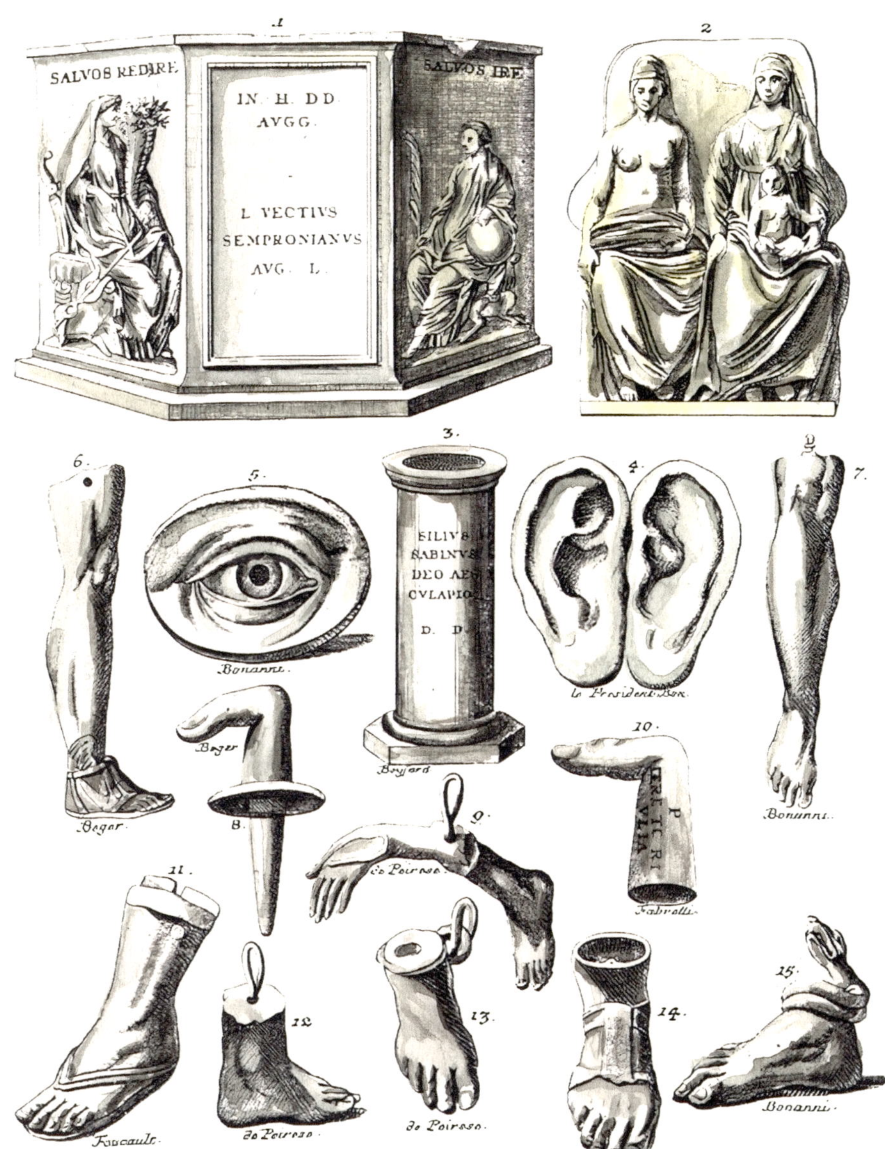

18, RUE ANTOINE-BOURDELLE - PARIS XVE

La Boîte de Soldats

— FIGURINES ET SOLDATS ANCIENS DE COLLECTION —

28, RUE VIOLET - PARIS XVᴱ

LA BOÎTE DE SOLDATS

28 rue Violet
M° Avenue Émile-Zola / Dupleix
01 45 78 89 44 / 06 03 78 28 82
boitedesoldats.fr

This wonderfully nostalgic specialist shop brings out my inner child. Since 1996, the shelves have been lined with antique soldiers and queens created by Vertunni, along with hundreds of figurines made of everything from lead to paper. An invaluable address for original gifts and for collectors.

N° 1559

N° 1583 N° 1584 N° 1585 N° 1586 N° 1587 N° 1588 N° 1589 N° 1590 N° 1591 N° 1592 N° 1593

AU FACTEUR CHEVAL

124 rue Saint-Charles
M° Boucicaut / Charles Michels
01 45 79 59 93
aufacteurchevalantiquites.com • @aufacteurcheval_antiquites

I like places that preserve traces of the past. Here, visitors are greeted by a storefront that reads "butter and eggs"—quite the opposite of what they'll find inside. In fact, this antiques store took up residence in a former creamery. The art deco interiors contain everything from furniture to a fine selection of books and a multitude of objects.

N° 1511

N° 1535 N° 1539 N° 1513 N° 1543

L'ÉQUILIBRE

5

108 rue Blomet
M° Vaugirard
01 48 42 30 46
lequilibreparis.com • @lequilibre.paris

This exquisite bakery dates from 1889 and is listed among the city's historic monuments. I'm in love with the decor, designed by Benoist & Fils. The large ceiling fresco and wall paintings never fail to make an impression, and nor do its baked goods, which are worthy of the finest restaurants. A special mention for the pastry selection, which changes with the seasons.

N° 1518 N° 1549 N° 1518

LE CAFÉ DU COMMERCE

6

51 rue du Commerce
M° Avenue Émile-Zola / Commerce
01 45 75 03 27
lecafeducommerce.com • @lecafeducommerce_paris

Le Café du Commerce is one of my favorite *bouillons*. Opened in 1921, this Parisian bistro, featuring a mosaic floor, has preserved its early-20th-century atmosphere (and reasonable prices). I order a steak tartare, prepared on the spot, from one of the tables located on the upper level, under the glass roof—the perfect place to watch the servers come and go, and eavesdrop on lively conversations.

N° 1510

N° 1511

N° 1512

N° 1513

N° 1576

N° 1505

N° 1506

N° 1507

N° 1508

N° 1509

TENNIS DE LA CAVALERIE – ASSOCIATION TENNIS SUFFREN

7

6-8 rue de la Cavalerie
M° La Motte-Picquet – Grenelle
01 41 09 17 69 / 06 60 87 90 62
tennis-suffren.fr

Perched atop an art deco building since 1925, this tennis court is without doubt the most beautiful in Paris, and definitely one of the most secret. The wooden lockers in the changing rooms call to mind old English clubs, and the honeycomb timbered roof is a marvel. The view of the Eiffel Tower and the Jardins du Trocadéro will take your breath away, especially when admired from the balcony.

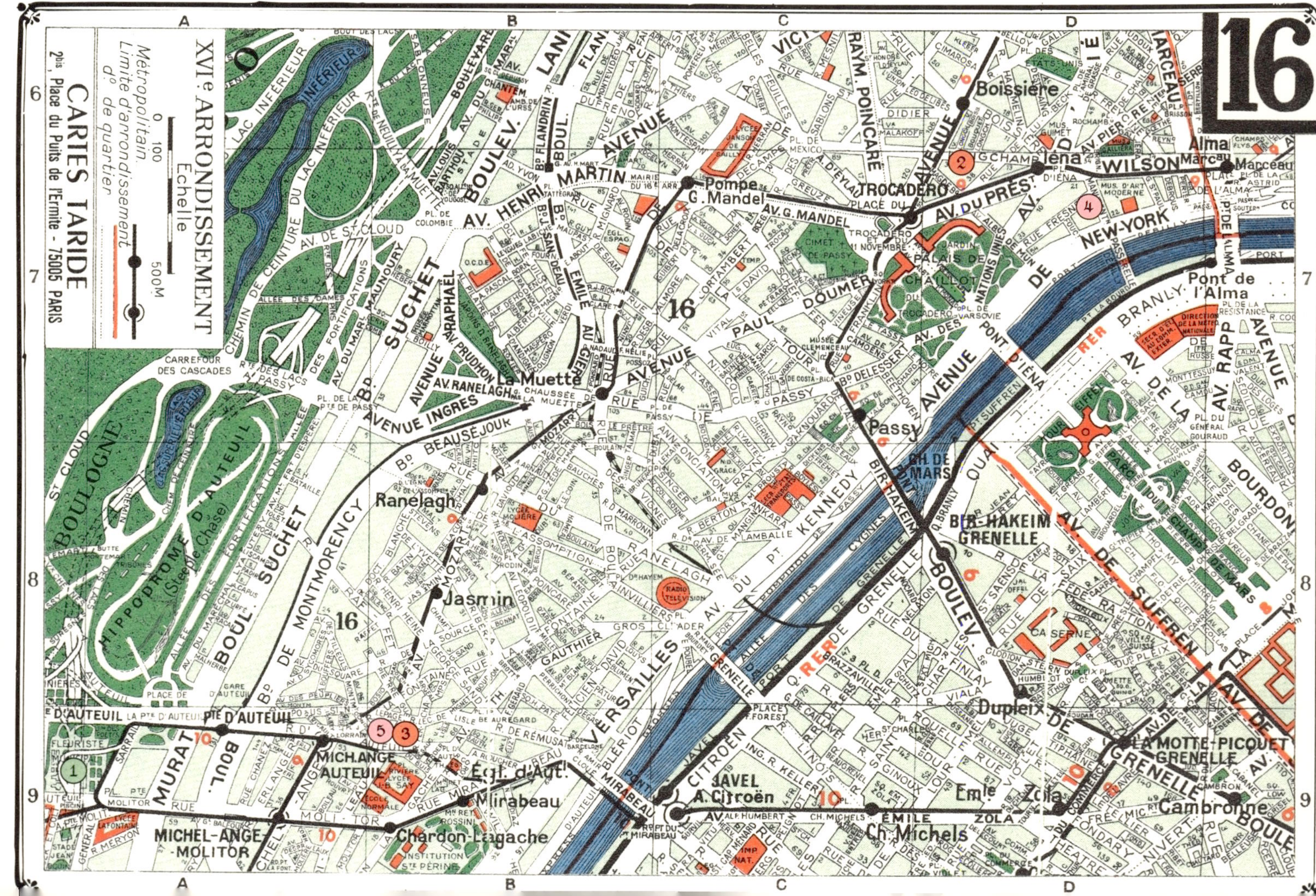
16
XVIe ARRONDISSEMENT
Echelle
0 100 500M
Métropolitain.
Limite d'arrondissement
d° de quartier
CARTES TARIDE
2bis, Place du Puits de l'Ermite - 75005 PARIS
AV. DE NEW-YORK
Pont de l'Alma
AV. RAPP
AV. DE LA BOURDONNAIS
AV. DE SUFFREN
La Motte-Picquet Grenelle
BOULEV. DE GRENELLE
Cambronne
Dupleix
Bir-Hakeim Grenelle
Passy
Trocadéro
Boissière
Iéna
Alma Marceau
AV. DU PRÉST. WILSON
RAYM. POINCARÉ
AV. G. MANDEL
Pompe
G. Mandel
Emle Zola
Ch. Michels
Javel A. Citroën
QUAI DE GRENELLE
QUAI BRANLY
PONT D'IÉNA
BIR-HAKEIM
AV. DU Pt KENNEDY
Radio Télévision
La Muette
Ranelagh
Jasmin
Mirabeau
Chardon-Lagache
Égl. d'Aut.
Michel-Ange Auteuil
Michel-Ange Molitor
Pte d'Auteuil
BOUL. MURAT
Bd SUCHET
AVENUE INGRES
AV. RAPHAEL
AV. RANELAGH
BOULEV. LANNES
AV. HENRI MARTIN
Bd DE MONTMORENCY
PONT MIRABEAU
VERSAILLES
HIPPODROME D'AUTEUIL (Steeple Chase)
BOULOGNE
LAC INFÉRIEUR
RER
16

16^{E} ARRONDISSEMENT

1. Jardin des Serres d'Auteuil
3 avenue de la Porte-d'Auteuil
2. Roy Chocolats
27 rue de Longchamp
3. Servant
30 rue d'Auteuil
4. Les Marches
5 rue de la Manutention
5. Auberge Le Mouton Blanc
40 rue d'Auteuil

JARDIN DES SERRES D'AUTEUIL

1

3 avenue de la Porte-d'Auteuil
M° Porte d'Auteuil
paris.fr/lieux/jardin-des-serres-d-auteuil-1780

Created in 1898, on the edge of the Bois de Boulogne, this garden features five main greenhouses containing more than 1,000 species, many of them rare. Modern greenhouses have been built within the Roland-Garros stadium complex. I like the French garden facing the Grille d'Honneur, and the small Jardin des Poetes, just beyond the greenhouses.

SERRES MONUMENTALES DU NOUVEAU FLEURISTE DE LA VILLE DE PARIS

JARDIN DES SERRES D'AUTEUIL

GRANDES SERRES DE PALMIERS
AVEC PAVILLON CENTRAL

Bâches gradins, coupe intérieure.

Châssis de couches, sur bâches en fer de plusieurs numéros, prêts à l'avance. Verres et mastics prêts à poser.

Châssis à tabatière de 24 grandeurs différentes avec enduit inoxydable. On fabrique sur commande les châssis de toute forme et de toute dimension.

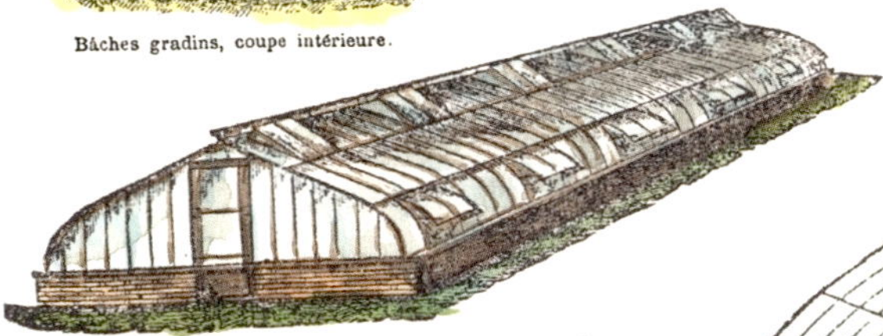

Serres à dalles métalliques (brevetées s. g. d. g.) dites serres Lefèvre

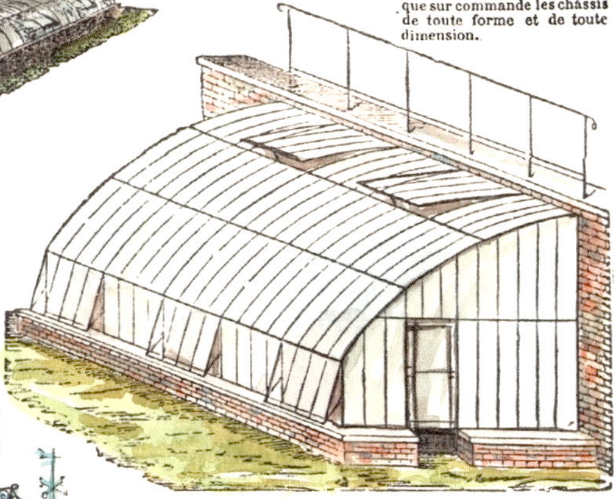

Croisées d'orangerie

Serres adossées.

3, AVENUE DE LA PORTE-D'AUTEUIL, PARIS XVIE

SERVANT

LE CONFISEUR D'AUTEUIL
CHOCOLATIER

Se trouve au **30 RUE D'AUTEUIL — PARIS XVIᴱ**

ROY CHOCOLATS

2

27 rue de Longchamp
M° Boissière / Iéna
01 47 27 34 36
roy-chocolatier.com • @roy.chocolatier

This boutique, opened by Madame Roy in 1948, has nurtured a passion for exceptional chocolate for the past 70 years. I have a penchant for the cacao almonds and the salted-butter-caramel *croustillants*, but the hardest thing is resisting the urge to buy everything in the store. The selection of tea and coffee, ground in-house, is also worth a look. This is a good place to find a small yet sophisticated gift.

N° 1641

N° 1650

SERVANT

3

30 rue d'Auteuil
M° Michel-Ange – Auteuil
01 42 88 49 82
chocolaterie-servant.com • @servantchocolatier

The confectioner at Auteuil opened in 1913 and became a genuine chocolate maker in 1932. Servant has been dedicated to chocolate and artisanal savoir faire ever since. With its wood paneling and orange awning, the boutique is absolutely charming. It's the kind of place that makes me want to be a child again, and climb up on the counter to thrust my hand into one of the large candy jars in search of a sweet treat.

N° 1606

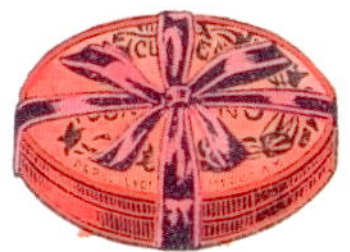

N° 1607

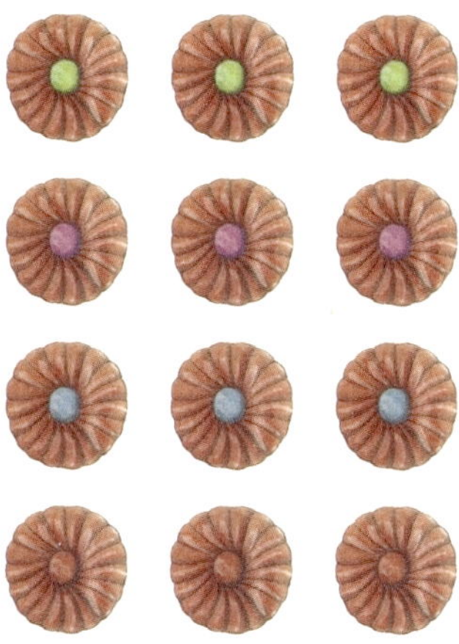

N° 1651

N° 1692

N° 1634

N° 1611

N° 1612

N° 1639 N° 1639

◈ LES MARCHES ◈

5 rue de la Manutention
M° Iéna
01 47 23 52 80
lesmarches-restaurant.com/en • @restaurantlesmarches

This surprising *routier*—a restaurant intended for truck drivers looking to take a break—near the Palais de Tokyo and the staircase on rue de la Manutention opened in 1934. It's a simple spot with a pretty terrace and classic bistro fare served à la carte. I often order the blanquette de veau and a tarte Tatin. Welcoming, generous, and friendly, this bistro serves up satisfying comfort food in a classic Paris setting.

N° 1658

◈ AUBERGE LE MOUTON BLANC ◈

40 rue d'Auteuil
M° Michel-Ange – Auteuil
01 42 88 02 21
aubergemoutonblanc.com • @lemoutonblanc_paris

There was a time when you might cross paths with Molière, Jean de La Fontaine, or Nicolas Boileau here. Opened in 1669, this inn is one of the oldest restaurants in Paris. In its warm, wood-accented interiors, diners feast on Norman specialties and French classics accompanied by a good wine. I come here whenever I happen to be passing through the neighborhood, or when I want to soak up the inn's literary spirit.

N° 1621

N° 1687

N° 1663

N° 1613

N° 1614

N° 1615

RESTAURANT - BISTROT ROUTIER

les Marches

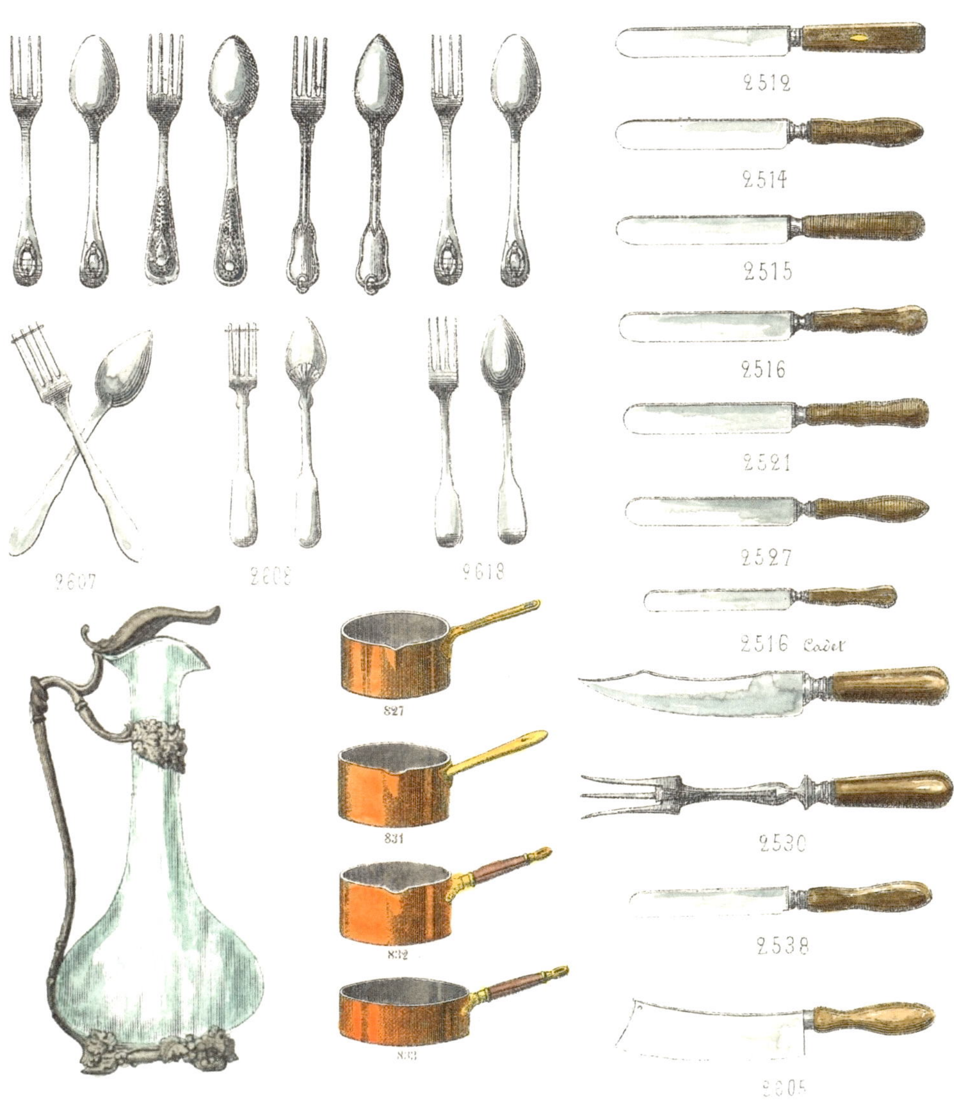

5 RUE DE LA MANUTENTION À PARIS

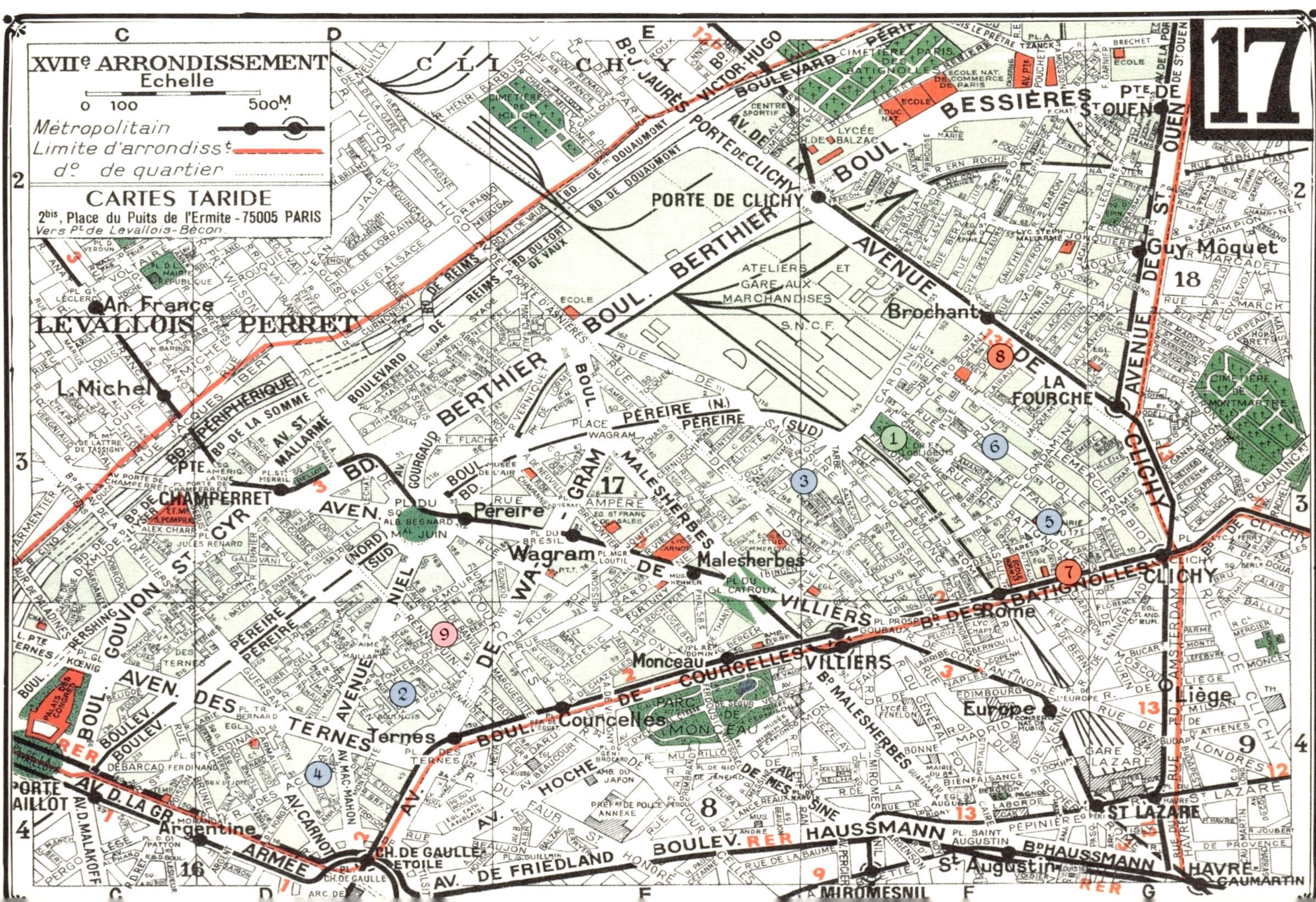

17
XVIIe ARRONDISSEMENT
Echelle
0 100 500M
Métropolitain
Limite d'arrondisst
do de quartier
CARTES TARIDE
2bis, Place du Puits de l'Ermite - 75005 PARIS
Vers Pt de Levallois-Becon
CLICHY
LEVALLOIS PERRET
An. France
L. Michel
PORTE DE CLICHY
BOUL. BERTHIER
AVENUE DE CLICHY
AVENUE DE ST OUEN
BOUL. BESSIÈRES
Pte DE St OUEN
Guy Môquet
Brochant
LA FOURCHE
ATELIERS ET GARE AUX MARCHANDISES
S.N.C.F.
CIMETIÈRE DE MONTMARTRE
CIMETIÈRE PARIS DES BATIGNOLLES
CIMETIÈRE DE CLICHY
LYCÉE H. DE BALZAC
BOULEVARD VICTOR HUGO
Bd J. JAURÈS
BD. DE DOUAUMONT
BOULEVARD PÉRIPHÉRIQUE
BD. DE LA SOMME
AV. ST. MALLARMÉ
PTE CHAMPERRET
AVEN. ST CYR
GOUVION
BOULEVARD BERTHIER
BD. GOURGAUD
Pereire
BOUL. PEREIRE (N.)
PEREIRE (SUD)
PLACE WAGRAM
AV. DE WAGRAM
Wagram
Malesherbes
BD MALESHERBES
Villiers
BD DE COURCELLES
Monceau
Courcelles
PARC DE MONCEAU
Ternes
AVENUE DES TERNES
AV. NIEL
AV. MAC-MAHON
AV. CARNOT
Argentine
AV. DE LA GR. ARMÉE
PORTE MAILLOT
AV. D. MALAKOFF
PALAIS DES CONGRÈS
PL. CH. DE GAULLE ETOILE
AV. DE FRIEDLAND
BOULEV. HAUSSMANN
Bd HAUSSMANN
St Augustin
MIROMESNIL
HAVRE-CAUMARTIN
ST LAZARE
GARE ST LAZARE
Liège
Europe
Rome
Bd DES BATIGNOLLES
CLICHY
Bd MALESHERBES
AV. HOCHE
RER
8
9
16
17
18

17E ARRONDISSEMENT

1. Square des Batignolles
   Rue Cardinet / Place Charles-Fillion
2. Féau Boiseries
   9 rue Laugier
3. Plein Cadre
   116 rue Cardinet
4. Atelier Midavaine
   54 rue des Acacias
5. L'Atelier d'Arthur
   3 rue Truffaut
6. Chez Ammar
   65 rue Nollet
7. Marché Biologique des Batignolles
   34 boulevard des Batignolles
8. Café Lanni – La Brûlerie de Paris
   125 avenue de Clichy
9. Le Bistrot Flaubert
   10 rue Gustave-Flaubert

SQUARE DES BATIGNOLLES

1

Rue Cardinet / Place Charles-Fillion
M° Pont Cardinet
paris.fr/lieux/square-des-batignolles-1761

I love coming to this little haven of greenery on summer mornings, for a stroll or to read a book on one of the benches. The babbling brook makes for a soothing soundtrack, adding to the bucolic, romantic atmosphere of the park. The square was created in 1863 with the aim of representing an elegant microcosm of nature, complete with a waterfall, stream, and picturesque path.

N° 1743

FÉAU BOISERIES

2

9 rue Laugier
M° Ternes
01 47 63 60 60
feauboiseries.com/en • @feauboiseries

Since 1875, this workshop has cultivated a unique savoir faire, handcrafting woodwork for all kinds of furniture and interiors. A richly decorated labyrinth leads visitors on a tour to discover the history of French decoration. You'll also find meticulously preserved antiques that serve as models for the artisans, who put their skills to work for leading interior designers.

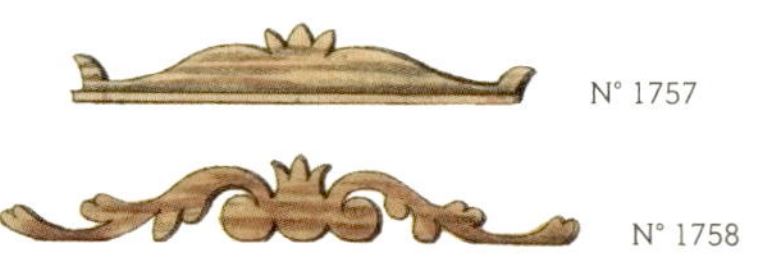

N° 1757

N° 1758

N° 1747

N° 1762

N° 1734 N° 1734

N° 1716 N° 1716

BOISERIES

FÉAU & CIE

AU 9, RUE LAUGIER

75017 PARIS

Fig. 166. — Assemblage à queue-d'aronde recouverte.

Fig. 167. — Assemblage d'onglet à clef.

Fig. 168. — Assemblage d'onglet à tenon et mortaise.

11. **Assemblage** d'onglet avec clef (**fig. 167**).
12. — d'onglet à tenon et mortaise (**fig. 168**).
13. — à enfourchement simple.
14. — à double enfourchement.
15. — d'un petit bois de croisée.
16. **Assemblage** d'un jet d'eau de croisée.
17. — d'un montant de porte avec panneau et traverse.
18. — d'un montant de porte à grand cadre avec panneau.

La collection de 18 modèles d'assemblage de menuiserie .... **26** »

Chaque modèle séparément du n° 1 à 14 .... **2** »
— — **du n° 15 à 17** **2 25**
— — **du n° 18** .... **3** »

N° 1796

N° 1717

N° 1710

N° 1768

N° 1740

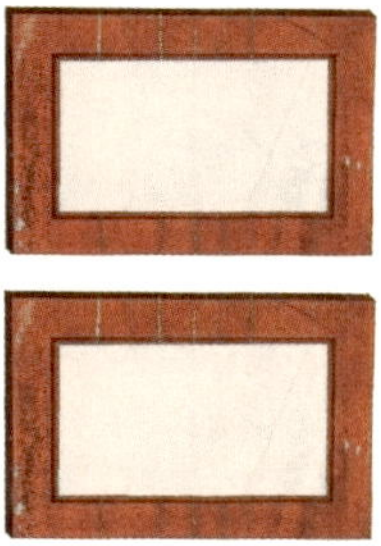

N° 1742

N° 1727

◈ PLEIN CADRE ◈

116 rue Cardinet
M° Pont Cardinet
01 42 27 50 53

I come here to have my drawings for exhibitions framed, as well as artwork bought at flea markets. All sorts of wood samples and pretty frames lie behind the typically Parisian, red storefront of this sleek boutique. Plein Cadre has been around since the 1980s and remains committed to offering its clients high-quality wood frames.

N° 1720

◈ ATELIER MIDAVAINE ◈

54 rue des Acacias
M° Ternes
01 43 80 68 94
ateliermidavaine.com •
@atelier_midavaine

When Louis Midavaine moved to Paris in 1918, Japanese art was in vogue; it inspired his own lacquerware furnishings and other art objects. Later, he set up his own studio, which became a benchmark in the discipline. His expertise and traditional techniques have since been handed down through generations.

N° 1720

L'ATELIER D'ARTHUR

3 rue Truffaut
M° Place de Clichy / Rome
01 55 06 12 01

It's hard to miss this bow maker's old-fashioned purple exterior on rue Truffaut. Through the windows, two artisans—Arthur and Alexandre—can be seen hard at work crafting bows in a wood decor that fires my imagination. Arthur set up shop here in 2004 to indulge his passion and perpetuate a craft whose roots go back to the 18th century.

N° 1712

N° 1703

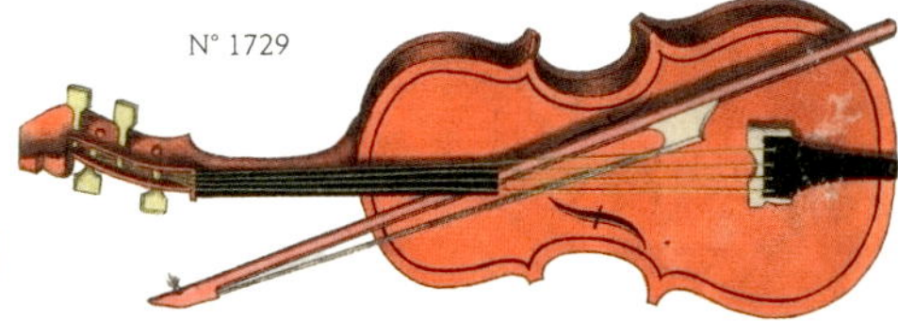

N° 1729

CHEZ AMMAR

65 rue Nollet
M° La Fourche / Pont Cardinet
06 25 03 06 34
@chez_ammar

Measuring just 118 sq. ft. (11 m^2), this pocket-sized vintage fashion boutique is bursting with treasures. Inside, you'll find men's clothing carefully selected by Ammar, the owner. It's rare to come across good vintage clothes stores for men, and this one never disappoints. This is where I get classic dandy pieces, quality suits made in France, Italian-made ankle boots, and painfully elegant accessories.

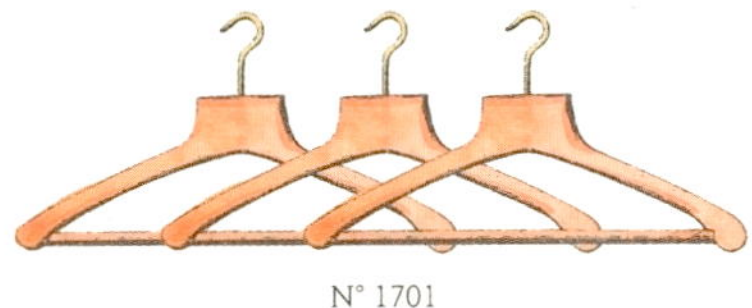

N° 1701

N° 1744

N° 1742

N° 1748

N° 1740

N° 1746

N° 1743

N° 1701

N° 1707

N° 1709

N° 1711

N° 1713

N° 1702

N° 1714

MARCHÉ BIOLOGIQUE DES BATIGNOLLES

7

34 boulevard des Batignolles
M° Rome / Place de Clichy
paris.fr/lieux/marche-biologique-des-batignolles-4514

N° 1703

N° 1715

Since the late 1990s, this friendly and entirely organic market has taken place every Saturday morning on boulevard des Batignolles. It makes for a lovely stroll, especially in summer, when I feel like getting out of my neighborhood and buying quality products. You'll find fruits and vegetables, as well as flowers, wine, soap, and honey, and everything is seasonal.

N° 1704

N° 1716

N° 1705

N° 1717

N° 1706

N° 1708

N° 1710

N° 1712

N° 1718

N° 1798

N° 1761

N° 1773

N° 1765

N° 1778

N° 1704

N° 1713 N° 1714 N° 1715

◈ CAFÉ LANNI – LA BRÛLERIE DE PARIS ◈

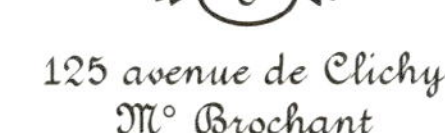

8

125 avenue de Clichy
M° Brochant
01 46 27 43 38
labruleriedeparis.fr • @labruleriedeparis

This tiny coffeehouse, founded in 1947, cultivates a tradition of roasting expertise. It offers more than 30 types of coffee bean in a charmingly eclectic, authentic setting. The aroma is what I love the most: it reminds me of mornings in my parents' kitchen, the air filled with the delicate odor of coffee from their steaming mugs.

N° 1702

N° 1789

◈ LE BISTROT FLAUBERT ◈

9

10 rue Gustave-Flaubert
M° Ternes / Pereire
01 42 67 05 81
bistrotflaubert.com/home/ • @bistrotflaubert

The storefront of this former gourmet grocery, with its early-20th-century design, is listed as a historic monument. In 1987, chef Michel Rostang acquired the boutique and turned it into the Bistrot d'à Côté, serving revisited classics of French cuisine. It has since been renamed Le Bistrot Flaubert. I like coming here in winter to appreciate the old-fashioned decor, or in summer to make the most of the terrace.

N° 1736

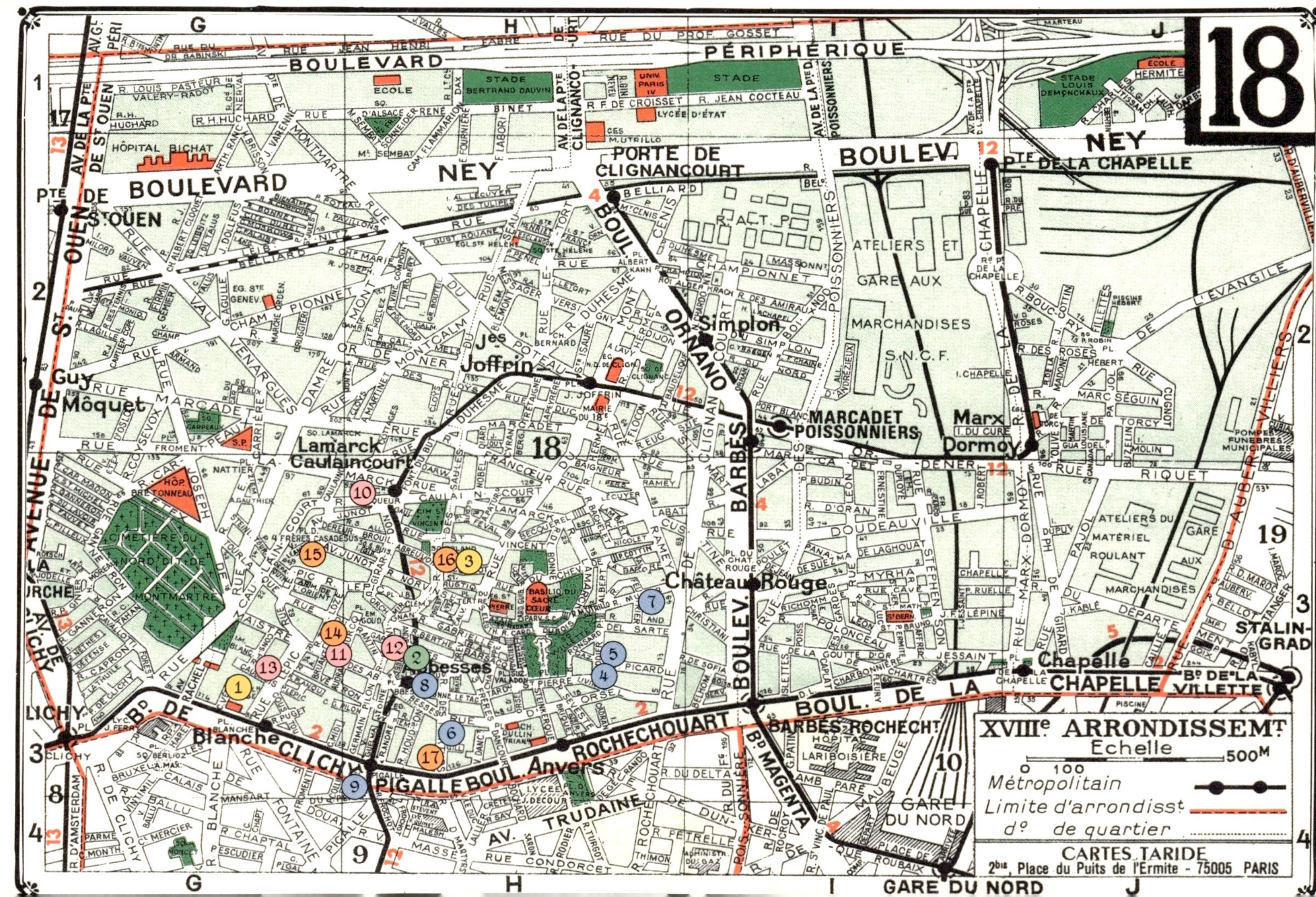

18
XVIIIe ARRONDISSEMT
Echelle
0 100 500M
Métropolitain
Limite d'arrondisst
dº de quartier
CARTES TARIDE
2bis Place du Puits de l'Ermite - 75005 PARIS
BOULEVARD PÉRIPHÉRIQUE
BOULEVARD NEY
PORTE DE CLIGNANCOURT
Pte DE LA CHAPELLE
Pte DE St OUEN
AVENUE DE St OUEN
BOUL. ORNANO
BOULEV. BARBÈS
BOUL. DE LA CHAPELLE
BOULEV. ROCHECHOUART
Bd DE CLICHY
Bd MAGENTA
Bd DE LA VILLETTE
Guy Môquet
Lamarck Caulaincourt
Jes Joffrin
Simplon
MARCADET POISSONNIERS
Marx Dormoy
Château Rouge
Abbesses
Blanche
PIGALLE
Anvers
BARBÈS ROCHECHT
Chapelle
STALINGRAD
GARE DU NORD
CIMETIÈRE DU NORD DE MONTMARTRE
HÔPITAL BICHAT
HÔP. BRETONNEAU
HÔPITAL LARIBOISIÈRE
BASILIQUE DU SACRÉ CŒUR
ATELIERS ET GARE AUX MARCHANDISES S.N.C.F.
ATELIERS DU MATÉRIEL ROULANT
GARE AUX MARCHANDISES
STADE BERTRAND DAUVIN
STADE LOUIS DEMONCHAUX
UNIV. PARIS IV
LYCÉE D'ÉTAT
POMPES FUNÈBRES MUNICIPALES

18^E ARRONDISSEMENT

1. Maison Boris Vian
6 bis cité Véron
2. Fotoautomat
53 rue des Trois-Frères
3. Musée de Montmartre
12 rue Cortot
4. Marché Saint-Pierre
2 rue Charles-Nodier
5. Mercerie Montmartre
20 rue Pierre-Picard
6. L'Objet Qui Parle
86 rue des Martyrs
7. De l'Autre Côté de la Butte
5 rue Muller
8. Librairie des Abbesses
30 rue Yvonne-Le-Tac
9. Sexodrome
23 boulevard de Clichy
10. Au Rêve
89 rue Caulaincourt
11. La Mascotte Montmartre
52 rue des Abbesses
12. Chez Camille
8 rue Ravignan
13. Café des Deux Moulins
15 rue Lepic
14. Studio 28
10 rue Tholozé
15. Hôtel Particulier Montmartre
23 avenue Junot
16. Au Lapin Agile
22 rue des Saules
17. Madame Arthur
75 rue des Martyrs

◈ MAISON BORIS VIAN ◈

6 bis cité Véron
M° Blanche
01 46 06 73 56
borisvian.org

Hidden behind the Moulin Rouge—practically backstage—you'll find the apartment where Boris Vian lived. To get there, take the little passage leading to the cité Véron, whose pretty entrance goes practically unnoticed in the busy Pigalle neighborhood. Visits must be booked through the Fondation Boris Vian, which has maintained the site since the author's death in 1959.

N° 1875

N° 1829

N° 1818

N° 1854

N° 1839

◈ FOTOAUTOMAT ◈

53 rue des Trois-Frères
M° Abbesses
06 88 75 83 50
fotoautomat.fr/en • @fotoautomat_france

On one of the steep streets leading up to the Sacré-Coeur basilica sits a vintage photobooth straight out of the 1960s (or the movie *Amélie*). Lift the curtain, make a face alone or with a friend, and capture the moment in four little silver gelatin portraits. A word of advice: go in the evening to avoid the line.

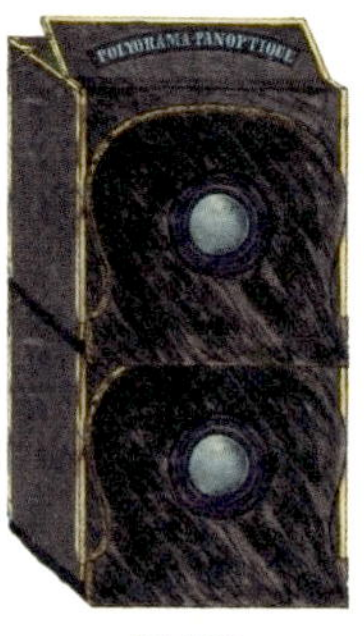

N° 1801

N° 1849

N° 1848

N° 1878

N° 1896

N° 1897

MUSÉE DE MONTMARTRE

3

12 rue Cortot
M° Lamarck – Caulaincourt
01 49 25 89 39
museedemontmartre.fr/en • @museedemontmartre

A slice of the countryside awaits visitors at this museum. Hidden in a pretty garden, the 16th-century house was once the haunt of many painters, including Suzanne Valadon. It is now a museum, and Valadon's still-intact studio is my favorite part: it feels as though the artist left the room just moments before we got there.

N° 1801

N° 1875

N° 1893

N° 1849

N° 1870

N° 1828

MARCHÉ SAINT-PIERRE

4

2 rue Charles-Nodier
M° Anvers
01 46 06 92 25
marchesaintpierre.com • @lemarchesaintpierre

Just down the hill from the Sacré-Coeur basilica lies Europe's largest textile market. Built in 1873, it is every sewer's paradise and stocks thousands of colorful fabrics of all kinds. I still remember the gentleman who, just a few years ago, operated the elevator, announcing each floor and opening the gates. I always come here to find beautiful textiles for my cushions and other creations.

N° 1823

MERCERIE MONTMARTRE

5

20 rue Pierre-Picard
M° Anvers
09 81 07 09 86

After buying my fabric, I head to this notions store, which reminds me of the 1970s. I come to buy braids for my cushions, find inspiration, and seek out little accessories for future creations. The store was originally located inside the Marché Saint-Pierre—they were created at the same time—before being separated out in the early 2000s.

N° 1818

N° 1827

N° 1823

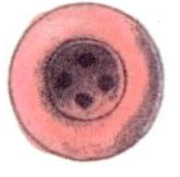

N° 1871

N° 1822

les Tissus de Qualité

MARCHÉ SAINT-PIERRE

2 RUE CHARLES-NODIER, PARIS

N° 1823

N° 1844

N° 1843

N° 1891

N° 1822

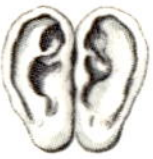

N° 1823

N° 1864

N° 1829

N° 1834

N° 1883

N° 1804

◈ L'OBJET QUI PARLE ◈

6

86 rue des Martyrs
M° Abbesses / Pigalle
06 09 67 05 30
lobjetquiparle.fr • @lobjetquiparle

Founders Guillaume and Catherine have a grand old time in their tiny antiques store—one of my favorite bric-a-brac shops in Paris. It's overflowing with everything imaginable: fabulous chandeliers, dishware, globes, curiosities of all sorts, reliquaries, and more. I never leave empty-handed. What's more, they have a talent for creating themed window displays that are always enchanting.

◈ DE L'AUTRE CÔTÉ DE LA BUTTE ◈

7

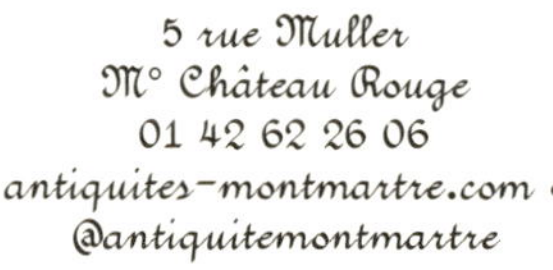

5 rue Muller
M° Château Rouge
01 42 62 26 06
antiquites-montmartre.com •
@antiquitemontmartre

This charming thrift store sits on a small street leading to the Sacré-Cœur basilica. The variety inside is staggering: vintage armchairs, lamps, glassware, and even antique stationery. Whenever I'm strolling through Montmartre, I'm always curious to see what beautiful, extraordinary objects Nathalie and Julien, the keen-eyed owners, have sourced.

❖ LIBRAIRIE DES ABBESSES ❖

30 rue Yvonne-Le-Tac
M° Abbesses
01 46 06 84 30
librairiedesabbesses.com • @librairiedesabbesses

I adore this kind of bookshop, where stacks of books climb to the ceiling and fill the air with their unique fragrance. The Librairie des Abbsesses has a poetic charm heightened by its location in a neighborhood that turned out the greatest poets and artists. I always follow the wise advice of the owner when choosing my next read.

N° 1825

❖ SEXODROME ❖

23 boulevard de Clichy
M° Pigalle
09 81 78 11 90

What would Paris be without its naughty side? Created in the 1980s in the heart of the Pigalle district, this is one of the oldest sex shops in the capital and the largest in Europe. This erotic supermarket has everything: clothing, all manner of objects and games—I don't think I need to spell it out for you. And it's open late.

N° 1815

N° 1801

N° 1804

N° 1802

N° 1805

N° 1803

N° 1806

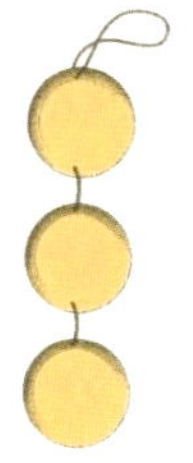

N° 1892

N° 1872

N° 1847

N° 1836

N° 1814

◈ AU RÊVE ◈

10

89 rue Caulaincourt
M° Lamarck – Caulaincourt
09 55 51 39 82
aureve.com • @aureve.montmartre

Musician Jacques Brel frequented this neighborhood bistro imbued with the Montmartre spirit. He allegedly wrote the song "Ne me quitte pas" here. Since 1921, Au Rêve has kept the dream alive for locals, artists, and other habitués. I always stop by when I'm in the area, to enjoy lunch or a drink immersed in the artistic ambience.

N° 1813

◈ LA MASCOTTE MONTMARTRE ◈

11

52 rue des Abbesses
M° Abbesses / Blanche
01 46 06 28 15
la-mascotte-montmartre.com/en • @lamascottemontmartre

This restaurant, open since 1889, has all the features of a typical Parisian brasserie: wicker chairs; a striped arbor; and Belle Époque interiors in wood, with green leather booths, bronze chandeliers, and period tiling. I come here for the delicious seafood platters, which are served *en service continu*, all day long.

N° 1866

N° 1859

N° 1887

N° 1896

N° 1800

N° 1807

CHEZ CAMILLE

(12)

8 rue Ravignan
M° Abbesses
01 42 57 75 62
FB: Chez Camille

Glasses have been clinking and hips have been swaying at Chez Camille since 1871. This pretty café with its bright yellow exterior channels Montmartre's artistic spirit. The owner, a fan of 1950s and '60s music, regularly hosts concerts amid the charming, slightly kitsch retro decor. I like to pop in here for a drink and some rock'n'roll.

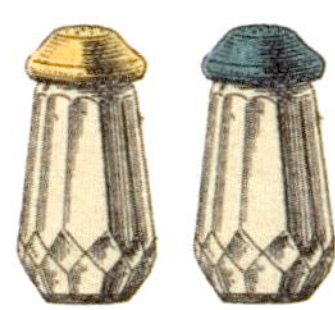

N° 1841

CAFÉ DES DEUX MOULINS

(13)

15 rue Lepic
M° Blanche
01 42 54 90 50
cafedesdeuxmoulins.com • @cafe.des.deux.moulins

As you pass by, you'll inevitably hear someone say, "Oh look, it's the Amélie Poulain café!" Besides providing the setting for this cult film, it also happens to be a typical Montmartre brasserie. Nothing has changed since it opened in the early 20th century: the old-fashioned bistro decor is still in place and the kitchen continues to serve classic French dishes.

N° 1881

N° 1857

N° 1894

N° 1820

STUDIO 28

14

10 rue Tholozé
M° Blanche / Abbesses
01 46 06 47 45
cinema-studio28.fr • @cinemastudio28

Established in 1928, this tiny cinema could recount a thousand anecdotes. When Luis Buñuel's *L'Âge d'Or* premiered in 1930, for instance, it was not to everyone's taste, and a fight broke out. Later, the cinema provided one of the settings for *Amélie*. To put it simply, this is a small theater with a grand history. I also come for the small café hidden in a quaint little courtyard at the back.

N° 1820

HÔTEL PARTICULIER MONTMARTRE

15

23 avenue Junot
M° Lamarck – Caulaincourt
01 53 41 81 40
hotelparticulier.com • @hotelparticuliermontmartre

Built in 1871, tucked away in an inconspicuous secret passage in the heart of Montmartre, this is one of the most beautiful places in Paris. Step through the gate for an enchanting escape to another world. Sip a cocktail in the lush garden or book a night in one of the five hotel rooms for what feels like a country retreat.

N° 1821

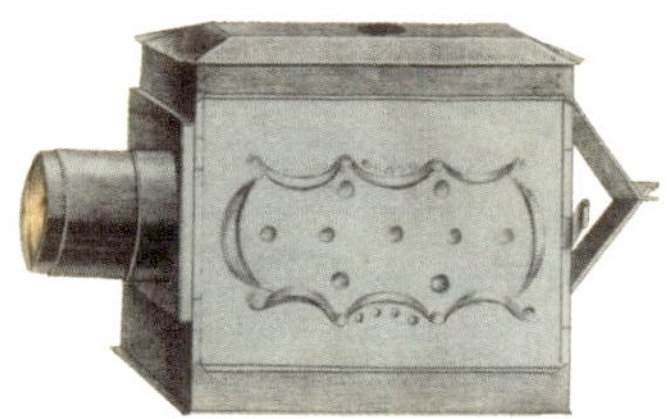

N° 1892

N° 1859

N° 1836

N° 1829

N° 1832

N° 1817

N° 1823

AU LAPIN AGILE

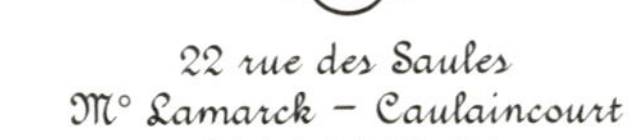

16

22 rue des Saules
M° Lamarck – Caulaincourt
01 46 06 85 87
au-lapin-agile.com/en • @au_lapin_agile

I am in love with this place. Built in 1860, just down the hill from Montmartre's vineyard, this legendary cabaret welcomed all the great painters who lived and breathed the neighborhood's bohemian spirit. In this colorful building that almost looks like it belongs in a Cézanne painting, artists give interactive performances in an authentic setting that has conserved the traces of its history.

N° 1877

N° 1871

MADAME ARTHUR

17

75 rue des Martyrs
M° Pigalle / Abbesses
07 68 78 68 01
madamearthur.fr • @madamearthur

Anyone passing through the area can't help but notice this venue's bright red exterior. Created in 1946, it was the first cabaret in Paris to host drag shows. I usually go for these performances, or else to get caught up in the evening musical events. I love the festive atmosphere here—it's sure to bring a smile to your face.

N° 1830

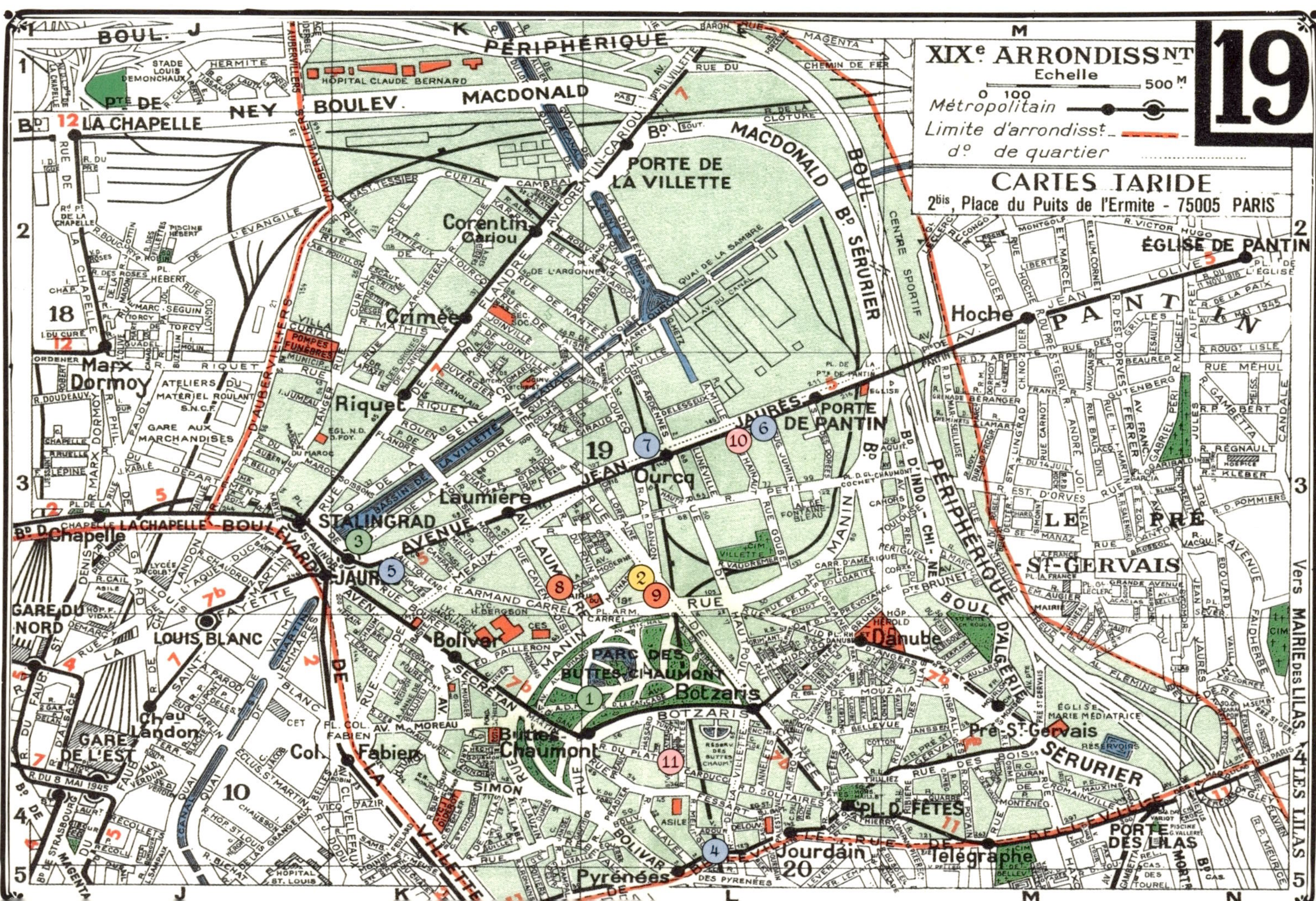

19
XIXe ARRONDISSNT
Echelle
0 100 500 M
Métropolitain
Limite d'arrondisst
d° de quartier
CARTES TARIDE
2bis, Place du Puits de l'Ermite - 75005 PARIS
Vers MAIRIE DES LILAS LES LILAS
PÉRIPHÉRIQUE
BOULEV. MACDONALD
Bd NEY
Bd LA CHAPELLE
PTE DE LA CHAPELLE
HÔPITAL CLAUDE BERNARD
PORTE DE LA VILLETTE
Corentin Cariou
Crimée
Riquet
Marx Dormoy
Stalingrad
Laumière
Ourcq
Jaurès
Porte de Pantin
Hoche
Église de Pantin
PANTIN
LE PRÉ ST-GERVAIS
Bolivar
Buttes-Chaumont
Botzaris
PARC DES BUTTES-CHAUMONT
Danube
Pré-St-Gervais
Place des Fêtes
Télégraphe
Porte des Lilas
Jourdain
Pyrénées
Colonel Fabien
Louis Blanc
Château Landon
Gare du Nord
Gare de l'Est
La Chapelle
BASSIN DE LA VILLETTE
Bd SÉRURIER
BOUL. D'ALGÉRIE
Bd D'INDO-CHINE
CENTRE SPORTIF
ATELIERS DU MATÉRIEL ROULANT S.N.C.F.
GARE AUX MARCHANDISES
POMPES FUNÈBRES
18
19
20
10

19^E ARRONDISSEMENT

1. Parc des Buttes Chaumont
   Entrances porte Fessart, porte de la Villette
2. Église Saint-Serge-de-Radonège
   93 rue de Crimée
3. Canauxrama
   13 quai de la Loire, bassin de la Villette
4. Atelier Cattelan
   2 rue Mélingue
5. Retouche de Qualité
   37 rue Bouret
6. Bellynck & Fils
   194 avenue Jean-Jaurès
7. Quincaillerie Mirus
   149 avenue Jean-Jaurès
8. Vieille France
   5 avenue de Laumière
9. Poilâne
   83 rue de Crimée
10. Au Bœuf Couronné
    188 avenue Jean-Jaurès
11. Le Bar Fleuri
    1 rue du Plateau

◈ PARC DES BUTTES CHAUMONT ◈

Entrances porte Fressart, porte de la Villette
M° Buttes-Chaumont / Botzaris / Laumière
paris.fr/lieux/parc-des-buttes-chaumont-1757

If you spend the summer in Paris, this is *the* park to visit for a picnic or a pleasant stroll. Opened in 1867, it is full of hidden treasures like the Temple de la Sybille—a small Roman-style monument perched at the park's highest point—and the beautiful waterfall that adds to the bucolic setting. The park is also home to Le Pavillon Puebla and Rosa Bonheur, both perfect for a drink and dancing at sunset.

N° 1992

◈ ÉGLISE SAINT-SERGE-DE-RADONÈGE ◈

93 rue de Crimée
M° Botzaris / Laumière
06 32 68 41 92 / 06 03 82 18 67
saint-serge.fr/fr/

This extraordinary Russian Orthodox church lies at the end of a small path, in peaceful seclusion. Built in 1917, after the Russian Revolution, it features wood paneling and warm colors, inviting visitors to step back in time, to the Russian Empire of the Czars with their eye-catching architecture. Coming to this inspiring place always makes me feel as if I've left Paris.

N° 1981

N° 1916

N° 1998 N° 1900

N° 1916

N° 1946

N° 1995

N° 1947

N° 1903

N° 1946

N° 1956

N° 1957

N° 1930

CANAUXRAMA

3

13 quai de la Loire, bassin de la Villette
M° Jaurès
01 42 39 15 00
canauxrama.com/en/ • @canauxrama

Canauxrama began plying the waters of the French capital in the 1980s. The company gives sailors at heart the opportunity to privatize or rent boats and navigate on the canals of Paris and on the Seine. There's always something magical about watching the beautiful shoreline glide slowly by on the long, quiet river. I often call on Canauxrama for special occasions.

N° 1979

N° 1933

N° 1917

N° 1999

N° 1956

N° 1960

N° 1955

N° 1974

N° 1961

N° 1950

N° 1951

N° 1952

N° 1953

N° 1998

N° 1954

N° 1955

N° 1956

N° 1957

ATELIER CATTELAN

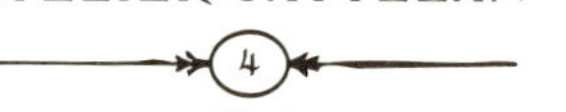

4

2 rue Mélingue
M° Pyrénées
01 42 08 58 18
cordonnier-haute-couture-chausseur-sur-mesure.com • @ateliercattelan

Founded in 1956, this luxury cobbler displays incredible craftsmanship. It offers custom shoes made with a selection of materials worthy of the most prestigious names in fashion. I bring my finest shoes here for repairs, but I also come for the best advice on how to care for them.

RETOUCHE DE QUALITÉ

5

37 rue Bouret
M° Jaurès
06 63 66 13 28

I never think twice when I need to have a garment mended: I head straight to Monsieur Zekhnine. And with good reason: he works on costumes worn by performers at the Paris Opéra, which earned him the silver medal for Meilleur Ouvrier de France (best craftsman). Since 1987, the founder's nimble fingers have delivered a quality service, from the most delicate repairs to restoring decor and vintage costumes.

CORDONNERIE
ATELIER CATTELAN
1956
Fig n°1
Fig n°2
AGRÉÉ PAR
LES PLUS
GRANDES
MARQUES
Fig n°3
Fig n°4
SE TROUVE AU
NUMÉRO 2 DE LA
RUE MÉLINGUE
— À —
PARIS XIXE
Fig n°5
Fig n°6

BELLYNCK & FILS

6

194 avenue Jean-Jaurès
M° Porte de Pantin
01 42 08 16 75
bellyncketfils.fr • @bellyncketfils

The painted facade alone is worthy of a postcard. Since 1936, Bellynck & Fils has specialized in cooking utensils for professionals and home cooks alike. When it opened, businesses could paste posters on the store's exterior, which the owners have carefully preserved. In fact, the same family still runs this legendary store on avenue Jean-Jaurès.

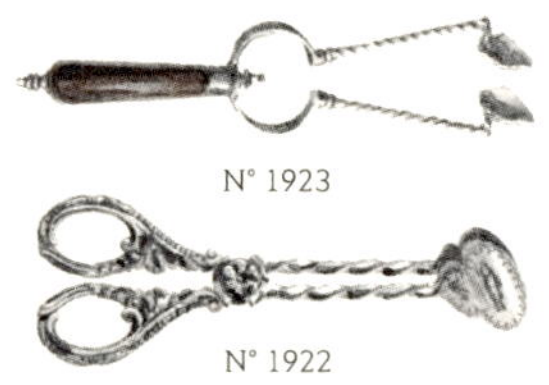

N° 1923

N° 1922

QUINCAILLERIE MIRUS

7

149 avenue Jean-Jaurès
M° Ourcq
01 40 40 01 78
quincailleriemirus.fr

This is the sort of bric-a-brac store that you simply can't leave empty-handed. Created in 1930, it is one of the oldest *quincailleries*, or hardware stores, in Paris, and has become a benchmark in the neighborhood. The concept is simple: there is a solution for everything here—thanks to the wise advice of the staff, who take their time with each client.

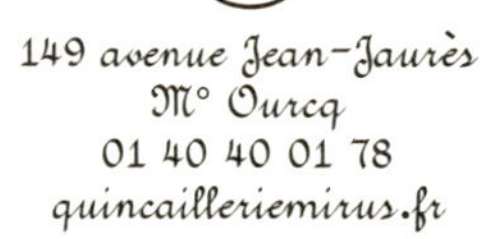

N° 1975

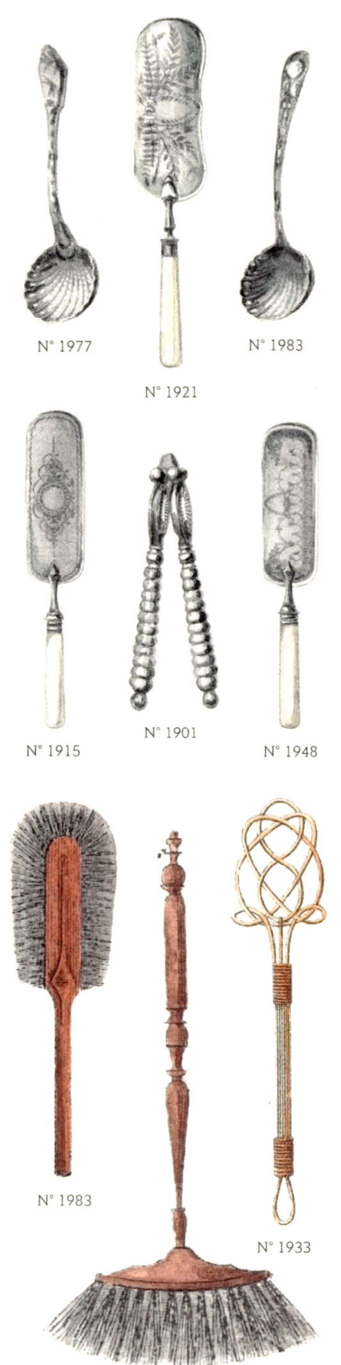

N° 1977 N° 1921 N° 1983

N° 1915 N° 1901 N° 1948

N° 1983 N° 1933 N° 1946

TOUT POUR LA CHARCUTERIE ET LA BOUCHERIE
MATÉRIEL POUR RESTAURANTS ET CANTINES

USTENSILES EN CUIVRE, ALU ET INOX

BELLYNCK

FOURNEAUX DE CUISINE DE QUALITÉ

PARIS XIXE : 194 AVENUE JEAN-JAURÈS

N° 1968

LA VIEILLE FRANCE

5 avenue de Laumière
M° Laumière
01 40 40 08 31
@la_vieille_france_1834

Nothing has changed since 1834; not the decor, nor the recipes, nor the company's desire to delight every Parisian. Using high-quality ingredients, they create exquisite versions of classic French pastries, such as éclairs, egg-custard flans, and Paris-Brests. Their specialty is the *Vieille France*: a puff pastry tart with applesauce, cinnamon, raisins, and nuts. Mouthwatering!

N° 1984 N° 1915

N° 1930 N° 1972

N° 1938 N° 1975

N° 1979

POÎLANE

9

83 rue de Crimée
M° Laumière / Botzaris
01 40 36 04 28
poilane.com/en/blogs/store/buttes-chaumont • @poilane

This superb boulangerie, featuring sumptuous interiors dating to the early 20th century, is tucked away just next to the Parc des Buttes Chaumont. Here, Apollonia Poilâne carries on and reinvents the craft she inherited from her father and grandfather. Everything is baked in the original wood-fired oven, including sourdough bread—perfect for a picnic in the park.

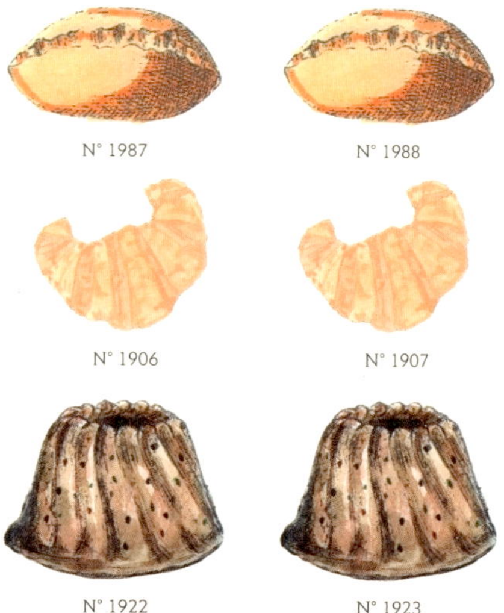

N° 1987 N° 1988

N° 1906 N° 1907

N° 1922 N° 1923

AU BŒUF COURONNÉ

10

188 avenue Jean-Jaurès
M° Porte de Pantin
01 42 39 44 44
boeuf-couronne.com/en • @auboeufcouronne_

Here, beef is given the royal treatment. Since the 1930s, this restaurant has served succulent meat of the highest quality in a splendid setting typical of the era. It stands out for its large selection of cuts and weights—there's something to satisfy every appetite. I often come here for dinner before a concert at the nearby Philharmonie de Paris—or just after one, if I'm feeling famished.

N° 1939

LE BAR FLEURI

11

1 rue du Plateau
M° Buttes-Chaumont / Botzaris
01 42 08 13 38
@fleuribar

Here, a meal of *poulet-frites* costs just 45 francs, or €6.86—that's right, the price hasn't changed since the bistro opened in the 1950s, even after France adopted the euro. This is the perfect restaurant for a quick bite to eat before going for a stroll in the Parc des Buttes Chaumont. Inside, regulars eat with gusto, amid the kind of old-fashioned decor that I love.

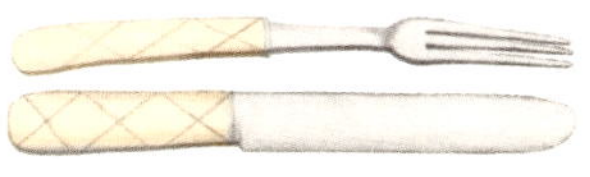
N° 1984

N° 1929

N° 1923

N° 1963

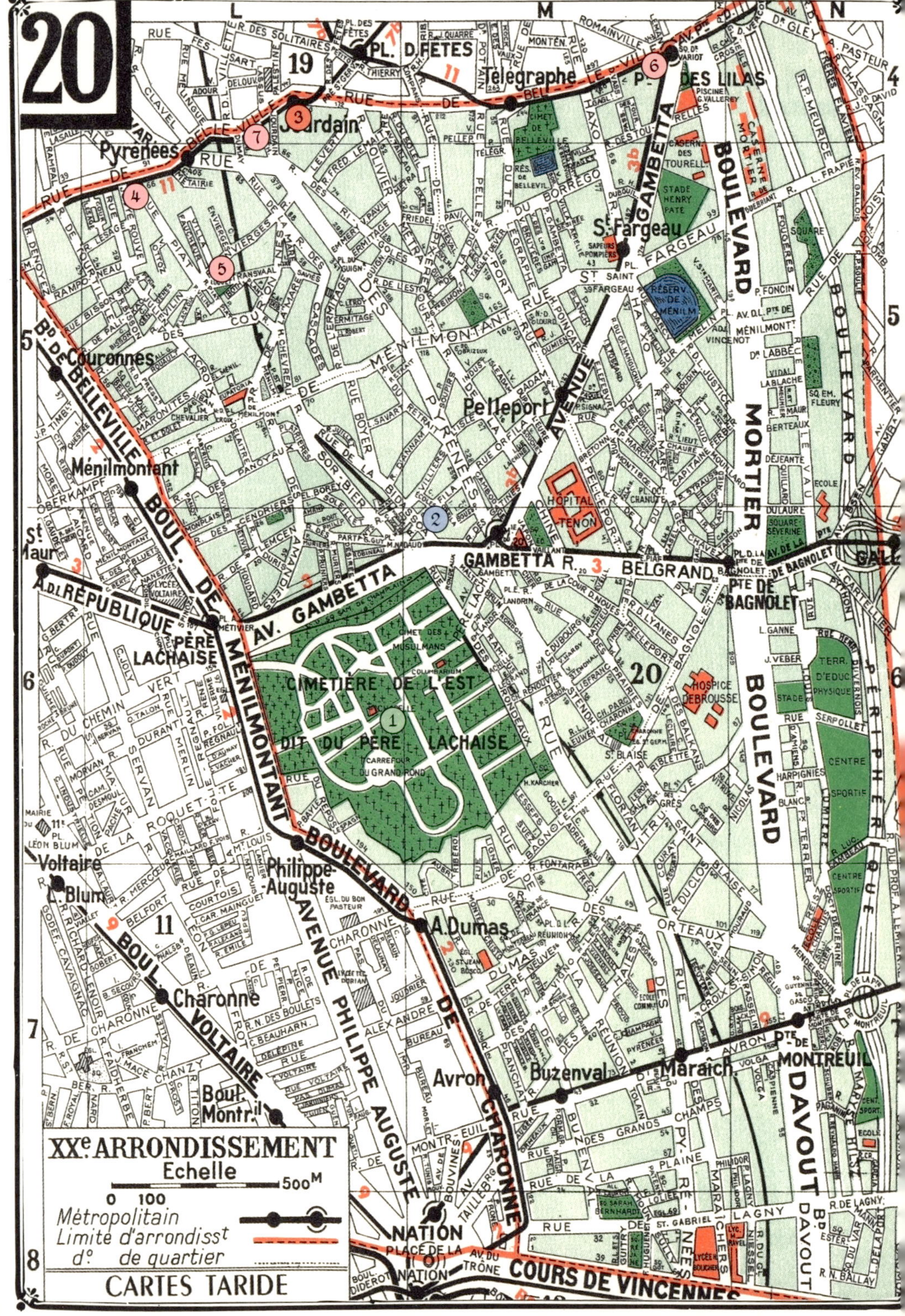
20
XXe ARRONDISSEMENT
Echelle
0 100
500M
Métropolitain
Limite d'arrondisst
d° de quartier
CARTES TARIDE
PL. D. FETES
Télégraphe
P. DES LILAS
Jourdain
Pyrénées
St Fargeau
Couronnes
Ménilmontant
Pelleport
Gambetta
St Maur
PÈRE LACHAISE
CIMETIÈRE DE L'EST DIT DU PÈRE LACHAISE
HOPITAL TENON
HOSPICE DEBROUSSE
Pte DE BAGNOLET
Philippe-Auguste
A. Dumas
Charonne
Voltaire L. Blum
Avron
Buzenval
Maraich.
Pte DE MONTREUIL
NATION
PLACE DE LA NATION
COURS DE VINCENNES
BOULEVARD MORTIER
BOULEVARD DAVOUT
BOUL. DE MÉNILMONTANT
BOULEVARD DE CHARONNE
AVENUE PHILIPPE AUGUSTE
AV. GAMBETTA
AVENUE GAMBETTA
Bd DE BELLEVILLE
BOUL. VOLTAIRE
A. DE LA RÉPUBLIQUE
PÉRIPHÉRIQUE
RUE DES PYRÉNÉES
RUE DE MÉNILMONTANT
RUE DE BELLEVILLE
RUE DE BAGNOLET
RUE D'AVRON
19
11
20

20E ARRONDISSEMENT

1. Cimetière du Père-Lachaise
Entrances porte des Amandiers, porte Gambetta, porte du Repos
2. Passementerie Verrier
10 rue Orfila
3. La Brûlerie de Jourdain
140 rue de Belleville
4. Le Baratin
3 rue Jouye-Rouve
5. Le Vieux Belleville
12 rue des Envierges
6. Le Clairon
328 rue de Belleville
7. La Cagnotte
114 rue de Belleville

◈ CIMETIÈRE DU PÈRE-LACHAISE ◈

1

Entrances porte des Amandiers,
porte Gambetta, porte du Repos
M° Père Lachaise / Gambetta / Philippe Auguste
paris.fr/lieux/cimetiere-du-pere-lachaise-4080

Opened in 1804, the Père-Lachaise cemetery—the largest of its kind in Paris—reads like a history book spread over 180 acres (73 ha). Parisians come here both to reflect and to stroll, particularly in summer, when the city's parks and gardens get crowded. I can spend entire afternoons here exploring hidden chapels or reading peacefully in the shade of the towering trees.

N° 2097 N° 2097

N° 2008

◈ PASSEMENTERIE VERRIER ◈

2

10 rue Orfila
M° Gambetta
01 46 36 49 01
passementerie-verrier.com/en • @passementerieverrier

I like unique places that preserve rare forms of savoir faire. Since 1918, this firm has been making textile ornamentation using exceptional materials. The incredible diversity of their creations—from period reproductions to modern pieces—will astound you. Imagine yards of thread passing through the artisans' hands as they weave patterns with precision.

N° 2092

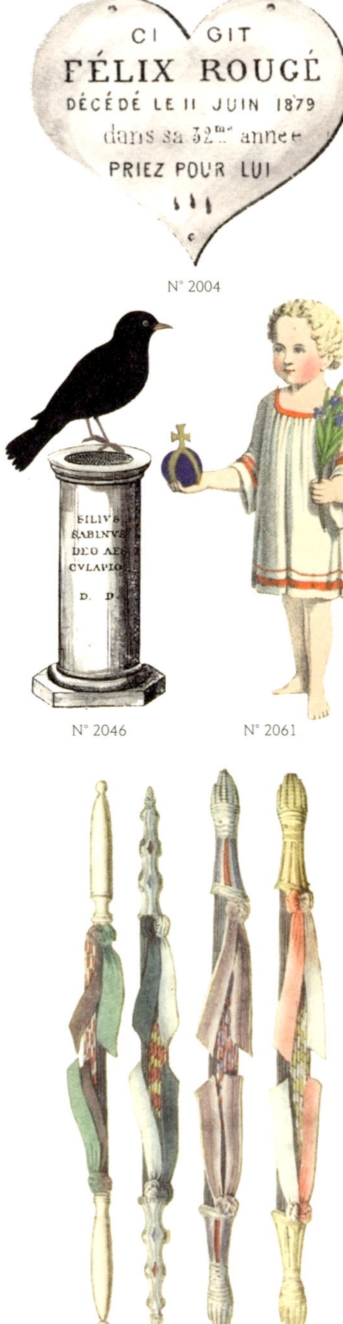

N° 2004

N° 2046 N° 2061

N° 2043

FABRIQUE DE PASSEMENTERIE D'AMEUBLEMENT

G. L. VERRIER FRERES & Cie

Société à Responsabilité Limitée au Capital de 10.000 Frs

10, Rue Orfila - PARIS-XXe

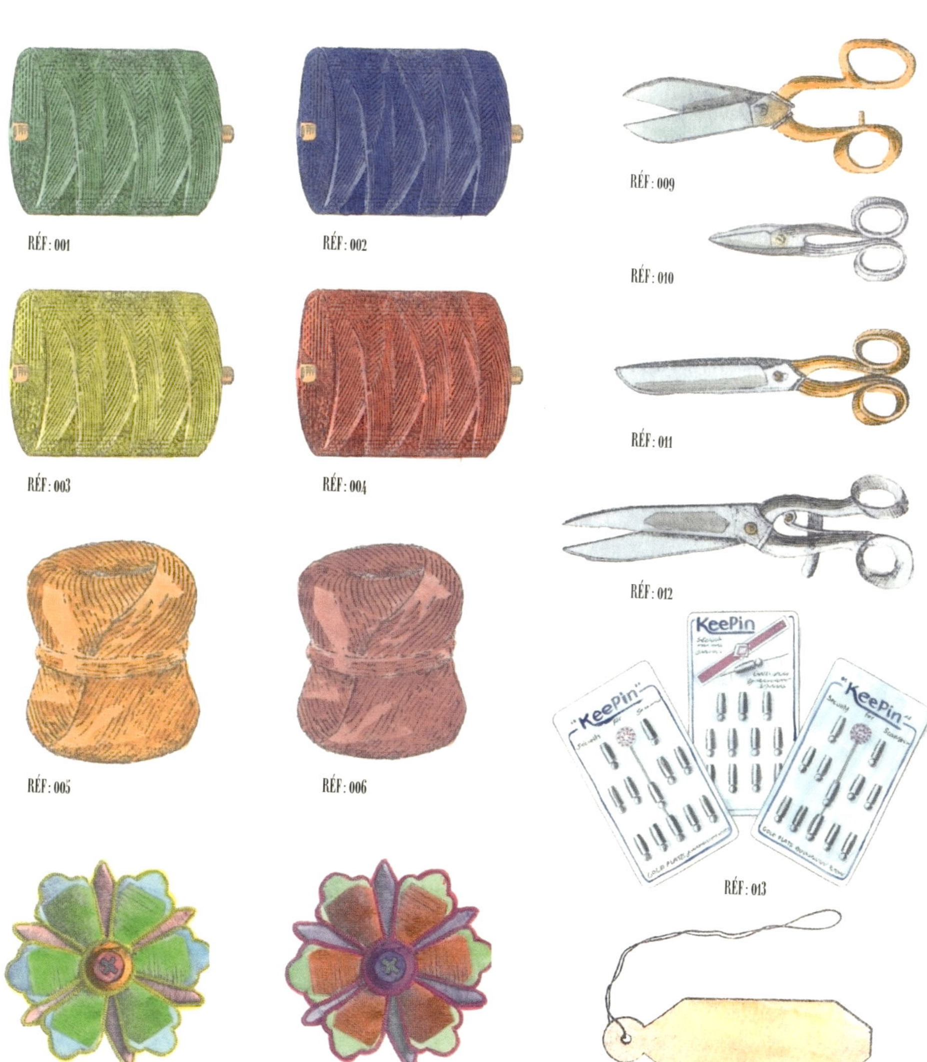

RÉF: 001
RÉF: 002
RÉF: 003
RÉF: 004
RÉF: 005
RÉF: 006
RÉF: 007
RÉF: 008
RÉF: 009
RÉF: 010
RÉF: 011
RÉF: 012
RÉF: 013
RÉF: 014

LE BARATIN

Restaurant - Vins de Propriétés

3 RUE JOUYE-ROUVE — PARIS XXE

N° 2058  N° 2055  N° 2086  N° 2087  N° 2088

N° 2028 N° 2029 N° 2021  N° 2022  N° 2023  N° 2024

N° 2036

LA BRÛLERIE DE JOURDAIN

3

140 rue de Belleville
M° Jourdain
01 47 97 92 77
FB: La Brûlerie de Jourdain

La Brûlerie de Jourdain has been filling the neighborhood along this commercial stretch of rue de Belleville with the scent of coffee since 1955. I love inhaling the aroma of freshly roasted beans and listening to them crackle. While you wait for your custom grind, admire the old scales or learn how to conjugate the verb *moudre* (grind) from the little poster next to the cash register.

N° 2081

LE BARATIN

4

3 rue Jouye-Rouve
M° Pyrénées
01 43 49 39 70

Le Baratin has been one of Belleville's most popular spots since 1987, and it is one of my very favorite places. The bistro cooking is perfectly executed—I ate the best beef cheek of my life here. Everything in this haunt for regulars and Parisians-in-the-know has remained the same since it opened. I like to sit at the pretty mahogany bar and watch the orders parade by throughout the service.

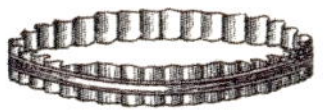

N° 2094

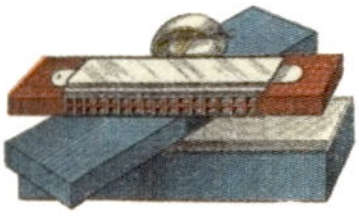

N° 2039

N° 2031

N° 2029

N° 2095

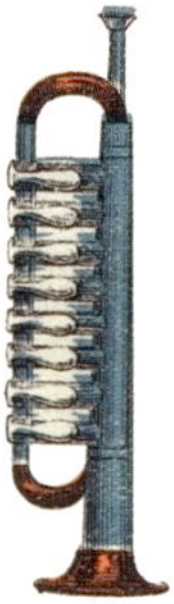

LE VIEUX BELLEVILLE

5

12 rue des Envierges
M° Pyrénées / Couronnes
01 44 62 92 66
le-vieux-belleville.com/en • @levieuxbelleville

N° 2044

N° 2017

Le Vieux Belleville puts a song in my heart. With accordions, traditional pop *chansons*, and a *guinguette* ambiance, it encapsulates all the gaiety and conviviality of Paris. In this café, open since 1992, music brings the neighborhood together around a glass of red wine and an Édith Piaf tune. Lyrics are handed out during dinner, so don't hold back.

N° 2086

N° 2040

N° 2045

N° 2054

N° 2048

LE CLAIRON

6

328 rue de Belleville
M° Porte des Lilas
01 43 64 66 84
leclairon.free.fr

While some places have no sense of identity, others affirm their originality from the get-go. From the old gas pumps and Triumph motorcycle above the refrigerators, to the beer tap installed in a BMW motor and the neon sign—which I love—above the bar, Le Clairon is upfront about its passion for motorcycles. This family business, open since 1989, has become a paradise for bikers. It's also perfect for a coffee break.

N° 2068

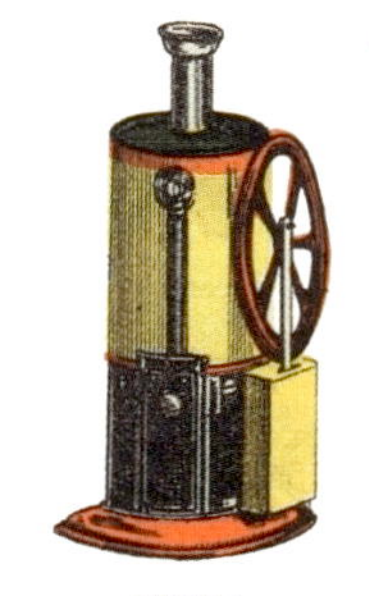

N° 2046

N° 2047

N° 2052

N° 2084

N° 2032

LA CAGNOTTE

7

114 rue de Belleville
M° Jourdain / Pyrénées
01 47 97 25 16
FB: La Cagnotte de Belleville

This lovely little spot has been tucked away on rue de Belleville since the 1970s. I come here for a café on the sunny terrace, followed by a local craft beer, before pushing the tables to the side and dancing until 2 a.m. Judith organizes a *boum* once a month, but the other evenings of the week are just as festive. La Cagnotte has also created its own literary prize.

N° 2076

N° 2093

N° 2061

N° 2069

AROUND PARIS

PUCES DE SAINT-OUEN

Rue des Rosiers, 93400 Saint-Ouen
M° Porte de Clignancourt / Garibaldi / Saint-Ouen
Friday 8 a.m.–12 p.m. & Saturday–Monday 10 a.m.–6 p.m.
pucesdeparissaintouen.com/en/ • @pucesdeparissaintouen

Since 1870, the Saint-Ouen flea markets have occupied a slice of Paris's northern edge like a miniature city, home to more antiques than residents. My parents were antiques dealers in the south of France, and they often brought me along on trips to the Paris flea markets as they scouted the stalls for treasures; when I moved to Paris twenty years later, returning to the *puces* I felt as if I had never left. I really like the **Marché Vernaison**, a little village with more than 200 vendors that feels worlds away from the capital. There's also the **Marché Dauphine**, the largest flea market, which brings together 150 merchants under a large glass roof, and the ever-charming **Marché Paul Bert**, where I find creative inspiration for new projects, objects, or decors. I never come with a specific goal in mind, but I always leave toting a precious find under my arm. Here are some of my favorite sellers.

MARCHÉ VERNAISON

marchevernaison.com • @marchevernaison

Lili et Daniel
Allée 1, Stand 6 • Liliane & Daniel Gantarksi
01 40 12 01 24 / 01 42 02 32 97
lilietdanielpuces@gmail.com
lilietdaniel.com • @lilipuces
Passementerie, beads, buttons, materials for jewelry making

Tombées du Camion
Allée 1, Stands 29–31 / Allée 3, Stands 107 & 108 bis
Charles Mas • 06 62 07 20 87
contact@tombeesducamion.com
tombeesducamion.com • @tombeesducamion
Antique and vintage objects, including toys, jewelry, light fixtures, decorative items, etc.

Syl's Antique Shop
Allée 1, Stand 44 / Allée 10, Stand 244
Michel Teboul • 06 08 64 90 38
teboul.sylvie@hotmail.fr • FB: Syl's antique Shop
Coffee grinders & coffee pots, pepper mills, enamel kitchenware, copperware

Marcel & Jeannette
Allées 3 & 6 (corner), Stand 108 / Allée 6, Stand 118
Virginie Chorro / Merry Liuzzo • 06 16 45 17 42 / 06 64 73 59 83 • merry.liuzzo@gmail.com
marceletjeannette.com • @marceletjeannette
Textiles, vintage fashion, work clothes, quilts, accessories (18th century to the present)

Laure de Villoutreys
Allée 6, Stand 101 • 06 63 16 03 17
lauredevilloutreys@gmail.com • @lespuceslaure
Antique and traditional fabrics, linens (18th century–1950s), clothing, accessories, decorative objects, sewing supplies

N° 2154 N° 2173 N° 2198
N° 2118 N° 2119
N° 2122
N° 2114 N° 2135
N° 2125 N° 2118
N° 2115 N° 2197

Bocquier Antiquités
Allée 6, Stand 99 • René Bocquier
06 09 63 85 93 • flaubertflaubert7@gmail.com
Upholstery fabrics, passementerie, household linens, curtains, lace

◈

Kévin Ricordel
Allée 6, Stand 112 • 06 63 28 21 62
kevin@cadresanciens.fr • cadresanciens.fr/en
@cadresanciens
Sale and restoration of antique picture frames and mirrors (16th–20th centuries), artwork framing service

◈

Charles Schwalberg
Allée 7, Stand 154 • 06 85 13 48 36
verrerie75@yahoo.fr • @schwalberg
Antique paintings and artworks, religious objects

◈

Francine
Allée 7, Stands 121 & 123
Francine Dentelles • 01 40 10 93 36
francinedentelles@gmail.com
@francinedentelles
Collectible lace

◈

De La Villette
Allée 8, Stand 160 • Frédéric Buquet
06 62 47 72 07 • antiques@delavillette.paris
delavillette.paris • @delavillette
Books, engravings, illustrations, photographs, objects, furniture (17th–20th centuries)

◈

Idées Broc, Le Vaisselier de Paris
Allée 8, Stand 163 • Gilles Plattner
06 88 07 96 57 / 06 51 18 83 07
ideesbroc@gmail.com • @ideesbroc.puces
Kitchenware, tableware, tea and coffee sets, earthenware

N° 2121 N° 2122
N° 2147 N° 2145
N° 2130 N° 2129
N° 2118
N° 2118 N° 2118
N° 2129 N° 2110

MARCHÉ AUX PUCES
— DE SAINT-OUEN —

SPÉCIMEN DE NUANCES DES DIFFÉRENTS MOULES À PÂTISSERIE EN CUIVRE VÉRITABLE

◈ MARCHÉ DAUPHINE ◈

132-140 rue des Rosiers
marche-dauphine.com/en/ • @marchedauphine

Dominique Saint-Martin
Stands 8-11 • 06 49 76 11 84
dominique.saint-martin@orange.fr
@dominiquesaintmartin
Antiques, textiles, dolls, bottles, crystal glasses, popular art objects, mother of pearl buttons, etc.

◈

Galerie Leyla Ahi
Stands 52-54 & 62 • Leyla Ahi
06 13 40 31 10 / 06 10 37 15 35
contact@galleryahi.com • galleryahi.com
@galerie_leyla_textiles
Antique textiles, costumes, and clothing from around the world, notably North Africa and the Middle East

◈

Belladone
Stand 55 • 06 21 79 34 99
belladone.vernaison@protonmail.com
@belladone_dauphin
Cabinet of curiosities

◈

Un Singe en Hiver
Stands 93-94 & 102-103 & 141 • Sylvain Seron
06 48 30 54 53 • info@unsingenhiver.com
unsingenhiver.com • @singenhiver
Antiques, furniture, garden decoration

◈

Daniel et Lili
Stand 128 • 01 40 10 83 46 • info@danieletlili.com
danieletlili.com • @danieletlili
Vintage jewelry, fashion accessories, crafts

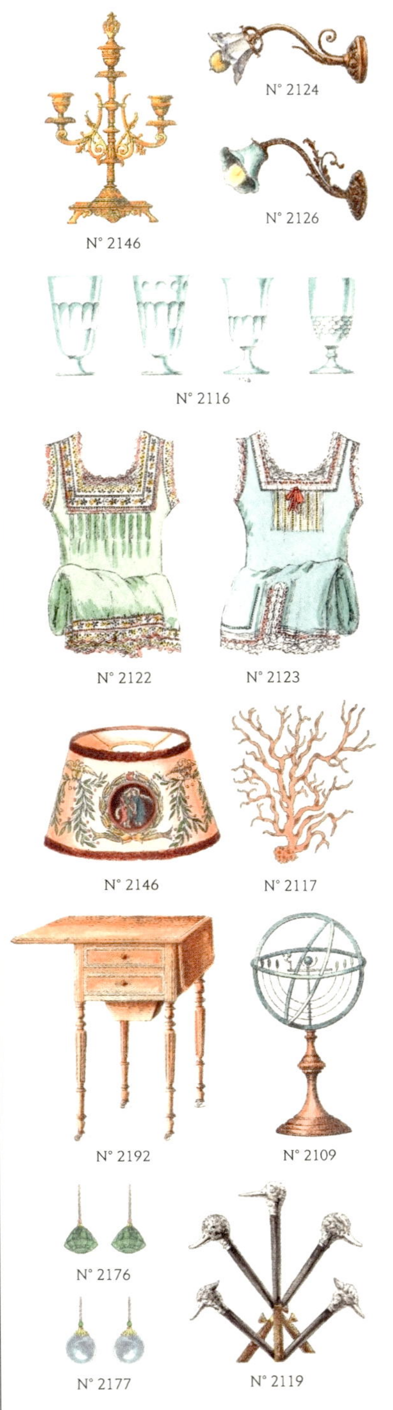
N° 2146 N° 2124 N° 2126
N° 2116
N° 2122 N° 2123
N° 2146 N° 2117
N° 2192 N° 2109
N° 2176 N° 2177 N° 2119

MARCHÉ AUX PUCES
— DE SAINT-OUEN —

GARNITURE DE THÉIÈRES, CAFETIÈRES, CRUCHES, SEAUX ET BROCS

◈ MARCHÉ PAUL-BERT ◈

96–110 rue des Rosiers & 18 rue Paul-Bert
paulbert-serpette.com/en • @paulbertserpette

Lila K: Winter Gardens
Allée 1, Stand 8 • 06 18 05 15 96
lila.k.antique@gmail.com • @lila_K_antiques
Chinoiseries, furniture, tableware, barbotine ware (set against blue walls painted with a winter garden of fruit trees and romantic flowers)

◈

Les Merveilles de Babellou
babellou@gmail.com

• Allée 1, Stands 12, 13, 14, 16
Isabelle Klein • 06 80 63 26 89
lesmerveillesdebabellou.com/en
@lesmerveillesdebabellou
Unique and designer vintage clothing, accessories, and jewelry

• Allée 1, Stand 15
François Casal • 06 10 37 40 24
Bar and garden furniture and accessories

• Allée 1, Stand 17
François Casal • 06 10 37 40 24
Antique restaurant and bar supplies, kitchenware, copper

• Allées 1 & 6 (corner), Stand 77
François Casal • 06 10 37 40 24
Display cases

◈

La Maison de Babellou
8 rue Paul-Bert • Isabelle Klein
06 80 63 26 89 • @lamaisondebabellou
Tableware, decoration, lighting, design, and furniture (19th–20th centuries)

◈

La Petite Maison
10 rue Paul-Bert • François Casal • 06 10 37 40 24
Charming furniture for home and garden (17th–19th centuries)

N° 2160
N° 2109 N° 2119
N° 2150 N° 2107
N° 2100 N° 2101 N° 2157
N° 2186
N° 2129

Elsa Halfen
Allée 2, Stand 121 • 06 76 01 55 46
elsahalfen@yahoo.com • @elsa_halfen
Antiques, objects of curiosity, decoration

◈

Bernard Tinivella
Allée 3, Stand 48 • Bernard Tinivella
07 63 39 07 08 • bernardtinivella@gmail.com
@bernard_tinivella
Neoclassical and Roman statues and sculptures

◈

LVS Antiquités
Allée 3, Stands 58 ter & 161
Virginie & Stéphane Baquet • 06 63 27 30 57
info@lvsantiquites.com • lvsantiquites.com
@lvs_antiquites_antique_frames
Picture and mirror frames
(17th–20th centuries)

◈

Multi Studio
Allée 3, Stands 163 & 165
Benoit Guineaudeau • 06 63 64 01 63
benoit.guinaudeau@hotmail.fr • @m.u.l.t.i.studio
Designer furniture (1920s–1970s), Italian futurist, brutalist, modernist, cubist design

◈

Pierre Bazalgues
Allée 4, Stand 211 • Pierre Bazalgues
06 13 26 53 30 • pierrebazalgues@neuf.fr
@pierre_bazalgues
19th-century curios and Gothic-style objects

◈

Antiquités Lahaye
Allée 5, Stands 204 bis & 245
Cécilia & Frédéric Lahaye • 06 71 58 60 41 /
06 08 71 96 74 • info@antiquiteslahaye.fr /
cc.lahaye@gmail.com / fredlahaye@live.fr
antiquites-lahaye.fr • @antiquites.lahaye
Botanical prints, furniture, chairs, lighting, curios, decorative objects (17th–20th centuries)

N° 2157 N° 2153 N° 2134 N° 2132 N° 2178 N° 2172 N° 2159 N° 2188 N° 2141 N° 2145 N° 2184 N° 2136 N° 2163

Bruno Le Yaouanc
Allée 5, Stands 208 & 210
Bruno Le Yaouanc • 06 86 49 05 96
bruno.leyaouanc@wanadoo.fr • @bruno.leyaouanc
19th-century French furniture

Art de Perse
1 rue Paul-Bert • Massoud Ekhteraei
06 67 23 71 64 • ekhteraei_leila@yahoo.com
Antique rugs and tapestries, passementerie, repairs

Sema
13 rue Paul-Bert • Nicolas Adjinsoff
01 40 11 25 69 / 06 03 29 30 32
Sale and installation of antique fireplaces, wood paneling, decorative objects and architectural pieces, metalwork, lighting, seats

MARCHÉ SERPETTE

110 rue des Rosiers

La Boutique de Sophie
Allée 3, Stand 1 • Sophie Cougoule-Devergne
06 98 83 64 04 • scdantik@gmail.com
@la_boutique_de_sophie
Italian and French chandeliers, furniture, home decor, antique restoration

EATING, DRINKING, AND ENTERTAINMENT

La Chope des Puces : Espace Django Reinhardt
122 rue des Rosiers • 01 40 11 28 80
contact@espacedjangoreinhardt.com
lachopedespuces.fr • @lachopedespuces
Animated bar-restaurant, featuring live gypsy jazz and swing jam sessions and concerts on Saturday and Sunday afternoons.

N° 2111 N° 2123
N° 2111 N° 2163
N° 2186 N° 2166
N° 2152 N° 2135 N° 2193
N° 2162
N° 2171 N° 2132

21, Rue Racine, 21

MAISON DE VENTE ET GRAND ATELIER DE MOULAGE

M. LORENZI

Mouleur en tous Genres

ET A FAÇON

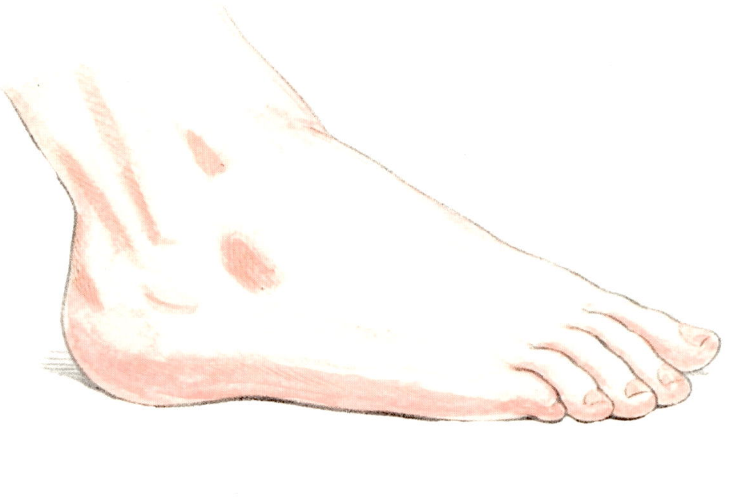

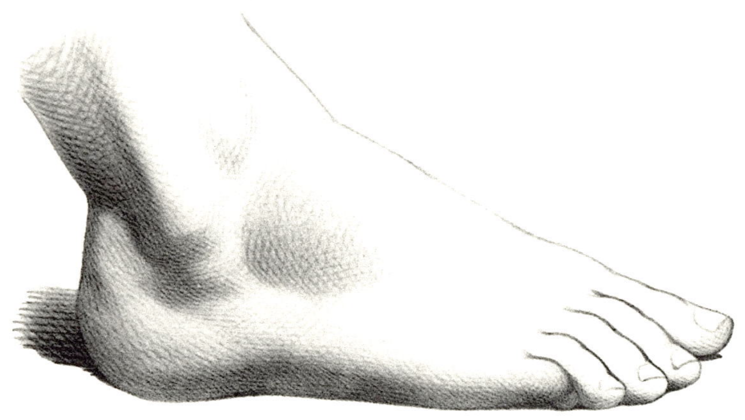

STATUETTES, TORSES, BUSTES, PIEDS, MAINS, MASQUES

Fournisseur des Écoles de Dessins

Spécialité de Camées & Médailles Artistiques

EXPÉDITION EN PROVINCE ET A L'ÉTRANGER

◈ LA BOÎTE D'ACCORDÉON LAURENT JARRY ◈

8 rue du Sergent-Bobillot, Montreuil
M° Croix de Chavaux
01 48 58 63 97
laboitedaccordeon.fr • @laboitedaccordeon

Since 1989, the accordion has reigned supreme at Laurent Jarry, where the music of old Paris hangs in the air. I'm fascinated by the stacks of accordions, the pearly keys waiting to be shined, and the velvet cases vying to embrace the most beautiful instrument in the neighborhood. This boutique-workshop exudes dedication, fine craftsmanship, and authenticity.

N° 2102

◈ ATELIER LORENZI ◈

60 avenue Laplace, Arcueil
RER Laplace
01 47 35 37 54
en.atelierlorenzi.com • @atelierlorenzi

Transporting visitors back to the nineteenth century, this house-studio looks like it was plucked from a small village in Provence. Since 1871, Atelier Lorenzi has perpetuated the technique of fine plaster casting, which can be used to make exact reproductions of sculptures from any historical period. During visits (on Thursdays and Fridays), owner Éric Nadeau passionately recounts the many stories that have unfolded here. This fascinating place takes me back to my own hours spent at the Louvre.

N° 2199

N° 2164

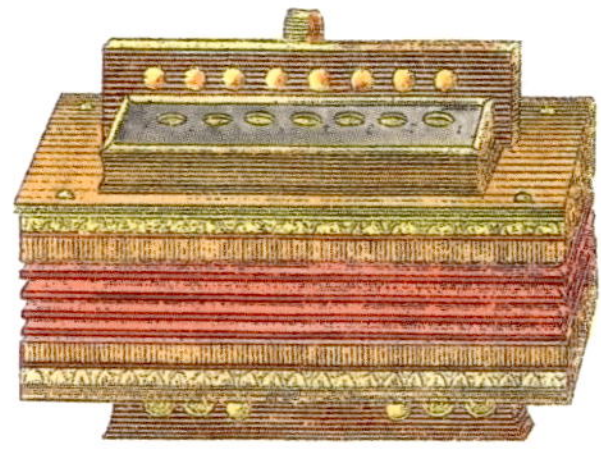

N° 2129

N° 2120 N° 2118

N° 2139

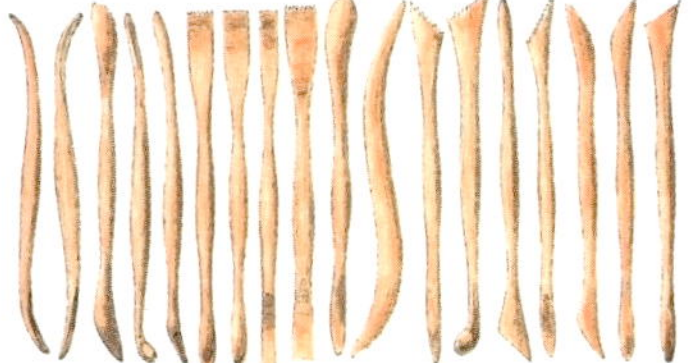

N° 2141

EXPLORING PARIS

UNUSUAL SITES

They're right there, above our heads, beneath our feet, behind a carriage door, on a wall, tucked away on a street corner, or even in a parking garage. Discovering one of these places, by accident or otherwise, feels like completing a step in a giant treasure hunt. That's what I love about Paris: the enduring surprise of sites that are unusual and unique, due to their history and location, but also the mysteries they hold.

HORLOGE DU PALAIS DE LA CITÉ

Corner of quai de l'Horloge & boulevard du Palais, 1er, M° Cité; RER Saint-Michel – Notre-Dame

Mounted on the facade of the Palais de la Cité—once at the heart of royal and judicial power (Marie Antoinette spent her last days in prison here)—the oldest public clock in Paris dates back to 1370. Its opulent Gothic design features a deep blue ground adorned with golden fleurs-de-lis: a symbol of French royalty.

"MÈTRE ÉTALON" STANDARD METER

13 place Vendôme, 1er, M° Tuileries & 36 rue de Vaugirard, 6e, M° Saint-Sulpice / Mabillon

Original standard meter bars in marble are installed on two walls of the capital. They date back to 1796–1797, when, during the Revolutionary period, France invented and adopted the metric system.

❖ SMALLEST STREET IN PARIS ❖

Rue des Degrés, 2e, M° Bonne-Nouvelle

This tiny street-staircase, barely 20 feet (6 m) long and 11 feet (3.3 m) wide, is the smallest in Paris. You won't find any front doors or shops here—just fourteen steps connecting rues Beauregard and de Cléry.

❖ ANGEL OF RUE DE TURBIGO ❖

57 rue de Turbigo, 3e, M° Arts et Métiers

To spot it, simply look up. This huge caryatid, spanning three stories, has overlooked rue de Turbigo since 1859. Designed by Auguste Émile Delange for a competition organized by the École des Beaux-Arts, the figure wears a tunic typical of Second Empire style. As for its meaning—that remains a mystery.

❖ AUBERGE NICOLAS FLAMEL, OLDEST KNOWN HOUSE IN PARIS ❖

51 rue de Montmorency, 3e,
M° Étienne Marcel / Arts et Métiers

This former refuge for the poor, now a restaurant, has been standing for more than 600 years. It was built in 1407 by rich Parisian Nicolas Flamel—who, according to legend, made his fortune as an alchemist—and its stone facade, along with the pious medieval inscription above the entrance, have bravely stood the test of time.

◈ KILOMETER ZERO PLAQUE ◈

*Parvis Notre-Dame – place Jean-Paul II,
4e, M° Cité; RER Saint-Michel – Notre-Dame*

At the foot of Notre-Dame cathedral, this small bronze plaque might easily go unnoticed. Yet the historic geographical landmark marks the kilometer zero for all the roads in France. For me, it represents both a point of departure and of homecoming—no matter how far you roam, Paris will always call you back.

◈ NARROWEST STREET IN PARIS ◈

*Rue du Chat-qui-pêche, 5e, M° Saint-Michel;
RER Saint-Michel – Notre-Dame*

Stepping into this street feels like walking along Diagon Alley. At just 6 feet (1.8 m) wide, it is the narrowest street in the capital. The name (which means "the cat that fishes") comes from a black cat who is said to have lived here with its master. Legend has it that the feline was skilled at fishing in the Seine.

◈ OLDEST TREE IN PARIS ◈

*Square René Viviani, 5e, M° Cluny – La Sorbonne;
RER Saint-Michel – Notre-Dame*

Each of its leaves is a page out of French history. Sent as a seed from America, this black locust was planted in 1601, during the reign of Henry IV, by Jean Robin. The latter gave his name to the species, also known as false acacia, hence its botanical name: *Robinia pseudoacacia*.

◈ LE BATEAU IVRE WALL ◈

Rue Férou, 6e, M° Saint-Sulpice / Mabillon

In a little cobbled street linking the Jardin du Luxembourg and Place Saint-Sulpice, Arthur Rimbaud's most famous poem—written when he was just 16—is displayed as a giant mural. The full 100 lines of "Le Bateau Ivre" ("The Drunken Boat") were hand-painted on an old stone wall, for the contemplation of poetry-loving strollers.

◈ JARDIN CATHERINE-LABOURÉ ◈

29 rue de Babylone, 7e, M° Vaneau / Sèvres – Babylone / Saint-François-Xavier

Concealed behind a tall stone wall, this former convent garden opens onto sweeping lawns lined with lindens and poplars. The orchard is home to apple, cherry, and hazel trees, among others. There's even a small vegetable garden for neighborhood children to enjoy. As soon as spring arrives, I like to picnic in the shade of the arbor dripping with grapevines.

◈ LAVIROTTE BUILDING ◈

29 avenue Rapp, 7e, M° Alma – Marceau; RER Pont de l'Alma

Rich ornamentation and numerous details make this one of Paris's rare art nouveau gems. Built between 1900 and 1901 by architect Jules Lavirotte, this charmingly fanciful masterpiece was awarded the prize for the most beautiful facade by the city that same year.

MAISON LOO, THE PAGODA PARIS

48 rue de Courcelles, 8e, M° Courcelles / Miromesnil

Having arrived in France in 1902, art dealer Ching Tsai Loo decided in 1925 to buy a hôtel particulier and turn it into a pagoda, in tribute to his native country, China. Tucked away in the Plaine Monceau district, this exceptional building, now a private museum, makes for a striking contrast with its typically Parisian neighbors.

AVENUE FROCHOT & VILLA FROCHOT

2 rue Frochot, 9e, M° Pigalle

Avenue Frochot is brimming with enigmas and oddities. Visitors are first greeted by an incredible art deco stained-glass work reminiscent of Hokusai's *The Great Wave off Kanagawa.* Created in the 1930s, the motif, chosen for its "Asian" style, adorned the facade of the Shanghai, a one-time Chinese cabaret.

Across the street stands the neo-Gothic Villa Frochot, built in 1823. Allegedly a hotspot for paranormal activity, its history is full of sudden deaths and inexplicable noises. And the mystery deepened when French singer Sylvie Vartan bought the house only to get rid of it shortly thereafter.

SMALLEST HOUSE IN PARIS

39 rue du Château d'Eau, 10e, M° Château d'Eau / Jacques Bonsergent

Squeezed in here since the early 19th century, this minuscule house is just 5 feet (1.5 m) wide. The ground floor is occupied by a business that manages to operate out of barely 13 square feet (4 m^2). The upper floor is said to have been used as a baby's room, where there was just enough space for a cradle.

AUTEL DU CULTE DE BOUDDHA

37 rue du Disque, 13e, M° Olympiades / Porte d'Ivry

A glowing red light guides visitors as they enter this parking lot on rue du Disque, where the Buddha altar lies hidden in the shadows. It is a mystical place where families and regulars gather in silence.

GANESH HINDU TEMPLE

17 rue Pajol, 18e, M° La Chapelle / Stalingrad

Founded in 1985 by a Tamal refugee, this was the first Hindu temple to open in France. The mystic setting and welcoming, incense-laden atmosphere enthrall visitors. Every year, celebrations are held for each Hindu holy day.

ROCHER DE LA SORCIÈRE

Passage de la Sorcière, access via 23 avenue Junot or 65 rue Lepic, 18e, M° Lamarck – Caulaincourt

This surprising rock-like structure is nestled on a small street in Montmartre. Legend has it that a lone elderly woman living in a house just next to it would frighten the neighborhood children, who transformed the passage's name from "de la sourcière" (dowser's passage) to "de la sorcière" (witch's passage). The huge block of stone is actually a defunct fountain.

◈ SMALLEST SQUARE IN PARIS ◈

Place du Calvaire, 18e, M° Abbesses

Perched at the top of the Butte Montmartre, just behind the famous place du Tertre, this minute square-terrace, strewn with cobblestones, is the smallest in Paris. It is named after a calvary erected near the Saint-Pierre basilica in 1805.

◈ WALLACE FOUNTAINS ◈

Throughout the city / wallacefountains.org

It's not unusual to come across one of these fountains on a stroll through Paris—there are about 700 of them in the capital. Richard Wallace, a British philanthropist who was inspired by London's drinking fountains, gifted 70 of them to the city of Paris between 1872 and 1879 to cope with water shortages.

◈ ASNIÈRES PET CEMETERY ◈

4 place Marguerite Durand, Asnières-sur-Seine, M° Gabriel Péri

This place is a little like Père-Lachaise, but for animals. Created by Marguerite Durand, the cemetery has been open to the public since 1899. Tens of thousands of cherished pets are buried here, along with celebrity animals and heroic police rescue dogs.

NEIGHBORHOOD STROLLS

I love Paris for its charming addresses, its intriguing tales, its nooks and crannies, and its hidden treasures. So, there's nothing I like better than wandering the city streets. There's always something to be discovered on a stroll: a beautiful house, secluded green spaces, or neighborhoods with a village atmosphere. To find them, you have sometimes to leave the wide boulevards behind, and slip down narrow streets or cross a park. And even though the hustle and bustle are never far away, you'll feel like you've experienced, for a moment, the peaceful side of Paris. Here is a list of some of my favorite walks.

SQUARE DE LA PLACE-DAUPHINE

Access via rue Henri-Robert or rue de Harlay, 1er, M° Pont Neuf / Cité

SQUARE DU VERT-GALANT

Access via place du Pont-Neuf, 1er, M° Pont Neuf / Cité

PASSAGE DE L'ANCRE

Access via 30 rue de Turbigo or 221 rue Saint-Martin, 3e, M° Réaumur – Sébastopol / Arts et Métiers

PASSAGE MOLIÈRE

Access via 157 rue Saint-Martin or 82 rue Quincampoix, 3e, M° Étienne Marcel / Rambuteau

HÔTEL-DIEU DE PARIS HOSPITAL GROUNDS

Access via parvis Notre-Dame – Place Jean-Paul II, 4e, M° Cité; RER Saint-Michel – Notre-Dame

PLACE DES VOSGES & HÔTEL DE SULLY

Access via southwest corner, Place des Vosges, 4e, M° Chemin Vert / Saint-Paul

COUR DU COMMERCE-SAINT-ANDRÉ

Access via 59–61 rue Saint-André-des-Arts, 19–21 rue de l'Ancienne-Comédie, or 130 boulevard Saint-Germain, 6e, M° Odéon

PASSAGE DAUPHINE

Access via 30 rue Dauphine or 27 rue Mazarine, 6e, M° Odéon

PLACE DE FURSTEMBERG

Access via rue de Furstemberg, 6e, M° Saint-Germain-des-Prés / Mabillon

CITÉ BERRYER

Access via 25 rue Royale or 24 rue Boissy d'Anglas, 8e, M° Madeleine / Concorde

CITÉ DE TRÉVISE

Access via rue Bleue or rue Richer, 9e, M° Cadet

COUR DES PETITES-ÉCURIES

Access via 61 bis–63 rue du Faubourg-Saint-Denis or 20 rue d'Enghien, 10e, M° Château d'Eau / Bonne Nouvelle

PASSAGE DELANOS
Private road, access via 148 rue du Faubourg-Saint-Denis or 25 rue d'Alsace, 10e, M° Gare de l'Est

PASSAGE DU DÉSIR
Private road, access via 84 rue du Faubourg-Saint-Denis, boulevard de Strasbourg, or 89 rue du Faubourg-Saint-Martin, 10e, M° Château d'Eau

PASSAGE REILHAC
Private road, access via 54 rue du Faubourg-Saint-Denis or 39 boulevard de Strasbourg, 10e, M° Château d'Eau

CITÉ DU FIGUIER
Access via 104–106 rue Oberkampf, 11e, M° Parmentier / Ménilmontant

CITÉ DURMAR
Private road, access via 154 rue Oberkampf, 11e, M° Ménilmontant / Parmentier

CITÉ INDUSTRIELLE
Access via rue Camille-Desmoulins or 113–115 rue de la Roquette, 11e, M° Voltaire

COUR DAMOYE
Access via 12 place de la Bastille or 12 rue Daval, 11e, M° Bastille / Bréguet – Sabin

COUR DE L'INDUSTRIE
Access via 37 bis rue de Montreuil, 11e, M° Rue des Boulets / Faidherbe – Chaligny

COUR DES BRETONS
Private road, access via 99 rue du Faubourg-du-Temple or 4 rue du Buisson-Saint-Louis, 11e, M° Belleville

PASSAGES ALEXANDRINE & GUSTAVE-LEPEU
Access via 27 rue Émile-Lepeu or 44 rue Léon-Frot / 31 rue Émile-Lepeu or 48 rue Léon-Frot, 11e, M° Charonne / Philippe Auguste

PASSAGE DU PLATEAU
Access via 8 rue du Plateau or 11 rue du Tunnel, 11e, M° Buttes-Chaumont

PASSAGES LHOMME & JOSSET
Access via 26 rue de Charonne / 38 rue de Charonne, 11e, M° Ledru-Rollin

PASSAGE SAINT-MAUR
Private road, access via 81 rue Saint-Maur, 11e, M° Rue Saint-Maur

CITÉ DEBERGUE
Access via 28–30 rue du Rendez-Vous, 12e, M° Porte de Vincennes / Picpus

COUR D'ALSACE-LORRAINE
Private road, access via 67 rue de Reuilly, 12e, M° Montgallet

IMPASSE CANART & PASSAGE DE LA VOÛTE
Access via 34–36 rue de la Voûte / 100–102 cours de Vincennes or 45–47 rue de la Voûte, 12e, M° Porte de Vincennes

IMPASSE MOUSSET
Access via 81–83 rue de Reuilly, 12e, M° Montgallet

RUE CRÉMIEUX
Access via 228–230 rue de Bercy or 19–21 rue de Lyon, 12e, M° Quai de la Rapée / Gare de Lyon

SENTIER DES MERISIERS
Access via 101 boulevard Soult
or 3 rue du Niger, 12e,
M° Porte de Vincennes / Picpus

VILLA DU BEL-AIR & SENTIER DE LA LIEUTENANCE
Access via 102 bis avenue de Saint-Mandé or 81 boulevard Soult, 12e,
M° Porte de Vincennes / Picpus

BUTTE-AUX-CAILLES DISTRICT
13e, M° Corvisart / Tolbiac

CITÉ FLEURIE
Access via 65 boulevard Arago, 13e,
M° Glacière / Denfert-Rochereau

CITÉ FLORALE DISTRICT
Access via rue Auguste-Lançon,
rue Boussingault, or rue Brillat-Savarin,
13e, RER Cité Universitaire

SQUARE DES PEUPLIERS
Access via rue du Moulin-des-Prés,
13e, M° Tolbiac

VILLA DAVIEL
Access via 7 rue Daviel,
13e, M° Corvisart

RUE DES THERMOPYLES
14e, M° Pernety

SQUARE DE MONTSOURIS
Private road, access via 8–12 rue Nansouty
or 51 avenue Reille, 14e, M° Porte d'Orléans;
RER Cité Universitaire

VILLA DES CHARMILLES
Access via 56 rue Castagnary,
15e, M° Convention

VILLA SANTOS-DUMONT
Access via rue Santos-Dumont, 15e,
M° Porte de Vanves / Convention

RUE MALLET-STEVENS
Private road, access via 9 rue du
Docteur-Blanche, 16e, M° Ranelagh

VILLAS DIETZ-MONNIN & ÉMILE-MEYER
Private roads, access via 6 rue
Parent-de-Rosan / 16 rue Parent-de-Rosan, 16e, M° Porte de Saint-Cloud

COUR SAINT-PIERRE
Private road, access via 47 bis avenue
de Clichy, 17e, M° La Fourche

ALLÉE DES BROUILLARDS
Access via place Dalida or 4–5 place
Casadesus, 18e, M° Lamarck – Caulaincourt

RUE DE L'ABREUVOIR
Access via place Dalida or 9 rue des Saules,
18e, M° Lamarck – Caulaincourt

VILLA LÉANDRE
Access via avenue Junot, 18e,
M° Lamarck – Caulaincourt

JARDIN DE LA BUTTE BERGEYRE
Access via rue Georges-Lardennois,
19e, M° Bolivar / Colonel Fabien

MOUZAÏA DISTRICT
Rue de Mouzaïa, 19e,
M° Botzaris

VILLA DE L'ADOUR
Private road, access via 13–13 bis rue
de la Villette or 14–16 rue Mélingue,
19e, M° Jourdain

CAMPAGNE À PARIS DISTRICT

Access via stairs on rue Mondonville, rue Georges-Perec, rue du Père-Prosper-Enfantin, or rue Camille-Bombois, 20e, M° Porte de Bagnolet

CITÉ AUBRY & VILLA RIBEROLLE

Access via 15 rue de Bagnolet / 35 rue de Bagnolet, 20e, M° Alexandre Dumas

CITÉ DE L'ERMITAGE

Access via rue de Ménilmontant, 20e, M° Ménilmontant / Jourdain / Gambetta

CITÉ DES ÉCOLES

Access via 13 rue Orfila or 28–30 rue Villiers-de-l'Isle-Adam, 20e, M° Gambetta

PASSAGE DES SOUPIRS

Access via 244 rue des Pyrénées or 47 bis rue de la Chine, 20e, M° Gambetta / Pelleport

PASSAGE PERREUR & VILLA PERREUR

Access via 42 rue du Capitaine-Marchal or 21–23 rue de la Dhuis / 22 rue de la Dhuis, 20e, M° Pelleport

PASSAGE PLANTIN

Access via 16–18 rue du Transvaal or 81 rue des Couronnes, 20e, M° Couronnes / Pyrénées

RUE DES VIGNOLES & SURROUNDING PASSAGES

Access via boulevard de Charonne, rue Planchet, rue de Buzenval, rue de la Réunion, or rue des Orteaux, 20e, M° Avron / Buzenval

RUE TACLET & VILLA GEORGINA

Access via 121 rue Pelleport / 36 rue de la Duée, 20e, M° Télégraphe / Saint-Fargeau

SQUARE DES GRÈS

Access via 55 rue Vitruve, 20e, M° Porte de Bagnolet

VILLA DE L'ERMITAGE & CITÉ LEROY

Access via rue des Pyrénées or rue de l'Ermitage, 20e, M° Ménilmontant / Jourdain / Gambetta

VILLA DU BORRÉGO

Access via 33–35 rue du Borrégo, 20e, M° Télégraphe / Saint-Fargeau

VILLA OLIVIER-MÉTRA

Access via 28 rue Olivier-Métra, 20e, M° Place des Fêtes

Numerous hidden courtyards and outdoor passages abound around the following streets:
rue Saint-Maur (10e/11e),
rue de Charonne (11e), rue Oberkampf (11e),
rue du Faubourg-Saint-Antoine (11e/12e),
rue de Belleville (19e/20e).

◈ COVERED PASSAGES ◈

Paris's covered passages transport visitors to the 19th century. Galleries were built between buildings during this period because the poorly lit and often muddy streets were far from conducive to the development of local businesses. Thanks to the construction of these early shopping arcades, numerous tearooms, small boutiques, and restaurants sprang up and flourished, attracting the Parisian bourgeoisie. Today, only 25 or so remain, but they have retained their authentic charm, their original decor, and their architecture. I love immersing myself in these places that are steeped in history and beauty. Here are my favorite covered passages.

GALERIES DU PALAIS-ROYAL

Entrances on place Colette, rue de Beaujolais, rue de Valois, rue de Montpensier, 1er, M° Palais-Royal – Musée du Louvre / Pyramides

GALERIE VÉRO-DODAT

Entrances at 19 rue Jean-Jacques-Rousseau & 2 rue du Bouloi, 1er, M° Palais-Royal – Musée du Louvre

PASSAGE DES JACOBINS

Entrances on place du Marché-Saint-Honoré, 1er, M° Tuileries / Pyramides

GALERIE COLBERT

Entrances at 6 rue des Petits-Champs & 4 rue Vivienne, 2e, M° Bourse / Palais-Royal – Musée du Louvre

GALERIE VIVIENNE

Entrances at 4 rue des Petits-Champs, 4–5 rue de la Banque, 6 rue Vivienne, 2e, M° Bourse / Palais-Royal – Musée du Louvre

PASSAGE BEN-AÏAD

Private road, visible from gates at 8 rue Bachaumont & 9 rue Léopold-Bellan, 2e, M° Sentier

PASSAGE CHOISEUL

Entrances at 40 rue des Petits-Champs & 23 rue Saint-Augustin, 2e, M° Quatre-Septembre / Pyramides

PASSAGE DES PANORAMAS

Entrances at 11 boulevard Montmartre & 10 rue Saint-Marc, 2e, M° Grands Boulevards

PASSAGE DES PRINCES

Entrances at 5 boulevard des Italiens & 97 rue de Richelieu, 2e, M° Richelieu – Drouot

PASSAGE DU BOURG-L'ABBÉ

Entrances at 120 rue Saint-Denis & 3 rue de Palestro, 2e, M° Étienne Marcel

PASSAGE DU CAIRE

Entrances on place du Caire and at 237 rue Saint-Denis, 34 & 44 rue du Caire, 33 rue d'Alexandrie, 2e, M° Réaumur – Sébastopol / Strasbourg – Saint-Denis

PASSAGE DU GRAND-CERF

Entrances at 145 rue Saint Denis & 10 rue Dussoubs, 2e, M° Étienne Marcel

PASSAGE DU PONCEAU
Entrances at 212 rue Saint-Denis & 119 boulevard de Sébastopol, 2e, M° Réaumur – Sébastopol / Strasbourg – Saint-Denis

PASSAGE VENDÔME
Entrances at 16 rue Béranger & 3 place de la République, 3e, M° République

ARCADES DES CHAMPS-ÉLYSÉES
Entrances at 76–78 avenue des Champs-Élysées & 59 rue de Ponthieu, 8e, M° Franklin D. Roosevelt

GALERIE DE LA MADELEINE
Entrances at 9 place de la Madeleine & 30 rue Boissy-d'Anglas, 8e, M° Madeleine

PASSAGE PUTEAUX
Entrances at 31 rue de l'Arcade & 28 rue Pasquier, 8e, M° Havre – Caumartin / Madeleine

PASSAGE JOUFFROY
Entrances at 10–12 boulevard Montmartre & 9 rue de la Grange-Batelière, 9e, M° Grands Boulevards

PASSAGE VERDEAU
Entrances at 6 rue de la Grange-Batelière & 31 bis rue du Faubourg-Montmartre, 9e, M° Le Peletier / Grands Boulevards

PASSAGE BRADY
Entrances at 46 rue du Faubourg-Saint-Denis & 33 boulevard de Strasbourg, 10e, M° Strasbourg – Saint-Denis

PASSAGE DU PRADO
Entrances at 18–20 boulevard Saint-Denis & 12 rue du Faubourg-Saint-Denis, 10e, M° Strasbourg – Saint-Denis

CITÉ L'ARGENTINE
Entrance at 111 avenue Victor Hugo, 16e, M° Victor Hugo

INDEX BY PLACE NAME

A

B

C

D

E

F

G

N

O

P

Q

R

INDEX BY CATEGORY

ART ATELIERS

ARTS & CRAFTS

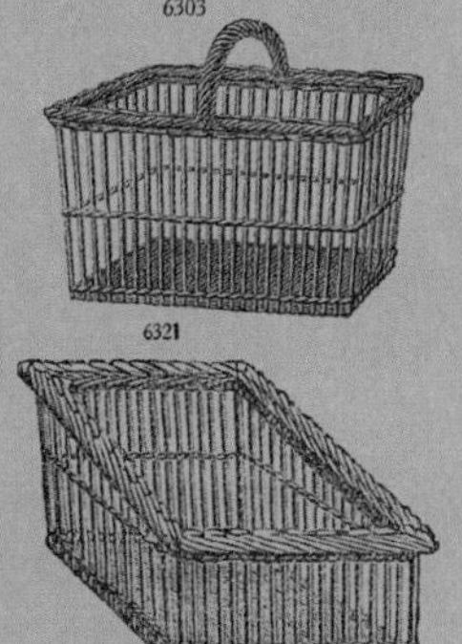

ARTISANS

BEAUTY & WELLNESS

Hairdressers & barbers

Products

Food markets

Gourmet groceries

Ice cream

Pâtisseries

Restaurants

Tea

Wine

HOTELS

KIDS

LIBRARIES

MARKETS

MUSEUMS & PLACES OF INTEREST

OUTDOOR ACTIVITIES

Cemeteries

Parks & gardens

Photobooths

River cruises

Street tours

RELIGIOUS INTEREST

SHOPS

Antiques & bric-a-brac

Books

Clothing & accessories

Department stores

Flowers

Home

Music

Party supplies

Pipes & cigars

Religious items

Notes for the reader

To know Paris is to understand that it holds countless surprises. I am continually discovering new addresses that embody the city's timeless essence. I invite you to keep exploring, and to make this guide your own by adding your favorite places in the space provided on the pages facing the map for each arrondissement.

Abbreviations:
M°: metro station
RER: train station served by suburban train service
@: Instagram
FB: Facebook

To reach a French telephone number from abroad, dial +33 and drop the first zero on the number provided.

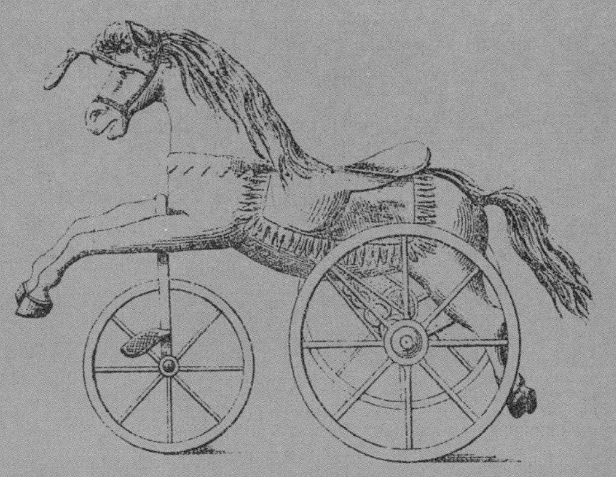

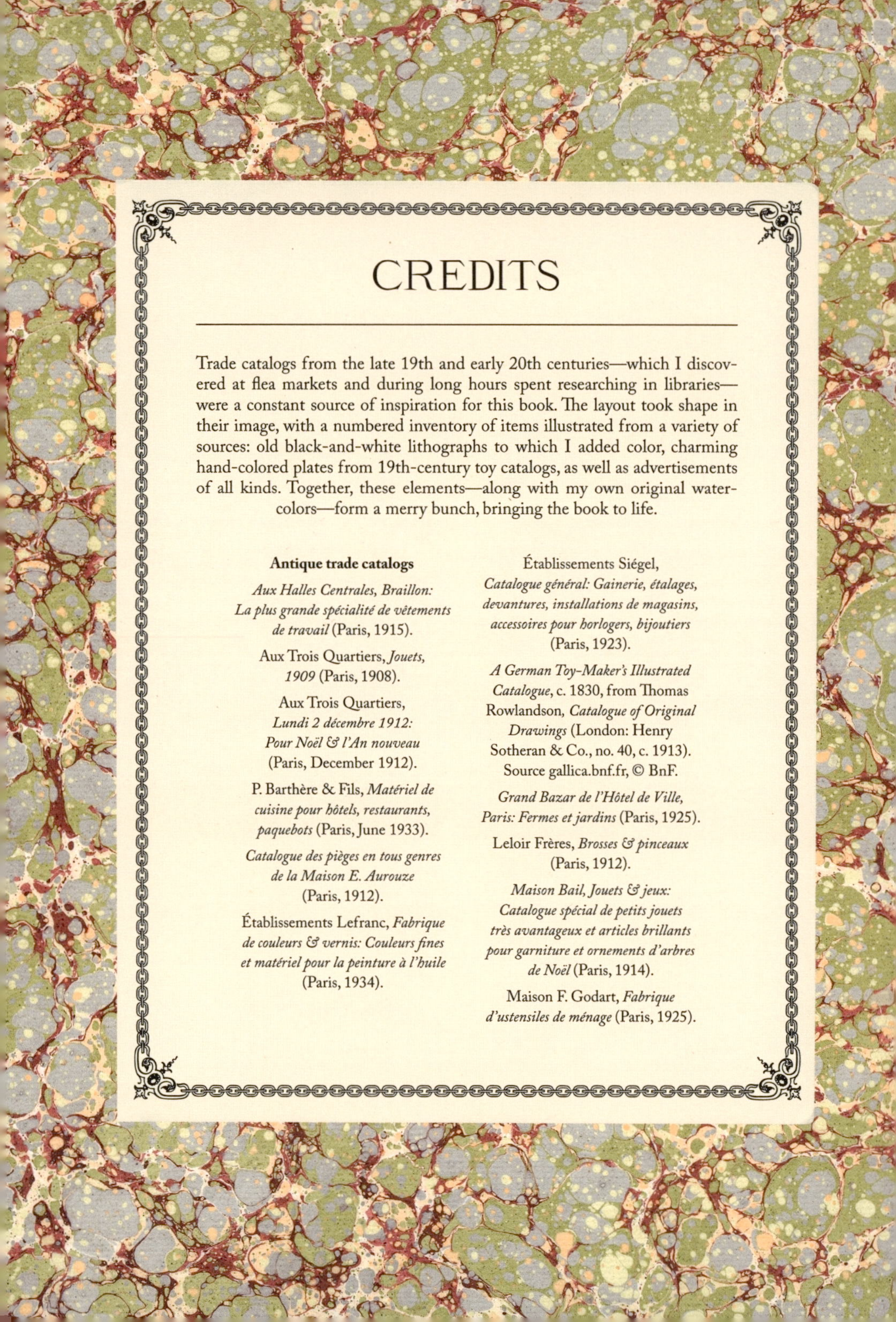

CREDITS

Trade catalogs from the late 19th and early 20th centuries—which I discovered at flea markets and during long hours spent researching in libraries—were a constant source of inspiration for this book. The layout took shape in their image, with a numbered inventory of items illustrated from a variety of sources: old black-and-white lithographs to which I added color, charming hand-colored plates from 19th-century toy catalogs, as well as advertisements of all kinds. Together, these elements—along with my own original watercolors—form a merry bunch, bringing the book to life.

Antique trade catalogs

Aux Halles Centrales, Braillon: La plus grande spécialité de vêtements de travail (Paris, 1915).

Aux Trois Quartiers, *Jouets, 1909* (Paris, 1908).

Aux Trois Quartiers, *Lundi 2 décembre 1912: Pour Noël & l'An nouveau* (Paris, December 1912).

P. Barthère & Fils, *Matériel de cuisine pour hôtels, restaurants, paquebots* (Paris, June 1933).

Catalogue des pièges en tous genres de la Maison E. Aurouze (Paris, 1912).

Établissements Lefranc, *Fabrique de couleurs & vernis: Couleurs fines et matériel pour la peinture à l'huile* (Paris, 1934).

Établissements Siégel, *Catalogue général: Gainerie, étalages, devantures, installations de magasins, accessoires pour horlogers, bijoutiers* (Paris, 1923).

A German Toy-Maker's Illustrated Catalogue, c. 1830, from Thomas Rowlandson, *Catalogue of Original Drawings* (London: Henry Sotheran & Co., no. 40, c. 1913). Source gallica.bnf.fr, © BnF.

Grand Bazar de l'Hôtel de Ville, Paris: Fermes et jardins (Paris, 1925).

Leloir Frères, *Brosses & pinceaux* (Paris, 1912).

Maison Bail, Jouets & jeux: Catalogue spécial de petits jouets très avantageux et articles brillants pour garniture et ornements d'arbres de Noël (Paris, 1914).

Maison F. Godart, *Fabrique d'ustensiles de ménage* (Paris, 1925).

Orfèvrerie argent: Paris (Paris, c. 1890).

J. Paturel & Cie, *Manufacture de ballons, jouets, articles pour fêtes: Marchands, forains, bazars* (Paris, 1931). Source: Ville de Paris / Bibliothèque Forney.

Le Printemps, *Au Printemps, Paris: Ameublements de campagne et de jardin, ménage, porcelaines* (Paris, May 1910).

Le Printemps, *Le Blanc au Printemps* (Paris, 1921).

Quincaillerie Anatole Elliott: Tarif général 1er Mars 1877 (Paris, March 1877).

Quincaillerie, articles de Paris, Anatole Elliott, Maisons A. Elliott & F. Gallimard réunies: Tarif album no.32, 1er août 1885 (Paris, August 1885).

Johann Martin Rau, *Musterbuch für Nürnberger Manufakturwaren*, lithographs by Friedrich Scharrer (1860s–1870s). Source: bavarikon.de.

G. Sennelier, *Catalogue général illustré: Fabricant de couleurs fines et matériel d'artistes* (Paris, 1896).

Spielzeug und Manufakturwaren-Musterbuch, lithographs by Friedrich Scharrer and August Kolb (Nuremberg, 1860s). Source: bavarikon.de.

Spielzeug-Musterbuch, lithographs by Friedrich Scharrer or August Kolb (Nuremberg, 1850s–1860s). Source: bavarikon.de.

Spielzeug-Musterbuch, lithographs by Friedrich Scharrer (Nuremberg, 1860s). Source: bavarikon.de.

Spielzeug-Musterbuch (Nuremberg, c. 1870). Source: bavarikon.de.

Viville, *Parfumerie de l'Opéra* (Paris, 1905).

***

Endpapers and pages 1, 302–304: marbled paper by Marie-Anne Hamaide.

Quotation page 5: Jean Cocteau, *Paris, Suivi de Notes sur l'amour* (Paris: Grasset, 2023).

Maps reproduced from a Cartes Taride guide, c. 1970s.

Page 199: *Natation sur le ventre – Natation sur le dos*, from Friedrich Eduard Bilz, *La nouvelle médication naturelle: Traité et aide-mémoire de médication et d'hygiène naturelles*, vol. 2 (Leipzig, [1898]). © Bridgeman Images.

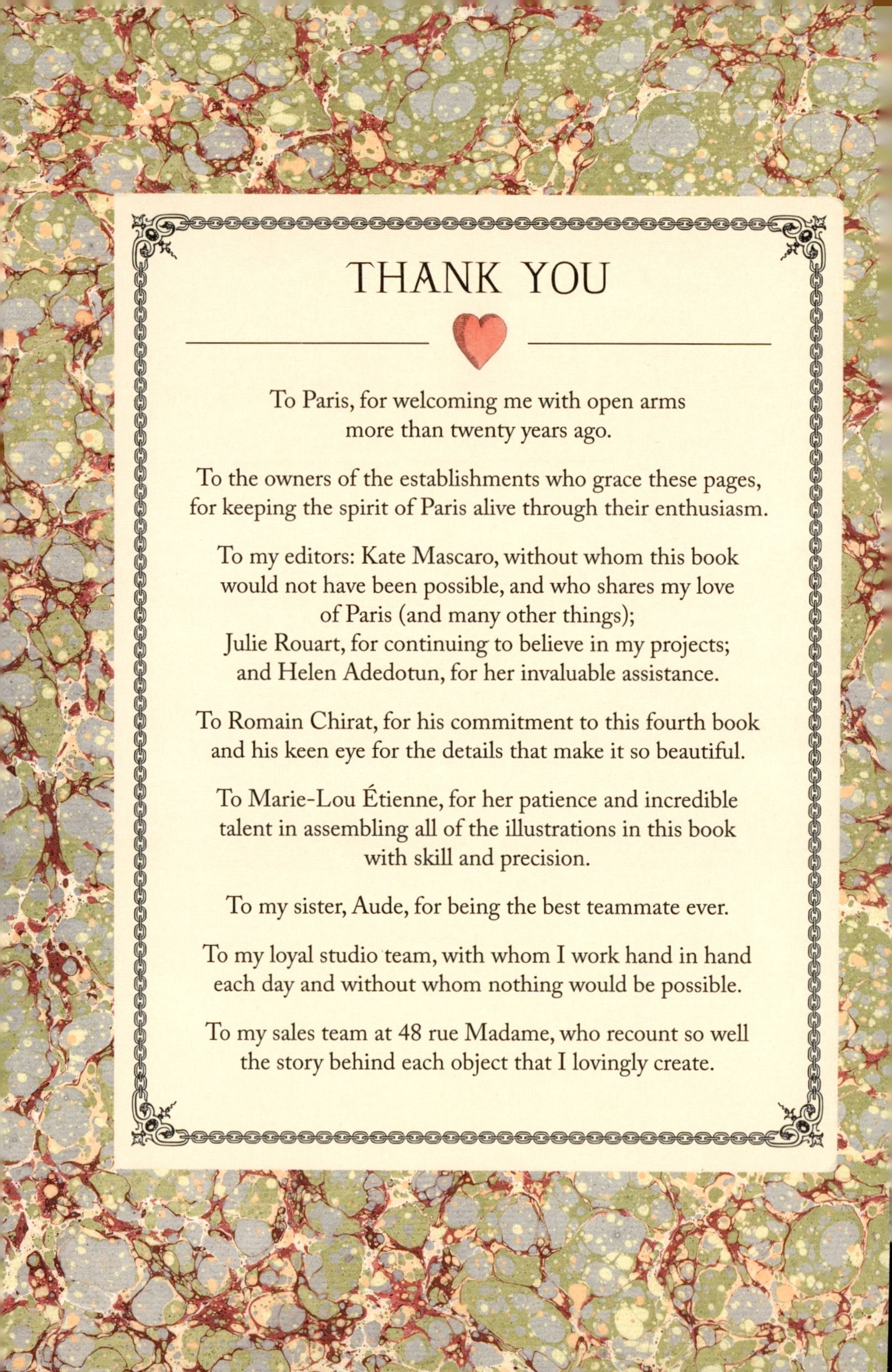

THANK YOU

To Paris, for welcoming me with open arms
more than twenty years ago.

To the owners of the establishments who grace these pages,
for keeping the spirit of Paris alive through their enthusiasm.

To my editors: Kate Mascaro, without whom this book
would not have been possible, and who shares my love
of Paris (and many other things);
Julie Rouart, for continuing to believe in my projects;
and Helen Adedotun, for her invaluable assistance.

To Romain Chirat, for his commitment to this fourth book
and his keen eye for the details that make it so beautiful.

To Marie-Lou Étienne, for her patience and incredible
talent in assembling all of the illustrations in this book
with skill and precision.

To my sister, Aude, for being the best teammate ever.

To my loyal studio team, with whom I work hand in hand
each day and without whom nothing would be possible.

To my sales team at 48 rue Madame, who recount so well
the story behind each object that I lovingly create.

French illustrator and designer Marin Montagut is fascinated by the craftsmanship of the past. Using watercolor to render the poetry of the world around him, he has created a collection of unique and whimsical decorative objects, which can be found in his Paris boutique. His creations are all handmade in France, in his studio in the 20th arrondissement. He is the author of *Extraordinary Collections: French Interiors, Flea Markets, Ateliers*, and *Timeless Paris: Ateliers, Emporiums, Savoir Faire*, and is coauthor with Ines de la Fressange of *Maison: Parisian Chic at Home*. He has collaborated with numerous prestigious French brands and institutions including Café de Flore, the Comédie-Française, Château de Versailles, Pierre Frey, and the Ritz Paris.

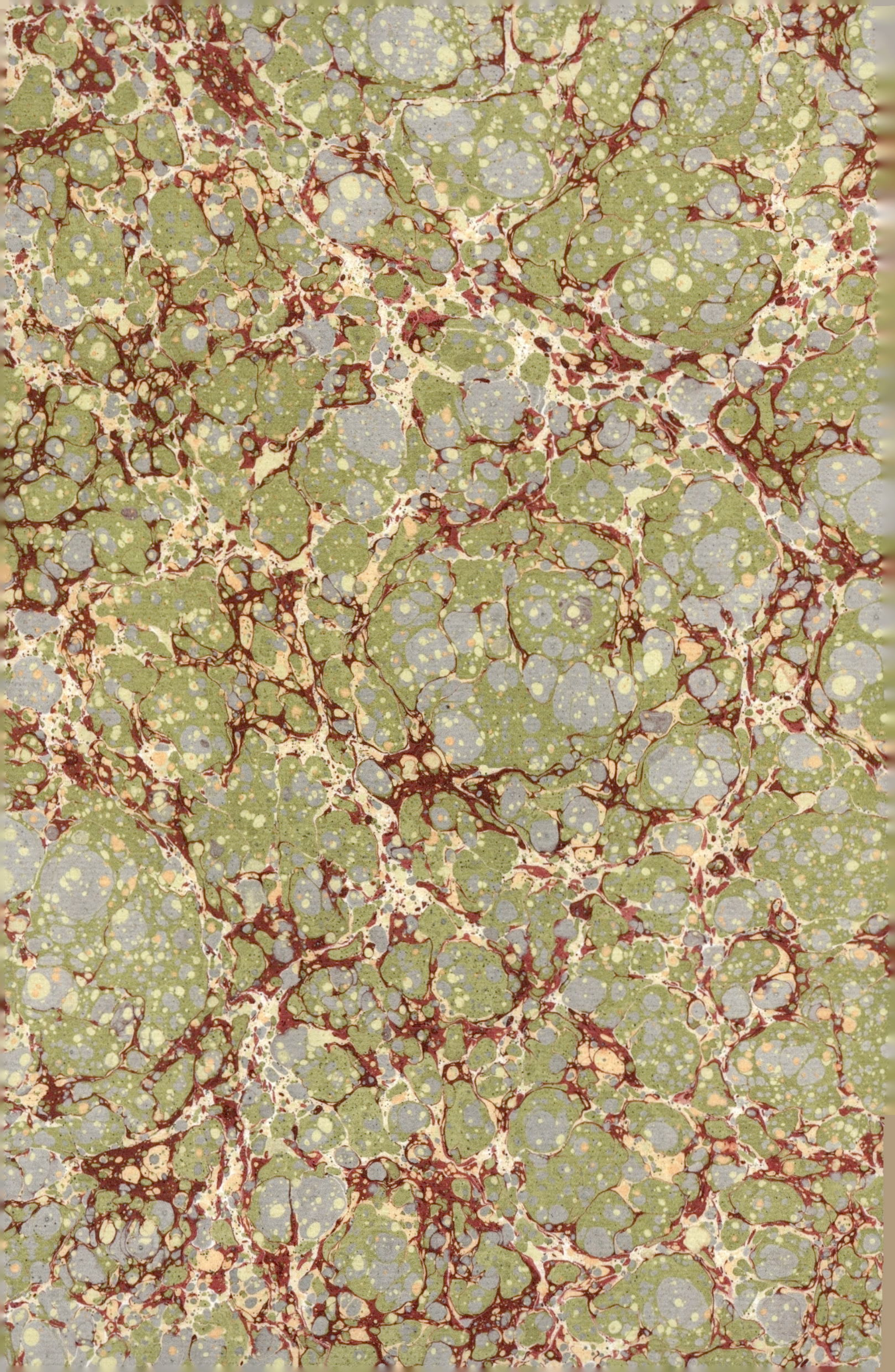